inFAMOUS 2

STRATEGY GUIDE OUTLINE

JUL 26 2011

SHOCK TO THE SYSTEM

The world has never been a simple place, merely a battleground between everyday heroes and villains. All that changed in an instant when the Ray Sphere turned Cole MacGrath into a superhuman and Empire City into a war zone. Now Cole finds himself on a quest to acquire enough power before the apocalyptic arrival of The Beast that has been foretold.

To harness his abilities and combat the coming threat, Cole needs both control and comprehension. He must understand how his powers work, as well as how to work them. Joining Cole on this journey in New Marais are faces both new and old, but it can be hard to distinguish friend from foe. It's important to remember that everyone has a hidden past, and each person hides his or her own agenda.

The road to a future is littered with choices and bodies. The choices that Cole makes and the bodies that he steps over to get to that future have yet to happen…

THE BEAST IS COMING

The End of Empire City

Cole MacGrath was just a bike messenger, a college dropout with nothing significant marking his life. That changed with one routine delivery. The fateful package contained a Ray Sphere, which exploded upon opening, killing thousands and decimating five square blocks of Empire City. Cole not only survived the blast, but also woke up with the power to control electricity. He didn't know who sent the package or how it had given him powers when it killed so many others, but he was determined to find out.

At the same time, Empire City went into lockdown as it tried to quarantine a plague that started spreading after the blast. To make matters more complicated, other people with powers, called conduits, began to appear in the city, and it was up to Cole to sort out who they were and how they were related to everything that was happening. He faced trial after trial, and even his best friend, Zeke, momentarily turned on him.

Eventually, Cole discovered the mastermind behind the explosion, a man named Kessler. The leader of a secret organization called The First Sons, Kessler had planned the entire event so that Cole would become powerful. In a vision of the future, Kessler told Cole about the coming of The Beast, a creature powerful enough to wipe life off the planet, and Cole was the only one who could stop it.

A month after the vision, Cole met Lucy Kuo, an NSA agent and fellow conduit who knew all about The Beast. Her mission was to help Cole prepare for the inevitable encounter. Kuo had a friend named Dr. Sebastian Wolfe, who worked on the Ray Sphere prototype. He could help Cole gain new powers; all Cole had to do was go to New Marais.

Just as Cole, Zeke, and Kuo were leaving for New Marais, The Beast showed up unannounced. Without enough power to stop it, Cole was thoroughly beaten. The group was able to escape, but Empire City was gone.

Continuing in New Marais

Humanity's only hope lies in New Marais. Traveling by ship down the coast, Cole, Zeke, and Kuo snuck into the city. New Marais was on lockdown and unfriendly to conduits. Once in the city, the trio saw why.

Joseph Bertrand III had New Marais in the palm of his hand, and he had used the public's fear to manipulate them into accepting his politics. Along with his personal Militia, Bertrand sought to remove conduits from New Marais and simultaneously protect the city from the mutated, violent freaks that came from the swamps.

In order to stop The Beast, Cole needs to reach Wolfe. To locate Wolfe, Cole must overcome Bertrand's Militia as well as the creatures from the swamp. Cole is facing yet another difficult mission. How will he ensure his victory? With brute, malicious strength, or with understanding and controlled power?

THE INFAMOUS

Cole MacGrath

Before the famous blast that rocked Empire City, Cole MacGrath was no one special. After the blast, Cole was thrust away from the life he knew and landed in a crumbling city. Empire City was changed forever by the blast, and so was Cole.

The device that caused the explosion gave Cole a strange ability. He could feel a connection with the electricity flowing through the entire city and soon learned to manipulate this energy to his will. But Cole wasn't the only person who had changed. In the wake of the blast, Empire City was thrown into chaos, and the law enforcement couldn't keep up. Reapers— mutated thugs, junkies, and drug dealers—took over the streets, while the city's homeless banded together to form the Dust Men, and they were looking to force their way up the city's ranks.

Through his struggles in Empire City, Cole discovered the truth behind the explosion. A man called Kessler planned the blast and spearheaded the construction of the object that gave Cole his new powers. During Kessler's final battle with Cole, he revealed his reasoning behind the events. Kessler was actually Cole from an alternate universe, a place where he married his love and had a family. But a massive creature known as The Beast destroyed Kessler's world. Everything he knew was gone. In order to prevent that from happening in Cole's world, Kessler had to make sure Cole had the strength to stop The Beast. Cole needed to gain power and be trained at all costs.

Cole defeated Kessler and vowed that he wouldn't let The Beast win.

He was contacted by NSA agent Kuo and continued his new mission to prepare for The Beast's coming as Empire City continued to adjust to life after the blast. But as Cole boarded a ship to New Marais, home to Dr. Wolfe and a new device that had the potential to enhance Cole's powers, The Beast appeared.

It was too soon, as Cole wasn't ready and The Beast was too strong, casting him aside and wiping Empire City off the map. Furious and disappointed with himself, Cole vowed once again he wouldn't let The Beast win. He continued to New Marais, unsure of what the former urban haven held for him.

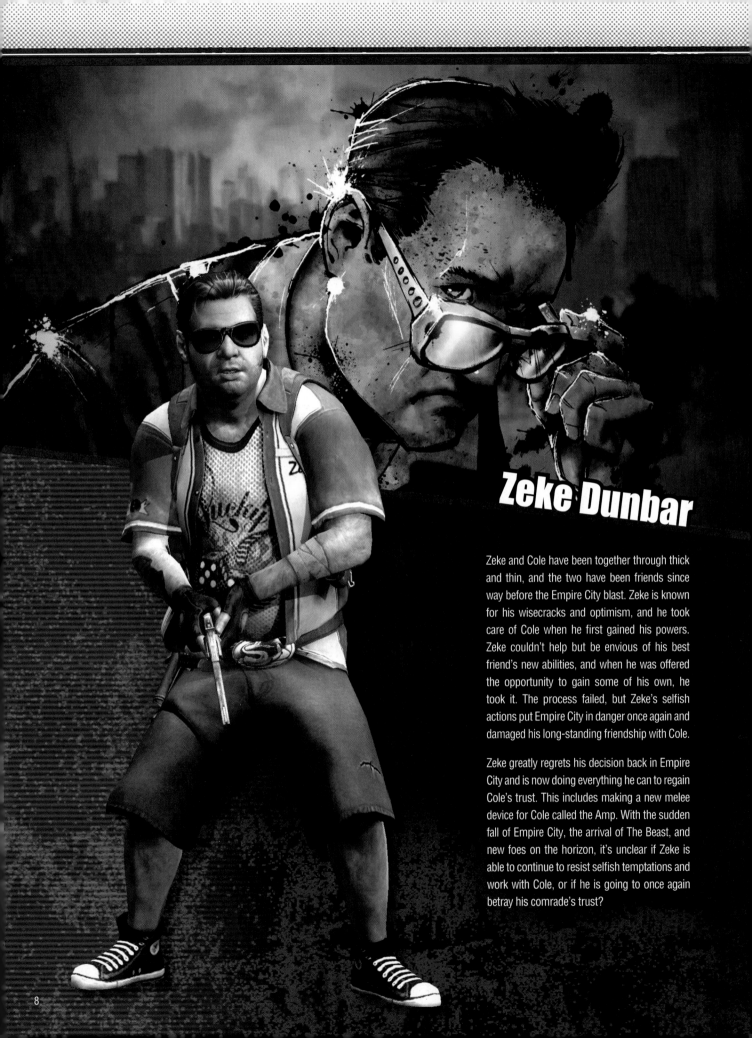

Zeke Dunbar

Zeke and Cole have been together through thick and thin, and the two have been friends since way before the Empire City blast. Zeke is known for his wisecracks and optimism, and he took care of Cole when he first gained his powers. Zeke couldn't help but be envious of his best friend's new abilities, and when he was offered the opportunity to gain some of his own, he took it. The process failed, but Zeke's selfish actions put Empire City in danger once again and damaged his long-standing friendship with Cole.

Zeke greatly regrets his decision back in Empire City and is now doing everything he can to regain Cole's trust. This includes making a new melee device for Cole called the Amp. With the sudden fall of Empire City, the arrival of The Beast, and new foes on the horizon, it's unclear if Zeke is able to continue to resist selfish temptations and work with Cole, or if he is going to once again betray his comrade's trust?

Lucy Kuo

NSA agent Lucy Kuo appeared in Empire City shortly after Cole's battle with Kessler. Her mission is to help Cole expand his powers and ensure that he is prepared for his imminent encounter with The Beast. Due to Kuo's connections with John White, the NSA agent who lost his life to a Ray Sphere while trying to help Cole, she is fully aware of Cole's situation and the risk she's taking by assisting him.

In order to enhance Cole's abilities, Kuo instructed the group to head to New Marais, where her contact, Dr. Wolfe, planned to help Cole expand his powers. However, The Beast appeared in Empire City before the ship bound for New Marais was able to leave. Kuo witnessed Cole's defeat to The Beast and rushed him and Zeke to New Marais before they disappeared with the rest of Empire City.

Kuo's sense of justice is strong, and though she's determined to prepare Cole at all costs, she'll do everything she can to prevent the loss of innocent lives. She's in awe of Cole's abilities and the good they can accomplish. As an NSA agent, Kuo has received combat training and is efficient with her side-arm, but without powers like Cole's, there is only so much she can do.

Shortly after arriving in New Marais, Kuo is given the power to do more to stop The Beast and to save New Marais. The process was forced upon her, and it was more painful than can be imagined, but in the end Kuo's powers as a conduit were awakened. She has control over ice and is ready to use the abilities thrust upon her for the greater good.

Nix

Nix was born and raised in New Marais. She has seen what it used to be and what Joseph Bertrand has done to transform the city. Nix lived on the outskirts of town with her mother, and although they were not the wealthiest around, they were happy. That all changed when Bertrand gathered people from outside the town. He lured them under false pretenses, and then used a Ray Sphere to vaporize them. All so he could awaken his powers.

Bertrand did gain awesome powers, but the blast also woke the powers lying dormant inside Nix. The life and family she knew were gone, and in their place was the ability to control oil and fire. From that fateful day onward, Nix sought out revenge against Bertrand for what he did to her family and her home.

Even before meeting Cole, Nix used her powers to tar and burn those who stood against her, whether they were Militia or monsters. Nix is passionate, strong, and often cruel. Vengeance is everything to her, and she is willing to dirty her hands time and time again to see Bertrand burn.

Nix feels a strong connection with Cole as a fellow conduit and as someone who shares a tragic past. She does all that she can to convince Cole to follow her down

35 k 670

200

Sebastian Wolfe

Dr. Sebastian Wolfe is a former member of the First Sons and a scientist who worked on the organization's Ray Sphere project. His involvement with the creation of the Ray Sphere has caused him great guilt, and to make amends, he is ready to help Cole enhance his powers. He is introduced to Cole in New Marais through NSA agent Kuo.

Upon meeting, he tells Cole about the power Ray Sphere Inhibitor, a device Wolfe created that has the ability to drain power instead of grant it. It also has the power to cure the hundreds of thousands of people infected with the plague caused by Ray Sphere blasts. But before Wolfe could help Cole any further, Joseph Bertrand abducted and tortured him for information. Whether Wolfe told Bertrand what

Joseph Bertrand III

Joseph Bertrand III rules over New Marais with an iron fist. He used public fear, the threat of The Beast, and the lack of information surrounding conduits to slip into power. Once there, Bertrand used his influence to gather up a Militia, which he commands to ruthlessly enforce his authority.

Bertrand campaigns to clean the city of the impure creatures that taint the streets of New Marais. To carry out his promises, he has ordered the Militia to eliminate the freaks that crawl out from the swamps and the ones like Cole who hide in human form. According to Bertrand, the swamp monsters and conduits damage the purity of the human race and must be eliminated.

But Bertrand is keeping a secret. Just like Cole, he too is a conduit seeking to expand his powers. What they are and what he wants to use them for is unknown.

The Beast

In Kessler's time, The Beast appeared and laid waste to all of humanity shortly after Kessler gained his powers. In order to prevent such a disaster from happening in other timelines, Kessler came to Cole and forced his powers into maturity much earlier than they had appeared in Kessler's time, hoping to give Cole more time to prepare for The Beast.

However, The Beast appeared much sooner than anticipated. Towering against the skyline of Empire City, The Beast annihilated the metropolis in mere minutes. It is able to manipulate gravity, crushing steel buildings and sucking citizens into an oblivion from which there is no escape. Although Cole survived an encounter with The Beast, he was not able to gather much information about it. It is still a mystery as to where it came from or what it is. The Beast remains at large and is moving down the coast from the ruins of Empire City to the flooded streets of New Marais.

New Marais

New Marais' history and culture have been long forgotten, swept away by the famous flood that rolled through the city. After that, New Marais became a haven for outsiders and outcasts. It was an urban exploration playground, lawless and full of adventures.

But over the past year, the city's districts have transformed once again. Fear spread after the Empire City explosion, and the public panicked as mutated creatures and conduits sprung up in New Marais.

The politician Joseph Bertrand took advantage of the situation and seized control of the city. Now the streets of New Marais are flooded with his Militia, rednecks looking for an excuse to dish out justice in the name of their city.

Every action has more than one approach. Cole can choose to save a civilian or kill them, Arc Restrain an enemy or Bio Leech them for energy, or go on a rescue mission with Kuo or cause havoc with Nix. Each decision Cole makes is judged, and at the end of the action or mission, he is given Karma. If he chooses the righteous path, he'll gain good Karma, whereas villainous actions give him evil Karma. Keep track of Cole's Karma with the Karma meter in the upper left corner of the screen.

The Good

Helping others before yourself, working for the greater good, and protecting as many lives as possible. That's what it means to follow the righteous path. Cole may find it difficult to stick to this mindset when it is often easier to play the villain, but he gains more popularity and support for it. Kuo helps encourage Cole to make the right choices and reminds him that only he has the power to save the world. If he doesn't take the right path, who will?

Being good does have its benefits. Cole gains ice powers that freeze enemies in their tracks and leave citizens unharmed. He also forms a deeper connection with Kuo, who shares the same beliefs.

The Bad

Taking justice into your own hands, not letting anything or anyone get in your way, and making use of the people around you then discarding them when you're done. That's what it means to follow the villainous path. Cole may find it easier to destroy everything in his path rather than finding a different route, but the public will not stand by a renegade vigilante destroying their lives. Choosing this path isolates Cole and increases his enemies to include the citizens of New Marais.

However, being evil does give Cole some advantageous powers. He acquires fire powers and can use Ionic Drain to heal himself while wiping out surrounding enemies. Cole also forms a deeper connection with Nix, who loves to encourage mayhem.

The Mission

Primary Missions

New Marais is Cole's last stand against The Beast. If he can't find a way to stop The Beast here, it's game over. Cole and his companions use primary missions to seek out ways to increase his power while uncovering The Beast's weakness. Marked in the city with white icons, these missions reveal more information on what Cole must do to stop the towering menace approaching New Marais and also show what Joseph Bertrand's purpose in the city is.

Side Missions

In addition to the primary missions, Cole also has side missions given by his comrades as well as the citizens of New Marais. Marked with yellow icons, these optional undertakings not only give Cole a greater understanding of the needs of the city, but also give him experience, Karma, and even special items such as Blast Shards.

Side missions come in three varieties, neutral, good, and evil. Neutral missions are marked in yellow and can be completed regardless of Cole's Karma ranking. Good missions are marked in yellow and blue and are only available to Cole when his Karma ranking is in the blue. On the other hand, evil missions, marked in yellow and red, are only available to Cole when his Karma ranking is in the red.

Game Screen

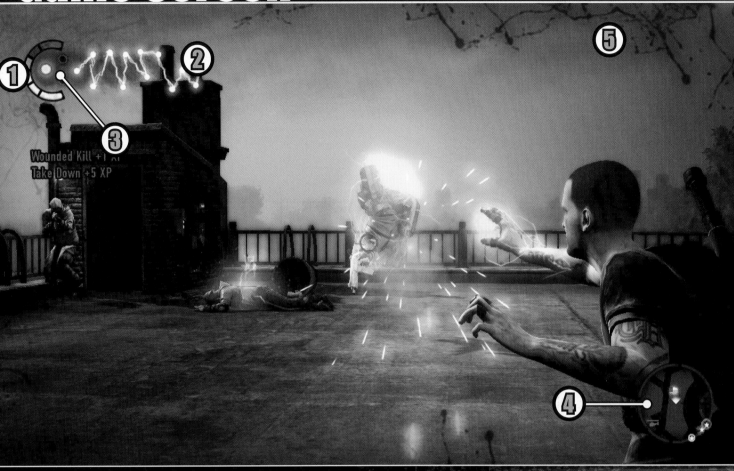

① Karma Meter

Keep track of Cole's current Karma ranking with the Karma meter. The blue bars are good Karma, and the red bars are evil Karma. The closer Cole's Karma ranking is to the outside of the meter, the more good or evil he is.

② Energy Meter

This series of electric cores ties together to form Cole's energy meter. Whenever Cole performs an attack, some of his energy is drained, and when it's all gone, he cannot use any electricity-based attacks. Refill Cole's energy by absorbing electricity from various objects, such as transmitters, lights, and cars.

③ Ionic Charge

The purple Ionic Charges are stored between the Karma meter and the energy meter. At first, Cole can only store one Ionic Charge, but by gaining upgrades, he can eventually store up to three. Ionic Charges are collected from fallen enemies, but it is random which enemy is going to drop one.

④ Minimap

The minimap in the bottom right corner of the screen displays Cole's immediate surroundings. The minimap also indicates where nearby missions are located with yellow icons, the general location of dead drops with blue bird icons, and even where enemies are with red icons. Karma opportunities also have their own icon on the minimap. To view a full map, press **SELECT**.

⑤ Blood

As Cole takes damage, the screen flashes and blood splatters along its edges. The more damage Cole takes, the harder it is to see. To recover health, take cover and avoid damage or absorb some electricity.

Electric Sources

Any objects that hold electricity can be drained to give Cole more energy and speed up his healing process. Use the ping ability to find electric sources and drain away!

Blast Shards

Blast Shards are glowing indigo collectables strewn all across New Marais. Gather these objects to extend Cole's energy meter. To help locate Blast Shards, use the ping ability to display nearby ones on the minimap.

Blast Cores

Blast Cores are the key to expanding Cole's powers and using the Ray Sphere Inhibitor. The only way to collect Blast Cores is to play the primary missions.

Medical Centers

If Cole succumbs to his injuries sustained battling the beasts and villains of New Marais, he reappears fully healed at the nearest Medical Center. Complete Side Missions to unlock additional Medical Centers throughout the city.

Pause Menu

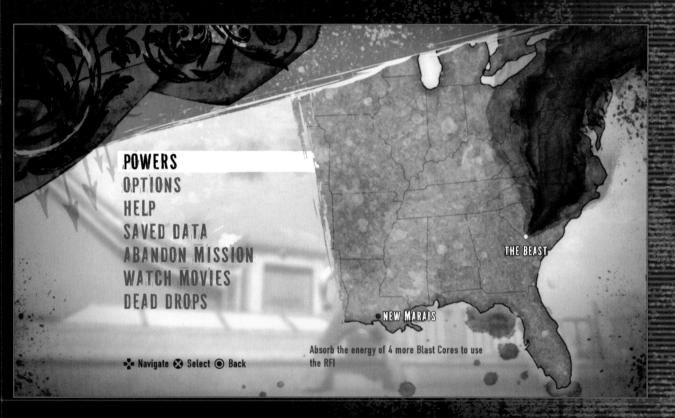

POWERS
OPTIONS
HELP
SAVED DATA
ABANDON MISSION
WATCH MOVIES
DEAD DROPS

Navigate   Select   Back

Absorb the energy of 4 more Blast Cores to use the RFI

THE BEAST

NEW MARAIS

The pause menu contains important information regarding Cole's progress. Use this menu to review all unlocked powers, adjust the game options, view the game controls, save the game data, access User-Generated Content, watch unlocked cinemas, and listen to collected dead drops.

For Cole, gaining super powers happened instantly, but mastering them continues to take time and dedication. The type of abilities and upgrades that Cole gains depends on his decisions. Moral and ethical actions unlock powers that support Cole's decisions, whereas malicious and evil actions unlock powers that help Cole spread destruction.

Whether they are used for good or evil, Cole's powers are centered around four basic abilities, Bolts, Blasts, Grenades, and Rockets. There are also two advanced abilities, Kinetic and Ionic. When Cole's energy meter is drained, there are several ways to refill his energy. He can gather energy from electrical sources, such as cars, lights, and transmitters, or he can drain energy from human bodies through Bio Leech. To Bio Leech, Cole has to knock down a civilian or Militia member, then lock-on and start draining. Cole also has the option of performing an Arc Restraint to humanely restrain a knocked down enemy, or using Pulse Heal to cure a downed ally.

CONTROLS

Menu Controls

| Select highlighted menu item | ⊗ |
| Previous screen/Return to main menu | △ |

Game Controls

Electric Drain [L2]

Aim Mode [L1]

Precision

Quick Swap Menu

Purchase Powers

Ionic Powers

[SELECT] Map

[R2] Kinetic Pulse/Lightning Tether/C...

[R1] Static Thrusters/Use Object/Lock...

△ Melee Finisher

▢ Melee Attack

◯ Drop/Cover/Dive Roll

⊗ Jump/Climb

START Pause Menu

L3 Move

R3 Move Camera

Aim Mode Controls

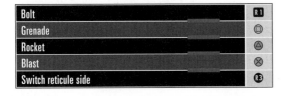

Bolt	R1
Grenade	▢
Rocket	△
Blast	⊗
Switch reticule side	R3

Ground Lock-On Controls

Bio Leech	▢
Pulse Heal	△
Arc Restraint	◯

NEUTRAL

Bolts

Bolts are small, condensed bursts of energy that are easy to aim. They do not take up much of Cole's energy meter and can be fired rapidly for massive damage.

ALPHA BOLT

This is the first Bolt power available to Cole. Although not nearly as strong as the rest of Cole's Bolt attacks, the Alpha Bolt is easy to fire and string together for a long series of electric shocks.

UNLOCK REQUIREMENTS: Available at start.

PINCER BOLT

The Pincer Bolt fires out three balls of electric energy, which come together to damage a single target. The Pincer Bolt does not fire as rapidly as some of the other Bolt attacks, but what it lacks in speed, it makes up for in brute strength.

UNLOCK REQUIREMENTS: Six Take Down stunts in the Evolution mission.

COST: 400 XP

ARTILLERY BOLT

The Artillery Bolt is as fast as the Alpha Bolt, but is effective even against long-range targets.

UNLOCK REQUIREMENT: 5 Climbing Assault stunts.

COST: 800 XP

Blasts

Use a Blast attack to release a shockwave of electric energy to knock Cole's enemies off balance or even off buildings.

ALPHA BLAST

The Alpha Blast is the first Blast attack available to Cole. It has enough strength to launch enemies off their feet, but should be followed up with other attacks to defeat a foe.

UNLOCK REQUIREMENTS: Available at start.

DETONATION BLAST

This Blast attack sticks to whatever it hits until it explodes, damaging everything around it. If Cole jumps when he is close to an exploding Detonation Blast, he can use the energy for a super jump.

UNLOCK REQUIREMENTS: Five Watch Your Step stunts.

COST: 600 XP

Grenades

Grenades create eruptions of charged energy. They are perfect for clearing out clusters of foes, but it is easy for innocent civilians to be caught up in a blast.

ALPHA GRENADE

The Alpha Grenade is Cole's first explosive. This basic grenade explodes shortly after it makes contact with its target.

UNLOCK REQUIREMENTS: Available at start.

CLUSTER GRENADE

The Cluster Grenade is the most powerful explosive available to Cole. After being thrown, this grenade splinters in-air and rains down small Sticky Grenades on everyone below.

UNLOCK REQUIREMENTS: 10 Precision Head Shock stunts.

COST: 5500 XP

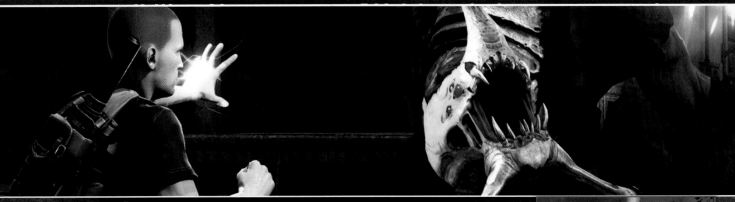

Rockets

Rockets are massive electric attacks that rip through targets. These are the most powerful and energy-consuming attacks within Cole's four basic powers.

ALPHA ROCKET

The Alpha Rocket contains massive amounts of kinetic energy that hits Cole's target like a ton of bricks. It has impressive long-range flight, but it isn't as strong as Cole's other rockets.

UNLOCK REQUIREMENTS: Available at start.

STICKY ROCKET

The Sticky Rocket launches at Cole's target and en-route, splits into homing charges that attach to nearby enemies.

UNLOCK REQUIREMENTS: Perform three Dead Eye stunts.

COST: 2600 XP

Misc. Powers

Cole has some additional powers that don't fit in with his other attack categories. Here are his miscellaneous powers.

CAMERA

Created by Zeke, Cole's camera is the only one in the world that doesn't break because of Cole's powers. With a 14.1 megapixel sensor and a 28mm wide-angle lens, this camera can take pictures near and far. It is made available during specific missions.

KINETIC PULSE

Cole can use his powers to lift objects containing electricity and launch them at targets. To lift an object, press and hold **R2**; to aim, move the right analog stick; and to throw, press ⊗.

UNLOCK REQUIREMENTS:
Complete the Forward Momentum mission.

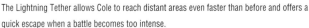

LIGHTNING TETHER

The Lightning Tether is an electrokinetic rope that pulls Cole toward whatever it latches onto. The Lightning Tether allows Cole to reach distant areas even faster than before and offers a quick escape when a battle becomes too intense.

UNLOCK REQUIREMENTS:
Complete the Easy Going mission.

PRECISION

While aiming, press and hold the up directional button to zoom in for precise firing. Precision slightly slows down time, allowing Cole to concentrate on his targeting, but it also drains his energy meter.

UNLOCK REQUIREMENTS: Complete the Good Gets Better mission.

Ionic Powers

Ionic powers are awe-inspiring. These attacks can wipe out entire militia units and then some. Civilians can easily get sucked into an attack if Cole isn't careful. With great power comes great responsibility!

IONIC VORTEX

The Ionic Vortex is the first Ionic power available to Cole. This ability creates a spinning vortex that tears through the world. Like all Ionic powers, Ionic Vortex requires the energy of an Ionic Charge.

UNLOCK REQUIREMENTS: Complete the Storm's Coming mission.

IONIC STORM

The Ionic Storm is a massive attack that uses an Ionic Charge to rip open the sky and call down a lightning storm, destroying everything in its path.

UNLOCK REQUIREMENTS: Complete The Final Piece mission.

Amp Upgrades

The Amp, created by Zeke and Cole, is customized to work with Cole's electrical powers. This melee weapon can be used even when Cole's energy meter is empty.

MELEE

Cole can use the Amp to melee targets. When melee attacks are strung together, they can fill up combo meters until Cole is able to unleash Finisher Attacks.

UNLOCK REQUIREMENTS: Available at start.

FINISHER ATTACKS

After landing a few hits on a target, Cole can launch a Finisher Attack to dish out severe damage. These special attacks are usually enough to eliminate standard enemies.

UNLOCK REQUIREMENTS: Complete the Evolution mission.

COST: 600

ULTRA ATTACKS

Ultra Attacks are even stronger than Finisher Attacks and can be executed after a long hit combo.

UNLOCK REQUIREMENTS: Complete the Storm's Coming mission.

COST: 1200 XP

ULTRA DRAIN

Ultra Drain sucks out energy from targets hit by an Ultra Attack. This power is a quick and easy way to fill up Cole's energy meter while in the middle of combat.

UNLOCK REQUIREMENTS: Complete the Good Gets Better mission.

COST: 1600 XP

QUICKER COMBOS

Once Quicker Combos is unlocked, Cole can earn Finisher Attacks and Ultra Attacks with even shorter hit combos.

UNLOCK REQUIREMENTS: Complete the Ray Field Energy mission.

COST: 3000 XP

Upgrades

As Cole completes more and more side missions, he unlocks special upgrades.

MEGAWATT DRAIN

Megawatt Drain increases Cole's Electric Drain speed by 50 percent.

UNLOCK REQUIREMENTS: Complete 10 side missions.

COST: 500 XP

IONIC CHARGE 2

Ionic Charge 2 increases Cole's Ionic Charge storage capacity to two.

UNLOCK REQUIREMENTS: Complete 20 side missions.

COST: 900 XP

GIGAWATT DRAIN

Gigawatt Drain increases Cole's Electric Drain speed by 100 percent.

UNLOCK REQUIREMENTS: Complete 30 side missions.

COST: 1200 XP

IONIC CHARGE 3

Ionic Charge 3 increases Cole's Ionic Charge storage capacity to three.

UNLOCK REQUIREMENTS: Complete 40 side missions.

COST: 1800 XP

PRECISION ENHANCED

Precision Enhanced increases the time dilation and zoom during Cole's Precision aiming mode.

UNLOCK REQUIREMENTS: Complete 50 side missions.

COST: 2100 XP

BLAST SHARD SENSE

Blast Shard Sense indicates the nearest Blast Shard on the edge of the minimap whenever Cole pings for electric sources.

UNLOCK REQUIREMENTS: Complete 60 side missions.

COST: 2500 XP

Bolts

MAGNUM BOLT

The Magnum Bolt is one of the most powerful Bolts available to Cole, but also one of the slowest.

UNLOCK REQUIREMENT: 10 Head Shock stunts & Champion Karma rank.

COST: 1200 XP

BOLT STREAM

The Bolt Stream unleashes a continuous series of condensed electric clusters and continues to fire while **R1** is held down.

UNLOCK REQUIREMENT: 10 Stick It To The Man stunts & Hero Karma rank.

COST: 2800 XP

Blasts

GRAVITON BLAST

Lift targets into the air and leave them temporarily vulnerable with this attack. Although not very damaging by itself, the Gravitation Blast is very effective when combined with other attacks.

UNLOCK REQUIREMENTS: A Rubber Rocket stunt & Champion Karma rank.

COST: 1200 XP

SHATTER BLAST

The Shatter Blast is an ice-based attack where Cole creates a collection of ice spikes, then blasts them at his target.

UNLOCK REQUIREMENTS: Choose Kuo in the Storm the Fort mission & Hero Karma rank.

COST: 2800 XP

Grenades

STICKY GRENADE

For an explosion Cole's foe is sure to never forget, use the Sticky Grenade. This long-range Grenade sticks to its target until it explodes. To keep it from sticking to a target, hold down ⓞ to make the grenade bounce off a wall or person.

UNLOCK REQUIREMENTS: Five Enviro Kill stunts & Guardian Karma rank.

COST: 1400 XP

ICE GRENADE

The Ice Grenade creates a cluster of ice spikes upon detonation. It doesn't have a wide area of effect, but it does a good job of knocking away targets caught in its path, giving Cole a little space.

UNLOCK REQUIREMENTS: Choose Kuo in the Storm the Fort mission & Champion Karma rank.

COST: 2600 XP

Rockets

REDIRECT ROCKET

The Redirect Rocket can be used two ways, as a standard rocket or as a homing strike. To have the Redirect Rocket follow a specific target, hit an object or enemy with a Bolt attack while the Rocket is mid-flight. This then causes the Redirect Rocket to adjust its flight to hit the same location as the Bolt.

UNLOCK REQUIREMENTS: Five Hit Flying Enemy stunts & Guardian Karma rank.

COST: 2000 XP

FREEZE ROCKET

The Freeze Rocket is sure to stop enemies in their tracks. This ball of subzero gas instantly freezes a target on contact and leaves them as a fragile, frozen shell.

UNLOCK REQUIREMENTS: Choose Kuo in the Storm the Fort mission & Hero Karma rank.

COST: 4100

Issue #0

Insider's Guide
to New Marais

Retaking
New Marais

User-Generated
Content

NSA Intel

Extras

Misc. Powers

ICE LAUNCH

The Ice Launch uses a frozen column of ice to lift Cole into the air. It raises Cole higher than a super jump.

UNLOCK REQUIREMENTS: Choose Kuo in the Storm the Fort mission & Champion Karma rank.

COST: 2400 XP

FROST SHIELD

An ice-powered shield that protects Cole from general attacks, the Frost Shield is an extra layer of defense.

UNLOCK REQUIREMENTS: Choose Kuo in the Storm the Fort mission & Hero Karma rank.

COST: 2500 XP

Ionic Powers

IONIC FREEZE

Ionic Freeze is an Ionic power that turns surrounding targets into blocks of ice. Waves of jagged ice move out from the ground in this terrifying attack. This frozen force only harms enemies, leaving citizens and allies unscathed.

UNLOCK REQUIREMENTS: Choose Kuo in the Storm the Fort mission & Guardian Karma rank.

Karmic Boosts

CIVILIAN SAFETY

As part of Cole's Good Karma, he gains boosts that help him continue to protect civilians. Civilian Safety makes it so the people of New Marais take almost no damage from Cole's attacks.

UNLOCK REQUIREMENTS: Guardian Karma rank.

GROUP HEAL

When Cole performs a Pulse Heal, he heals just one downed person. With Group Heal, Cole heals the targeted person and any surrounding injured people.

UNLOCK REQUIREMENTS: Champion Karma rank.

BOLT RECHARGE

Cole's energy meter recharges slightly after hitting an enemy with any Bolt attack.

UNLOCK REQUIREMENTS: Hero Karma rank.

Bolts

SKULL BOLT

The Skull Bolt gives Cole a critical-hit explosion for every successful headshot.

UNLOCK REQUIREMENT: Five Hit Clueless Enemy stunts & Outlaw Karma rank.

COST: 1200 XP

SCYTHE BOLT

Launch five connected balls of electricity to clothesline an enemy with the Scythe Bolt. It's extremely powerful and lets Cole eliminate clustered enemies with one shot.

UNLOCK REQUIREMENT: A 4-in-1 Blow stunt & Infamous Karma rank.

COST: 2800 XP

Blasts

PUNCH BLAST

The Punch Blast has a much narrower area of effect than the standard Blast. However, it is extremely powerful and more effective at staggering or knocking down enemies.

UNLOCK REQUIREMENTS: A Blast Party stunt & Outlaw Karma rank.

COST: 1200 XP

NIGHTMARE BLAST

The Nightmare Blast is unlike any other Blast power in Cole's possession. This attack surrounds targets with a cloud of ash and smoke, blinding and disorienting them. It leaves enemies very vulnerable to subsequent attacks.

UNLOCK REQUIREMENTS: Choose Nix in the Storm the Fort mission & Infamous Karma rank.

COST: 2400 XP

Grenades

DOUBLE GRENADE

After detonating once, the Double Grenade bounces upward and explodes a second time.

UNLOCK REQUIREMENTS: A CARnage stunt & Thug Karma rank.

COST: 1400 XP

NAPALM GRENADE

The Napalm Grenade is a vicious display of power. This grenade explodes on impact, giving no time for targets to escape. Victims are thrown skyward when exposed to the Napalm Grenade's flaming shockwave.

UNLOCK REQUIREMENTS: Choose Nix in the Storm the Fort mission & Outlaw Karma rank.

COST: 2800 XP

Rockets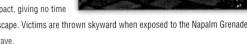

TRIPWIRE ROCKET

The Tripwire Rocket is actually two high yield charges connected by a sensitive tether. It can clothesline clustered enemies, letting Cole kill two foes with one rocket.

UNLOCK REQUIREMENTS: Choose Nix in the Storm the Fort mission & a Rocket Party stunt & Thug Karma rank.

COST: 2000 XP

HELLFIRE ROCKETS

Hellfire Rockets are a series of explosive missiles that pound into a target or continue to strike clustered enemies for stacked damage.

UNLOCK REQUIREMENTS: Choose Nix in the Storm the Fort mission & Infamous Karma rank.

COST: 4100 XP

Misc. Powers

FIREBIRD STRIKE

The Firebird Strike launches Cole forward at rapid speed, generally ending his flight with a concussive explosion. This ability is useful when Cole needs to follow targets or when he wants to escape from a firefight.

UNLOCK REQUIREMENTS: Choose Nix in the Storm the Fort mission & Outlaw Karma rank.

COST: 2500 XP

SPIKERS

Spikers are small swamp creatures that Cole has encountered before in New Marais. As part of Cole's Evil Karma, he can summon a squad of these monsters to fight by his side.

UNLOCK REQUIREMENTS: Choose Nix in the Storm the Fort mission & Infamous Karma rank.

COST: 3000 XP

Ionic Powers

IONIC DRAIN

The Ionic Drain uses an Ionic Charge to drain all surrounding citizens and enemies of their life force. The energy then goes directly into Cole to recharge his energy meter and health.

UNLOCK REQUIREMENTS: Choose Nix in the Storm the Fort mission & Thug Karma rank.

Karmic Boosts

BYSTANDER BONUS

Being evil does have benefits, including the Bystander Bonus, which gives Cole 1 XP for every civilian defeated.

UNLOCK REQUIREMENTS: Thug Karma rank.

BOLT CHAIN

The Bolt Chain lets Cole damage more enemies with fewer attacks. Targets hit with any Bolt attack cause an electric chain to reach out to nearby foes and objects.

UNLOCK REQUIREMENTS: Outlaw Karma rank.

BIO LEECH OVERLOAD

The Bio Leech Overload rewards Cole for sucking the life out of targets. After performing a Bio Leech, Cole has unlimited electricity for a short time.

UNLOCK REQUIREMENTS: Infamous Karma rank.

INSIDER'S GUIDE TO NEW MARAIS

Spread over two islands, New Marais' diverse neighborhoods contain some interesting flavor; from the neon-soaked Red Light District in Villa Cochon, to the slums of Ascension Parish, to the still-submerged houses of Flood Town. Somewhere in this city, Dr. Wolfe has the answers Cole needs—especially the most important one of all. How can they stop The Beast?

It was easy for the rest of the country to write off New Marais as a lost cause after the flood and rampant looting. But despite the anarchy that followed, the city managed to put itself back together—but only just barely.

Even though police still patrol the city's streets, the real power lies with the Militia. Led by billionaire industrialist Joseph Bertrand III, they have steadily increased their grasp on the city by rallying people behind their xenophobic cause.

Expose the oppressive Militia's secret agenda and gather their opponents to Cole's side. Nothing can be allowed to stand in the way of destroying The Beast.

Cole is ready to leave the tragic memories of Empire City behind him. No longer his home, it has nothing more to offer him in his quest to defeat The Beast. He looks to the future, preparing to leave with Zeke and Kuo on the last evacuation ship. The destination is New Marais to the south, where they hope to find Dr. Wolfe—the inventor of the Ray Sphere.

Suddenly, a massive explosion rocks the center of Empire City. Fireballs erupt skyward, raining debris, and the city Cole once called home is consumed in flames. Despite Kuo's insistence that they leave, he leaps from the deck to the pier below.

Cole can't see the source of the chaos from where he landed on the pier. Use the right analog stick and follow the on-screen instructions to look up, then left.

INVESTIGATE THE EXPLOSION

Heading back to the docks along the pier, a crowd of desperate civilians thrashes against the locked gates. Trapped on the other side with some horrible presence approaching, they need Cole to blast the gate open.

Hold **L1** to aim and press **R1** to fire electric bolts at the gate's lock in the center.

As Cole starts sprinting past the panicked masses, a series of explosions in the distance brings down several buildings. Out of the flames, a bus is sent soaring through the air and into one of the cargo ships waiting to depart. As the ship sinks into the bay, the pier shudders and the planks ripple from the force of the city's destruction.

SHOOT FIRST, ASK QUESTIONS LATER

Arriving at the end of the pier, Cole can finally make out the multi-story silhouette of the towering, but nevertheless distinctly human-shaped, source of the disturbance. Aim and fire Cole's bolts at the creature to get its attention.

Turning to face the source of the attacks, the monstrosity knocks Cole off his feet with the twisted remains of a large statue. Cole gets to his feet only to turn and find himself face-to-face with his greatest fear: The Beast.

PREMATURE CONFRONTATION

Merely irritated, The Beast focuses its energy to create a swirling vortex that draws in everyone and everything around it. Cole manages to stay airborne but is still vulnerable to the pull of The Beast. Continue to assault The Beast with bolts but remember to move away when it extends its arms in an attempt to suck Cole in. Blasting loose large, molten chunks of the monster's form secures Cole only a brief breather as he drops back down to the pier. Trapped by the flames behind him and cornered by The Beast, Cole has no choice but to unleash his potent Ionic Storm. Do this by pressing down on the d-pad.

There's no time to lose, so fire off Cole's bolts as quickly as possible at The Beast. Keep an eye on its hands as it gathers its energies for a massive attack, and step clear when it comes crashing down.

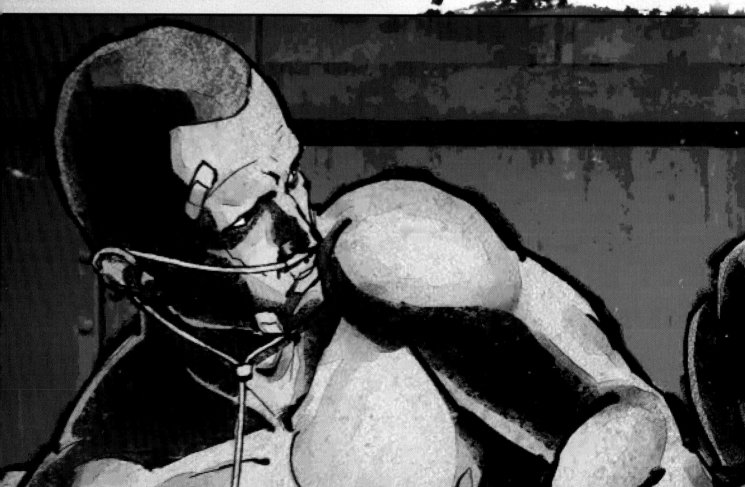

RETURN TO THE SHIP

The Beast is blasted into submission and collapses, but there's no time to celebrate. The violent exchange has strained the pier to its structural limit, and it begins to break apart.

Cole must sprint back to the ship before the pier collapses and drops him into the lethal waters below. Press ⊗ to leap safely over the gaps in the pier and onto the ship's deck.

A FISTFUL OF COLE

Before he can rejoin Zeke and Kuo, Cole is seized mid-air by an invisible force. Cole is easily trapped within the grasp of The Beast while suspended and helpless.

As Cole is crushed by its grip, he can only strike out blindly with his bolts. Press **R1** repeatedly to try to stun The Beast and make it release its hold on Cole. After landing a few solid blows, Cole can once again summon his Ionic Storm.

The massive effort to combat The Beast leaves Cole drained and near death. Unconscious for days aboard ship, Cole awakens to discover that his efforts were in vain—The Beast had reconstituted itself and annihilated what remained of Empire City.

With nowhere to go but onward, their boat fled down the coast to New Marais. As Cole, Zeke, and Kuo traveled south, so did The Beast, leaving a trail of destruction as town after town fell in its wake.

With New Marais in their sights, Kuo acquires a smaller boat to sneak in through the swamps. The entire city has been under lockdown since a group simply called The Militia seized power. The only way in is past their blockade, and it's up to Cole to break it.

Cole, Kuo, and Zeke cautiously approach the New Marais coast. Ahead, Kuo spots the Militia blockade and the artillery preventing their docking. Now equipped with Zeke's invention—the Amp—Cole disembarks and heads toward the Militia's mortar emplacement.

THE AMP

The Amp provides Cole with a melee attack suitable for close-range encounters when his enemies draw in too close for electric bolt attacks. Press ◎ to attack with the Amp.

APPROACH THE ARTILLERY

The closer Cole gets to the mortars, the more chunks of the rotting pier collapse under his feet. To safely cross, Cole must first jump and then hold **R1** mid-air to use his Static Thrusters and slow his descent.

STATIC THRUSTERS

Static Thrusters allow Cole to safely extend the distance of his leaps over hazardous obstacles. They also allow him to slow his descent for a precise landing from great heights.

SLEEP WITH THE FISHES

The nature of Cole's electrical abilities means that he cannot come into contact with bodies of water. Doing so shorts out his abilities, and damages him in the process. If Cole finds himself submerged, there is only a limited amount of time for him to get back on dry land before his light goes out for good.

BREAKING INTO NEW MARAIS

BEATING GREETINGS

Once Cole gets back on dry land, a pair of Militia riflemen wastes no time opening fire on him. Test out the Amp and beat them into submission without breaking a sweat.

Swiftly dispatch two more Militia on the metal platform ahead. Zeke radios in to see if Cole's okay. If Cole has taken too much damage, he can both heal and recover energy by draining any nearby sources of electricity.

Approach the power meter with the blue lights at the edge of the platform. Stand close and hold **L2** to drain it and replenish Cole.

ELECTRIC DRAIN

Press **L3** or **L2** to send out a pulse that detects and highlights electrical sources. Such sources near Cole emit a brief flashing electric field as an indication, and these are shown on the mini-map as blue lightning bolt icons.

LOWER THE BRIDGE

With the platform secure, there's still the raised bridge to address. Kuo directs Cole's attention to the generator across the water. He can lower the bridge by recharging the generator, but he must proceed with caution. The Militia contingent standing in his path is mixed in among the innocent civilians. These desperate and homeless victims of the floods have set up camp in this ramshackle shantytown.

SHANTYTOWN SUFFERING

Charging the generator lowers the bridge without any risk to the refugees. Overcharging the generator lowers the bridge at the cost of triggering explosions that consume Militia guards and innocent civilians alike. Regardless of Cole's decision, he encounters critically injured civilians lying in agony as he crosses the bridge.

GOOD KARMA OPPORTUNITY: MEDICAL EMERGENCY

Medical Emergencies are the first of several varieties of Karma Opportunities that Cole encounters in New Marais. Icons on the mini-map identify the kind of situation and type of Karma earned. A blue circle borders opportunities that earn Good Karma, while those netting Evil Karma are red.

Cole can channel his powers to heal the afflicted with a Pulse Heal. Approach an injured civilian and hold **R1** to lock onto him or her. While locked, hold ⬆ to charge up a depolarizing pulse to restore the natural rhythm of the person's heart. This compassionate act earns Cole Good Karma in addition to 3 XP (Healing Touch).

OUT OF THE FRYING PAN

Even if Cole indulges in his evil impulses, he can still help others—as a way to help himself. Heal the wounded for the XP, then swiftly execute them so Cole's Karma level doesn't drift too far toward good. This trick also works with Abductions and Muggings.

SPARE THE STRICKEN

Those poor displaced refugees have suffered long enough under the oppression of the Militia, cut off from aid and forced to scrape out a meager existence on the fringe of New Marais. Keep a close eye on the row of colored lights on top of the generator. Once it reaches the green level, immediately stop firing bolts. Charging it further triggers an explosive overload when it reaches the red.

Following the compass marker to the mortar emplacement puts Cole in the patrol path of several heavily armed Militia troops. Take the high ground by climbing or using the ladder to catch them off-guard. Be ready to sidestep incoming rockets when their burning exhaust lights up the area.

With the immense power at his fingertips, Cole has no use for waiting. If he's to defeat The Beast, he can't be afraid to use any means necessary.

If anything, any bystanders caught in the blast would receive the swift release of death that so many in Empire City were deprived of. Continue firing bolts until the generator lights up red, and then revel in the ensuing chaos.

SINK THE FERRYBOAT

Beyond the camp, a ferryboat outfitted to the teeth with mortars bombards a wooden bridge with heavy shells. An enemy on the top deck is equipped with

a rocket launcher while a pair of rifle-bearing grunts opens fire from a pier.

Target the volatile gas tank on the right side of the pier and watch as the ferryboat balloons

into an immense fireball and sinks. With the path clear, Cole can leap from the floating wreckage to a series of wooden barriers to a nearby metal platform. Take a moment to refill Cole's Power Cores by draining the high voltage stations.

A GRIND IS A TERRIBLE THING TO WASTE

The blinking orange beacon here signals one anchored end of a thick, low-gauge metal cable. Cole can travel swiftly across these Grindwires simply by jumping onto them.

GRINDWIRES

Pressing forward increases Cole's speed for even greater jumps. These powered cables are among the fastest ways that Cole can travel. Not only does he reach impressive top speeds, but he can also turn

back to reverse course on a dime. However, if the power is out in the area, Cole must run along the cables like any other surface.

Speed across and arrive safely on another metal platform. The Militia has installed a stationary gun turret here that can make short work of Cole with its high rate of fire. Take cover behind objects by moving close and pressing ⊚.

TANKS FOR THE ASSIST

While using cover, aim and fire at the gas tanks littering the area nearby. The resulting explosion is sure to neutralize the gunner but leave the turret intact. Turrets left operational can be manned again easily, so the wisest course of action is to destroy them.

WHACK-A-COLE

Although Cole is relatively safe behind cover, he is exposed when aiming from this position. Adjust the camera to center it on his target to keep his exposure to a minimum before attacking.

TURRET TAKEDOWNS

Move close to a turret and press **R1** to disable it. Cole sends a surge of electricity into the mechanism, igniting the gunpowder and causing the entire machine to explode into pieces. He earns 10 XP for each Disabled Turret.

Proceed ahead to the next Grindwire and ride it over the water, but be prepared for the cables to end just short of safety. Time Cole's jump and guide him onto the next metal platform with Static Thrusters.

Watch the right side as Cole nimbly jumps between the yellow pipes toward the next platform. Cole should reach it before the guards in that area are drawn to the commotion. With the element of surprise, Cole can eliminate the two guards before they have a chance to man the turret. From here, Cole can finally make it into New Marais via a final Grindwire.

REWARD: 500 XP

After docking, Kuo disembarks to lead Cole to Wolfe. Unfortunately, Wolfe informs them over the radio that the Militia has already been to his lab. They ransacked it and absconded with the hidden Blast Core intended for Cole.

RETRIEVE THE BLAST CORE

Kuo wastes no time taking point, so Cole needs to follow close as they journey to Wolfe's lab. She appears as a waypoint on the mini-map. It seems word of Cole's arrival has already reached the Militia on the main island. At the first intersection, Cole is immediately identified and targeted for termination.

SECOND STORY ENDINGS

Acquire the targets positioned on the second-floor balconies. Be prepared to sidestep rocket launcher attacks from the closest aggressor.

EXPLOSIVE COVER-UP

Use the various vehicles as cover from the rifle fire, but be prepared to move at a moment's notice. The explosive impact of an incoming rocket is more than enough to ignite a car's gas tank and harm Cole as he's knocked back by the blast.

Fight explosives with explosives by launching Cole's grenades. Aim with **L1** and press ⬤ to hurl the explosive balls of electrical energy. After disposing of the rocket-launching goon first, eliminate the other two Militia riflemen.

GRENADES

Cole throws his grenades in arcs at his targets, requiring him to account for distance when adjusting the height of his aim. Because the grenades explode after a slight delay, be sure to lead Cole's targets so they move into the imminent explosion.

BRINGING DOWN THE HOUSE

Don't put Cole or any bystanders in unnecessary danger by trying to trade shots with the riflemen out in the open. Instead, duck under their balcony and blast away from the bottom.

The Militia can't get a bead on Cole while he's directly beneath, and it's only a matter of time before the balcony gives out from under the Militia riflemen's feet. For his creativity, Cole is awarded a bonus 10 XP (Enviro Kill).

HAVING A BLAST

Kuo then ducks into an alley where a pickup truck is blocking the way. There's no time to phone a tow truck, but fortunately Cole's electric blast is the next best thing. Hold **L1** to aim and press ⊗ to fire off a wave of electric energy to knock the truck aside.

BLAST

Cole's electric blast is a versatile ability for both offense and defense. In addition to clearing obstacles, it's useful for flooring enemies, stripping their shields, or deflecting rockets.

ROOFTOP RUMBLE

Beyond the alley, three more Militia open fire from balcony positions. After taking them out, Wolfe contacts Kuo in desperate need of assistance.

Rushing to assist him, she tasks Cole with retrieving the Blast Core from the Militia guarding it on the nearby rooftops. Ascend and take them out, noting that several soldiers fire from protected positions atop watchtowers.

NON-STOP FLIGHTS

Keeping the Militia off their game is as easy as knocking them off their feet with a blast. Besides stunning Cole's enemies, a handy application during high elevation combat is to simply blast the opposition off the roof down to the streets below—provided they're close enough to the edge. Each freefalling enemy Cole takes out this way nets him 15 XP (Watch Your Step).

As Cole approaches the glowing Blast Core, a cry for help rings out from the alley below. Someone is being mugged!

GOOD KARMA OPPORTUNITY: MUGGINGS

To stop a mugging in progress, simply incapacitate the muggers by any means at Cole's disposal. Be careful not to injure the victim, or Cole risks generating more Evil Karma than Good earned for this selfless act. Success is rewarded with 5 XP (Hostage Rescued).

To obtain the Blast Core, walk up to the glowing crate marked on the mini-map and press **R1** when close enough. Cole briefly manages to speak to Kuo and Wolfe before a massive fireball erupts at the lab, lighting up the rooftop several blocks away and sending waves of explosive projectiles arcing through the sky.

RUSH TO WOLFE'S LAB

Quickly leap onto the nearest Grindwire and speed to the lab. Ensure maximum speed by using Cole's Static Thrusters to glide over the gaps between Grindwires. Watch out for Militia patrols on the rooftops when Cole closes the distance.

MAD SCIENCE 101

Arriving at the rooftop ruins of the lab, Cole finds Wolfe trapped beneath rubble. After being rescued, Wolfe admits to Cole that Kessler had convinced him of the threat The Beast posed. To that end, he developed the Ray Sphere that gave Cole his powers.

Realizing that Kessler had been right in his motives but wrong in his methods, Wolfe still believes that Cole needs to expand his abilities to defeat The Beast. He then introduces Cole to the Ray Field Inhibitor (RFI).

Essentially an anti-Ray Sphere, the RFI drains away powers rather than gives them. However, it relies on Blast Cores to power it. These glowing batteries for the energy powering genetic mutation are scattered around the city. Each of them releases this energy into the nearest Conduit.

Cole wastes no time harnessing the Blast Core's energy to expand his powers and become stronger, but he blacks out in the process from the strain. He awakens to the sight of Zeke warding off the Militia with his pistol. Zeke informs him that Kuo is already chasing after the foes who took Wolfe.

RISING TO THE OCCASION

Still unsteady after the massive infusion of energy, Cole senses he has a new power that Zeke encourages him to exercise. To activate the Kinetic Pulse, hold **R2** near an object and press ⊗ to launch it. The parking lot across the street makes an excellent training area, complete with cars and a lone Militiaman. Drop down to street level and use the Kinetic Pulse to lift a car and pummel Cole's target, earning 15 XP for taking down an enemy with a thrown object (Special Delivery).

Traveling to the waypoint that appears on the mini-map presents Cole with his first Evil Karma Opportunity.

Kuo radios Cole to suggest that he head to a rooftop in the northwest region of the island. From this location, he can salvage some of the fallout from the explosion at Wolfe's lab before the Militia acquires it.

EVIL KARMA OPPORTUNITY: SUPPRESS POLICE

Three man teams of the New Marais police force go on patrol regularly. Cole can feed the chaos of the city by striking them down in the line of duty, earning him Evil Karma.

MISSIONS

New missions are marked on the map with an exclamation point icon. White icons represent story missions. Yellow icons indicate Side Missions. Green icons are User-Generated Content (UGC) missions.

LOST AND FOUND

When Cole arrives, Kuo is nowhere to be found, but she radios in with instructions to secure a messenger pigeon. While Wolfe worked as an informer within the First Sons, he used these pigeons to relay reports to his NSA contact—Kuo. When the Militia destroyed his lab, the pigeons fled and are now flying freely all around the city.

DEAD DROPS

The dead drop recordings intended for Kuo are now up for grabs. Throughout New Marais, Cole may spot pigeons carrying audio files that shed light on the truth behind the First Sons.

The pigeons are indicated on the mini-map by blue bird icons. The blinking red beacons on their parcels also highlight them as they circle overhead. Shoot them down and press **R1** when close to them on the ground to acquire the recording and net Cole 50 XP.

BAG THE BIRD

The pigeon Kuo wants Cole to track down is circling the nearby clock tower. Follow its icon on the mini-map to that area. Kuo points out that Cole needn't kill the bird and can use his electric blast to knock it out of the sky.

Before dropping down to street level to retrieve the data, Zeke suggests that Cole should descend in style. Cole can perform a Thunder Drop by pressing ⊙ while falling to strike the ground upon landing with an intense burst of electrical energy.

WATCH THAT DROP

Pigeons don't always land at street level, depending on their position when Cole knocks them out. If it becomes difficult to determine a bird's location based on the mini-map, try getting to higher ground and then look for balconies or ledges where it might have landed for the telltale red light blinking on its collar.

Walk up to the pigeon and press **R1** to retrieve the recording. After it finishes, Kuo also asks Cole to try to track down some Rayacite. These glowing rocks were created when exposed to the radiation from the Ray Sphere and appear as smaller versions of the Blast Core.

▮▮▮▮ GATHER WOLFE'S RAYACITE

Kuo knows a great deal about Rayacite because she worked closely with an NSA contact in Empire City, John White. Both of them were identified by the government as having the same Conduit gene as Cole that makes them receptive to the Ray Sphere's radiation.

Known to Cole as Blast Shards, these rocks were all stored in Wolfe's lab before it went up in flames. Now they're scattered all throughout the city, often in hard-to-reach places. Their curious magnetic properties cause them to stick to the sides of buildings, so be prepared to work to reach them.

BLAST SHARDS

Cole can increase his maximum number of Power Cores by collecting Blast Shards. Once he collects enough, a new Power Core is added, which increases the maximum amount of energy that Cole's body can store at once.

To locate Blast Shards, click **L3** to display them on the mini-map as blue circles. Each Blast Shard found rewards Cole with 5 XP, and he earns an additional 5 XP when another Power Core is added.

The nearest Blast Shard is on the third floor of a building to the southwest facing the tower.

A second is along the side of building's fourth floor opposite the first. Scale the building face to the right and climb up to find a third Blast Shard. Upon collecting the third, Cole increases his Power Core total by one.

REWARD: 500 XP

While getting accustomed to his greater capacity, Cole is contacted by Zeke. During their last visit to New Marais shortly after the flood, Zeke got into a spot of trouble with some shady characters. Now these questionable associates have reached out to Zeke to seek the services of Cole—whom they refer to as "The Electric Man."

Meet with Zeke in the southwest at an abandoned boat lot to get more details on what exactly this favor is.

KARMA'S A BITCH

Demand for Cole and his abilities are at an all-time high since word of his arrival in New Marais has spread. Upon meeting with Zeke, he reports that both a cop and a junkie have sought him out because of his association with Cole. He now has a choice between two nearby Side Missions.

KARMA SIDE MISSIONS

Some districts offer the choice between two different Side Missions—one good, one evil. Completing either wrests control from the Militia and secures the district. However, once Cole chooses one, he is then locked out of completing the other.

Good Side Missions appear as blue variations of the normal Side Mission marker, while Evil Side Missions show as red variants. Many of these missions are only accessible when Cole meets the Good or Evil Karma requirements to accept it.

BODY HEALER OR SOUL STEALER?

The choice Cole makes between these two Side Missions can push his Karma significantly in either direction. To assist the police officer and earn Good Karma, continue to "Good Samaritan" (below). To help out the junkie and earn Evil Karma, continue to "Taking Out the Trash" (on the next page).

GOOD SAMARITAN

A lone officer waiting for backup that might never arrive is hoping Cole's heroic reputation isn't just hearsay. He reports that Militia members are rounding up and executing people they suspect of being deviants. He's outnumbered and outgunned, so his only hope rests with Cole.

Turning to the direction of the commotion, Cole sees three hostages being forced to step off the roof to their deaths by Militia members. Defeat the executioners before they can dispatch the helpless hostages.

HEAL THE CIVILIANS

A number of wounded victims lay dying near the mansion down the street. Head to the waypoints marking their locations on the mini-map and Pulse Heal them. The first two can be found along the path leading from the main gate that runs alongside the right of the building.

3 of 3 Hostages

A LONG WALK OFF A SHORT ROOF

After resuscitating them, continue to the rear of the property, where another casualty of blind persecution rests. Upon reviving him, voices from the rooftop above bark marching orders.

SOLE SURVIVOR

At least one hostage must survive to complete this mission. If all the hostages are lost, Cole fails.

ASSIST THE OFFICERS

Having secured the mansion, Cole is directed by Kuo to a firefight down the street that has erupted between Militia and the police. Come to the aid of law enforcement at the waypoint on the mini-map.

SHOCKING SHACKLES

Defeat the three Militiamen there, then lock onto one of them by holding **R1**. While locked on, press ◎ to Arc Restrain one per Kuo's request, so he can be interrogated later. Now that Cole's done the heavy lifting, the cops can take it from here.

TAKING OUT THE TRASH

A sharply dressed gentleman waits for Cole by the front of the nearby bait and tackle store. He claims to have discovered a pair of brothers working as Militia spies. One lies injured behind the store by the water.

DRAIN TO SUSTAIN

Lock onto him when close by holding **R1**, then press ◎ repeatedly to perform a Bio Leech. This ability allows Cole to refill his Power Cores by harvesting the life energy of his victims. It garners him Evil Karma and earns 1 XP (Drain).

LEECHING LIABILITY

The Bio Leech is a frightening ability that strikes fear into the hearts of ordinary citizens, but Cole's enemies aren't nearly as faint of heart. While performing a Bio Leech, Cole is still vulnerable to damage. When Cole is near death in combat, consider it a last resort only when no electrical sources are near.

The second brother is located near a shack, just across the water. Hold **R1** to bring up a photo of him to refresh Cole's memory. Direct Cole toward the waypoint on the mini-map. Once he gets close enough, his target cries out for help and summons assistance from a waiting cadre of Militia.

Prioritize Cole's targets and eliminate the rocket-launching Militiamen first. Once all of them have neutralized, proceed to the grassy clearing to the left of the shack where the second brother cowers in fear. Eliminate him to complete the mission.

REWARD: 100 XP

An array of Side Missions scattered throughout the city are now available to Cole. Bring up the map at any time with **Select** to locate the Side Mission nearest Cole. Although entirely optional, it's necessary to complete Side Missions to wrest control of New Marais away from the Militia.

All of the game's Side Missions and the requirements to unlock them are listed in a dedicated section of this guide, on pg. 120.

SIDE MISSIONS UNLOCKED

New Marais Tea Party, Tourist Trap, Overcharge—New Marais, Going Overboard

EVIL KARMA OPPORTUNITY: SILENCE STREET PERFORMERS

After Cole finishes up, Zeke complains about a street performer raising a racket with his bucket drumming. He considers it a favor to himself and the other annoyed citizens if Cole can shut him up. Silence the drummer with as much or as little force as desired to earn Evil Karma.

EVOLUTION

Kuo is banking on Cole developing his powers—and fast—to counter the ever-looming threat of The Beast. She directs Cole to the eastern end of the island, adjacent to the aqueduct separating Ascension Parish from the St. Charles Cemetery.

SIX SHOOTER

Based on previous conversations with Wolfe, Kuo believes that the key to Cole unlocking further abilities requires more than just the Blast Core. In order to broaden his powers, Cole must stress his body through practice and mastering his current abilities. Kuo has already spotted a Militia squad in the neighborhood, shown by the waypoint on the mini-map.

GOOD KARMA OPPORTUNITY: ABDUCTIONS

En route to the marked targets, Cole runs into an abduction that is under way. An armed Militia unit is escorting some innocent civilians who are being detained under trumped-up charges. Neutralize the guards and free the wrongfully imprisoned victims to earn Good Karma and 5 XP for each hostage rescued.

THREE FOR THE PRICE OF ONE

After defeating at least six of the Militia hunkered down by the cul-de-sac, Cole can purchase the Pincer Bolt using his accumulated XP. Press right on the d-pad to bring up the Powers Menu.

Make sure **R1** is highlighted, then press ⊗ to access the list of upgrades. Highlight Pincer Bolt and press ⊗ to purchase it for 400 XP. Exit the Powers Menu and try out the Pincer Bolt.

OLDIE, BUT A GOODIE

Zeke compliments Cole on it but comments that the standard Bolt seemed more "classic." Fortunately, Cole can easily switch between powers using the Quick Swap menu. Hold left on the d-pad to open it and tap **R1** to cycle through the available Bolt powers. Switch to the normal Alpha Bolt and fire one off, then switch back and fire a Pincer Bolt to complete the mission.

REWARD: 500 XP

FINISHER ATTACKS

Finisher Attacks can now be purchased with XP from the Powers screen. They give Cole the ability execute a devastating finishing blow against enemies when using his Amp. Fill the meter in the lower-left corner of the screen by landing melee hits in quick succession. Press ⚠ when the meter is halfway filled and its icon lights up to performer a finisher attack.

Kuo still hasn't turned up any leads on Wolfe's location, and things are looking grim. She thinks their best hope is trying to kidnap Bertrand—the leader of the Militia—at a rally he's holding at St. Ignatius Cathedral. He's sure to know where Wolfe is being held.

BERTRAND TAKES THE STAGE

Bertrand has assembled an impressive crowd before St. Ignatius, comprised of a varied mix of diehard followers and curious onlookers. He minces no words as he addresses them all from his podium.

He is convinced that the devil walks among the citizens of New Marais and that it is the greatest threat their city has ever known. This demon that levies the accusations against is none other than Cole.

Bertrand's hate-mongering puts Zeke ill at ease, and he motions for them to leave. However, Cole is quick to remind him that they can't risk the chance of Bertrand breaking Wolfe and extracting his vital knowledge.

SPEAK OF THE DEVILS

While Bertrand touts his Militia as the only thing standing between the people and the freaks, one such creature is spotted in the scaffolding overhead. A panic spreads through the crowd, and people begin fleeing in every direction, terrified and desperate. Cole now finds himself dead center in the middle of a furious fracas between Militia and Swamp Monsters.

Eliminate all the Swamp Monsters with extreme prejudice. Pepper them with long-range electric attacks while Cole is still beyond their reach, then switch to melee tactics as they draw nearer.

SWAMP MONSTERS

These fearsome creatures are the most common variety of the Corrupted. Simple-minded and vicious, they rely on base animal instincts and rush headlong upon acquiring a target.

Their mutated claw appendages are used to bludgeon their victims with wide, powerful swipes. The amount of damage they deal is compounded when a group of them corners Cole.

PRIORITY TARGETS

Although specifically commanded by Bertrand to cope with the Swamp Monster attack, the Militia at the cathedral do not hesitate to pull the trigger when Cole moves into their sights.

Successfully completing the mission only requires that Cole defeat the attacking Swamp Monsters. Lure the creatures away from the Militia to avoid putting Cole into the line of fire.

ESCAPING IN STYLE

Once Cole has taken care of the Swamp Monsters, Zeke urgently points out that Bertrand is escaping via his personal limo. This could be the only chance Cole gets at finding out where Wolfe is, so it's vital that Cole prevents Bertrand from escaping.

CATCHING A RIDE THE HARD WAY

Chase after the waypoint marker on the mini-map showing the limo location. Cole fails the mission if he loses Bertrand, and the screen displays a countdown indicating how much time Cole has left to close the gap.

Once Cole is within striking distance of the limo, follow the on-screen prompt to press ⊗ and mount the limo. In the ensuing cutscene, Bertrand brushes off Cole's threats. Before Cole can make good on his words, the skid of the Militia helicopter appearing from behind clotheslines him.

THE WHIRLYBIRD GETS INFIRM

The helicopter unleashes its arsenal of twin machine guns and rocket pods at Cole. Move quickly to avoid being gunned down, and try to keep the clock tower between Cole and the helicopter.

HELO. GOODBYE.

It can be incredibly taxing to trade blows with the helicopter. Rather than exhaust Cole's energy trying to land attacks upon the nimble aerial adversary, there's a simple way to down the chopper in a single blow.

While out of the line of fire, use Cole's Kinetic Pulse to lift a car. As soon as the helo swings into view, launch the car at it and watch as both explode in a massive overhead fireball.

REWARD: 500 XP

SIDE MISSIONS UNLOCKED

The Sidekick, Gunboat Diplomacy, Masquerade

BOMB SCARE

Bertrand may have gotten away during Cole's encounter with the helicopter, but Zeke thinks he has a lead on Wolfe's location. A mysterious device made with advanced technology has been spotted at street level. Meet with his source in the southeast, down the street from the large plantation.

ADVERTISING THE THREAT

The wall across the street from the concerned citizen has drawn the attention of several bystanders. A conspicuous electronic device pulses with a purple light. As Cole approaches, it flashes increasingly quickly before exploding.

NO DRAIN, NO GAIN

The surviving informer locates another bomb down the alley just around the corner, as indicated on the mini-map. Rush to it as quickly as possible

before it goes off and deactivate the detonation mechanism. Hold **L2** to use Cole's Electric Drain to sap the bomb and disable its detonator.

Having disabled the threat, Cole takes a closer look and identifies the bomb's payload as a Blast Shard. Press **R1** next to it to retrieve the shard and add it to Cole's collection.

GOOD KARMA OPPORTUNITY: SAVE VICTIM FROM BOMB

This Blast Shard-powered bomb is the first of many scattered throughout the city by some unknown menace. Throughout New Marais, citizens from all walks of life are drawn to the flashing lights, unaware of the danger they represent.

Save these overly inquisitive onlookers by draining the bombs before they explode. Cole earns Good Karma and a Blast Shard for his noble efforts.

EVIL KARMA OPPORTUNITY: STEAL BLAST SHARD

Zeke radios in to Cole to point out a citizen across the street carrying a Blast Shard. Kuo cautions Cole that there are plenty to be found throughout the city without harming innocent civilians.

Nevertheless, the Blast Shards are too dangerous to be kept in the hands of an ignorant public. Increasing his Power Cores is the fastest way for Cole to expand his abilities and defeat the Beast.

The ends justify the means when the fate of the entire city is on the line. Neutralize the citizen and walk up to their collapsed form to claim their Blast Shard and earn Evil Karma.

SEE THE WORLD BURN

If Cole is feeling confident in his power, he can forgo the Blast Shard reward for defusing and instead gain Evil Karma by detonating the bomb himself by firing a bolt at it.

REWARD: 500 XP

WOLFE HUNT

Kuo has managed to track down Wolfe's interrogator, who's currently winning big at the blackjack tables. Unfortunately, she already called attention to herself when the interrogator made a pass at her.

STALK THE INTERROGATOR

Now it's up to Cole to keep tabs on the interrogator from the rooftops and watch for when he leaves the casino. An ideal observation position overlooking the casino marks the mission start point on the map.

THIS LITTLE LIGHT OF MINE

Cole waits for the interrogator's winning streak to dry up. The target exits the building at night with flashlight in hand—now it's time for Cole to give chase.

Stick to the rooftops and stay out of sight, or else risk spooking the target. Keep track of him by observing his marker on the mini-map and noting the bouncing beam of his flashlight as he travels.

CLEAR THE ROADBLOCKS

Once Cole has tracked the target to his final destination, Kuo is ready with a commandeered vehicle to extract Wolfe. Unsurprisingly, he's being held deep in Militia territory behind several roadblocks. Cole must clear the road of these obstructions if Kuo has any chance of maneuvering a vehicle out of the hot zone.

A waypoint on the mini-map directs Cole to the roadblock's location and turns into a flashing circle when he gets close enough. Eliminate all the Militia to clear the roadblock, then proceed to the next as indicated on the mini-map.

As Cole hurries down the street, a subterranean disruption moves past him with surprising speed, throwing up chunks of concrete along the way. It overtakes him, and he can see some sort of commotion ahead followed by explosions.

Cole arrives at the next checkpoint to find that someone or something has already beaten him to the punch. The roadblock's Militia are all lying dead on the ground by the burnt husks of several vehicles. As Cole draws closer to investigate, a new variety of Corrupted erupts from the concrete.

BOSS Ravager

Cole has only a split-second to avoid the Ravager's initial charge. Perform a dodge roll by pressing ⊙ while moving the left stick to either side.

Despite their common enemy, the Ravager shows no hesitation in attacking Cole. Keep a safe distance, because this Corrupted moves very quickly both above and below ground. It also spits a barrage of explosive acid missiles that inflict heavy damage. As soon as its jaws drip with green fluid, it's time for Cole to start taking cover.

This beast's armor protects it from Bolts, requiring the skilled application of Grenades and the Kinetic Pulse. Despite its strength, the Ravager reacts like a coward when taking damage, burrowing beneath the ground and disappearing from the mini-map.

UNDERGROUND SENSATION

Look for the telltale wake the Ravager leaves in the concrete while tunneling and anticipate when it emerges. If Cole loses complete track of the Ravager, head to a rooftop and wait for it to surface and reappear on the mini-map.

UNDER PRESSURE

Steer clear of the Ravager when it rears up on its hind legs, because this means it's about to pin Cole to the ground. Press **R1** repeatedly while pinned to blast the Ravager until it releases its hold.

PROTECT THE TRUCK

After felling the beast, Kuo instructs Cole to return to the safe house. She is waiting with Wolfe in a pickup truck that is tucked away in the alley. After Cole hops aboard the bed of the truck, there's only a brief moment for pleasantries before Militia backup arrives, forcing them to beat a hasty retreat.

FLATBED FIREWORKS

Target the beds of Militia trucks with Cole's grenades to quickly take out their occupants in a single blast. Try not to waste any, because Cole and the truck are vulnerable while he uses his Electric Drain to replenish his energy

CRUISE CONTROL

It seems like the entire Militia has come out in force. Pickup trucks loaded with Militia riflemen dart out of side streets and alleys as Cole passes.

Try not to get too caught up in eliminating pursuers, since each turn brings further reinforcements. The mini-map is a good indicator of imminent threats, such as clusters of Militia waiting at the next intersection.

Cole and his allies seem to have lost their pursuers, but suddenly a big rig truck comes out of nowhere to careen head-on into Cole's truck. In the chaos following the crash, the Militia takes Kuo away while Wolfe lays dead. Cole barely manages to drag himself into the safety of a storm drain before passing out.

REWARD: 500 XP

SIDE MISSIONS UNLOCKED

Change the Channel, Trick Photography, Those Who Trespass Against Us, Malpractice, Past Decisions

---

DESPERATE TIMES

Cole is still disoriented and discouraged as he returns to consciousness in the storm drain. Zeke is glad to hear his friend's voice, but Cole isn't in a mood to chitchat. Zeke cuts the conversation short but soon after contacts Cole, asking to meet when he has the chance to discuss some new intel he's discovered.

INSPECT THE SHACKS

Meet Zeke on a rooftop in the southern part of the island to find the mission marker and start the mission. Zeke reports that he's got a lead on Kuo's location. His sources claim she's being held in one of the old bootlegger shacks.

EVIL KARMA OPPORTUNITY: SILENCE PROTESTERS

En route to the bootlegger shacks in the swamplands, Cole encounters a group of citizens exercising their First Amendment right to freedom of assembly by expressing their discontent.

These rabble-rousers with picket signs in hand are certainly brave to stand up for themselves, but also foolish to do so unarmed. Put a stop to their protest by whatever means necessary to earn Evil Karma.

Look for the first shack on an island in the shallow waters immediately to the south. Press **R1** at the front door to search for Kuo.

RAISING A STINK

Finding the first shack empty, Cole heads to the next shack on the main island when a trio of previously unseen Corrupted arrives suddenly to attack. These Gasbags don't stop for anything and self-destruct when close enough.

AT HARM'S LENGTH

Keep Gasbags at a safe distance with Cole's blasts before eliminating them to ensure he isn't caught in the explosion once they're defeated.

BULLETS IN BULK

Numerous Militia guard the second shack. Besides the common grunts, there are riflemen atop the watchtowers, rocket launcher Militia on the ground, and a turret. Keep tabs on the nearest electrical sources, because Cole takes a lot of fire here. The most dangerous threat of all is a new class of Militiaman—the Militia Minigunner.

MILITIA MINIGUNNER

Only the biggest and toughest members of the Militia get promoted to this position. It takes raw strength to carry a heavy machine gun and the many pounds of ammo it requires. Take cover and avoid engaging them from open or flat ground.

After determining Kuo is not in this shack, the next shack on the list is located on an island in the shallows to the southwest. En route to it, Cole is assaulted by a combined force of Gasbags and Swamp Monsters. Dispatch them quickly while conserving Cole's electricity for the fight ahead.

Several Militia backed by two turrets hold the position, and there are few electrical sources nearby. Conserve Cole's energy and eliminate the soldiers as efficiently as possible.

MEET NIX

Finding it empty, Cole's attention is drawn to a series of explosions on an island to the west shrouded in fog. Head to the waypoint marked on the mini-map to investigate. As his surroundings become increasingly indistinct, Cole hears the sound of heavy breathing coming closer.

He suddenly finds himself face to face with a Conduit capable of teleportation. She attacks without warning but quickly ceases when she recognizes Cole. Although the woman refers to herself as a fan of his, Cole only cares about the Blast Core she's holding. She is willing to turn it over, but only after Cole helps her with something. He quickly agrees and lets her lead the way.

GOT A LIGHT?

Follow the waypoints to try to keep up with Nix as she heads back to the main island. She stops to ensnare a squad of Militia in writhing tendrils of oil at her command. She instructs Cole to use his powers to light up her captives.

After this demonstration of how their powers interact, Nix has something bigger in mind. She doesn't go into detail, only beckoning Cole to ascend to the rooftop stealthily without alerting the Militia guards.

OIL SPILL AND CLEANING UP

Let Nix seize the guards and finish them off as Cole heads toward the waypoints indicating the location of oil drums on the rooftops. Approach each and press **R1** to help Nix tip the drums to dump oil on the Militia banners.

Once all four oil barrels have been emptied, Nix tells Cole to set them all ablaze with his electrical attacks. The inferno encircles the square, sending Militia and civilians alike into a riotous panic. While they're distracted, descend into the blaze and decimate the Militia.

TOP OFF THE TANK

Replenish Cole's energy at the nearest rooftop source before dropping down to street level. Once he's engaged in battle with the Militia amidst the ferocious flames, it can be difficult to seek out electrical sources.

When Bertrand's forces have been completely wiped out, Nix turns over the Blast Core and departs after a flirtatious exchange. Zeke warns Cole about Nix and suggests that Cole should meet up with him before using the Blast Core.

REWARD: 500 XP

SIDE MISSIONS UNLOCKED

Crossfire, Jail Break (Good), Flying Cars (Evil), Tough Critic

STORM'S COMING

Cole shows up for the meeting early and waits for Zeke to show. It's certainly a surprise to Cole when Zeke arrives in full Militia regalia. He's been attempting to gather information while undercover, with little luck so far.

With no time like the present, Cole activates the Blast Core and promptly blacks out. He awakens some time later with a new power in his arsenal.

IONIC POWERS

Zeke notes that the Militia troops in the square are stirring up trouble, presenting an opportunity for Cole to see what his new powers are.

Combat the Militia forces until one falls to the ground glowing with the distinctive purple light of Ray Field energy. Zeke speculates that he must have been exposed to Ray Sphere energy during Wolfe's testing.

TWISTER AND SHOUT

Walk over to his body and pick up the Ionic Charge, find either some citizens or Militia to serve as Cole's unwilling guinea pigs, and activate the Ionic Vortex by pressing down on the d-pad.

After this impressive demonstration, Zeke radios in to let Cole know Nix has shown up again looking for him.

REWARD: 500 XP

ULTRA ATTACKS

Cole's melee repertoire now benefits from the purchase of Ultra Attacks in the Powers screen. Even the toughest of Cole's enemies crumple to the ground when struck with these attacks. To unleash them, string together a long hit combo until the meter in the lower-left of the screen is completely full, then press ▲.

Return to Zeke's hideout on the nearby roof. Through his Militia contacts, Zeke has tracked down a plantation on the south side of town where Bertrand has hidden Kuo. Zeke and Nix agree to mount a rescue mission, but they have wildly different plans.

Zeke suggests that Cole rescue a squad of captive police officers and enlist their aid in storming the plantation. Nix wants to assault the Militia hard and fast, ramming the plantation with a trolley car filled with explosives. While faster, this bold action comes at the heavy cost of collateral damage to the innocents being held captive within. Cole has a tough decision to make.

COPS AND BOMBERS

Here is another chance for Cole to gain a serious boost to his Good or Evil Karma. To take the Good route and save the cops, continue to "Leading the Charge" (pg. xxx). To side with Nix and gain Evil Karma, continue to "Boom!" (pg. xxx).

LEADING THE CHARGE

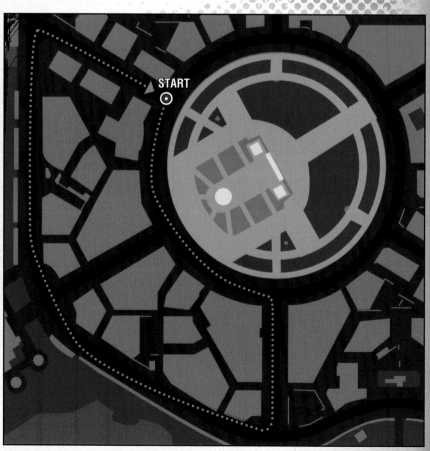

Head to the blue marker located closest to the Cathedral. Nix calls Cole on the way in an attempt to sway him toward her rescue plan. Ignore her and activate the marker to begin the mission.

CAPTIVE CONVOY ASSAULT

Bertrand has the Militia parading a cage full of captured police officers through the streets as a demonstration of his authority over New Marais. As Cole watches from his rooftop vantage point, the Militia convoy turns the corner onto the road circling the Cathedral.

The Militia convoy contains a helicopter, two semi-trucks full of Militia soldiers, and a pickup truck with two Militia rocket launcher soldiers in the back. An intimidating force to be sure, so a careful approach is required.

LONE AIRWOLF

The helicopter is the biggest threat in the convoy, so deal with it first. Once the helicopter is in range, hit it with a few bolts to get the pilot's attention and then lead it away from the convoy. Fire a barrage of Sticky Grenades to take the chopper down, or use Kinetic Pulse to throw a car and defeat the whirlybird in one blow.

HEAD 'EM OFF AT THE PASS

The Militia convoy follows a set route; don't worry if it gets too far away from Cole while he's dealing with the helicopter. Once the helicopter is down, simply take to the roofs and follow the mini-map to quickly cut off the rest of the convoy and continue Cole's assault.

JUST KEEP TRUCKING

Return to the rooftops and intercept the convoy. From above, take down the Militia soldiers standing guard on the roof of the semi-trucks.

Next, take down the Militia rocket launchers in the pickup truck at the rear of the convoy. Either zap the Militia soldiers with bolts from afar, or toss a few grenades into the bed of the truck to put them down for a dirt nap. Be sure to destroy the pickup truck as well, since it is a required target within the convoy.

NO MAN LEFT BEHIND

While decimating the Militia soldiers in the convoy, keep an eye on the mini-map for any soldiers that may have been knocked out (but not killed) by area attacks such as grenades or blasts. Even if the soldier is separated from a convoy truck, he must be defeated before Cole can successfully complete the mission. Militia soldiers remaining are marked with a red star on the mini-map.

SEMI CONDUCTOR

Last but not least, Cole needs to defeat the Militia soldiers inside the two semi-trucks. The Militia troops cluster in tight groups within the trucks, which makes them prime targets for Cole's grenades.

Strafe alongside the openings in the semi trailers and lob a few grenades into the crowd of Militia soldiers. If Cole runs out of juice or begins taking too much damage from the Militia, just back away and use any of the city's electrical resources to recharge.

When Cole has defeated all of the Militia soldiers, the convoy rolls to a stop. Jump on top of the truck containing the caged police and approach the electrical box at the front of the trailer. Repeatedly press **R1** to break the lock and free the police.

PUSH TO THE PLANTATION

With Cole's personal police force, follow the mini-map waypoint and head to the plantation located in the southwest corner of the map.

GO ON AHEAD!

The recently freed officers automatically head to the plantation. Regardless of where the convoy route stops, feel free to take any path toward the plantation. The cops are waiting for Cole when he arrives.

ASSAULT ON PLANTATION 13

Once Cole reaches the plantation, the cops storm through the front gate, eager for revenge on their captors! Allow the cops to face the brunt of the

defenders while Cole hangs back. The area is swarming with Militia soldiers, including a nest of rocket launcher troops on the balconies.

Use the iron fence surrounding the plantation for cover. Hang off one the large stone columns on either side of the plantation entrance and snipe the rocket launcher Militia from afar.

When the crowd of enemies has thinned out, head into the plantation yard. Zeke chimes in over the two-way radio that Kuo is being held in a service shed to the right of the plantation entrance. Follow the new mini-map marker to the shed, and press the **R1** button to open the door…

EXTRACTING KUO

Even if Cole sides with Nix, freeing Kuo from her captivity happens the same way. Turn to "The Mortar, The Scarier" (on the next page) for the rest of the mission.

BOOM!

Meet with Nix by the streetcar she's rigged with high explosives. All that's left for Cole to do is charge the trolley's motor with enough electricity to drive it straight through the main gates of the plantation.

Hop aboard the trolley and fire bolts at the generator atop it toward the front. The row of lights shows how much power the trolley is operating on.

Pay attention to the upper right-hand corner where the Trolley Bomb's status is indicated. Overcharging the trolley's generator or allowing the trolley to take too much damage can cause the bomb to go off prematurely.

Cole now has the challenge of multitasking between keeping the trolley moving by charging its generator and fending off the numerous Militia soldiers that open fire along the route. When in doubt, eliminate the threats before sending the trolley further ahead.

After crashing spectacularly through the gates, Nix and Cole must fight through the hordes of Militia troops guarding the compound. The blinking waypoint indicates where Kuo is being held, but there is fierce resistance getting there.

SPIN THEM RIGHT ROUND

Don't be stingy in using the Ionic Vortex to clear out tight groups of Militia, since Cole is likely to find another Ionic Charge from one of the many fallen Militia.

When the crowd of enemies has thinned out, head into the plantation yard. Zeke chimes in over the two-way that Kuo is being held in a service shed to the right of the plantation entrance. Follow the new mini-map marker to the shed, and press the **R1** button to open the door…

THE MORTAR, THE SCARIER

…or not. A huge explosion rocks Cole before he can open the door. The Militia has set up a mortar cannon inside a nearby gazebo to ruin Cole's day.

Run to cover and snipe the soldier operating the mortar with a bolt or grenade, then head into the gazebo once the soldier is dead. Walk up to the mortar cannon and press **R1** to permanently disable it.

However, Cole's mortar troubles are just beginning, as Zeke chimes in that two more cannon positions have been spotted at the rear of the plantation. Continue south from the gazebo, keeping the large trees between Cole and the second mortar cannon.

Wait for the mortar operator to fire off a round, then rush his position and use the Amp to quickly end his bombing run.

MORTAR MADNESS

The Militia mortars are as accurate as they are deadly. When approaching the mortar positions, try to keep trees and other large pieces of cover between Cole and the mortar.

If Cole must head out into an open area, make sure to stay on the move. The Militia is sure to drop a mortar on Cole's head the second he comes to a stop.

FREEING KUO

It appears that the shack is just the front entrance for a massive underground laboratory. Here, Cole finds Kuo out cold and chained up to some bizarre contraption. He frees Kuo and brings her to the surface, but unknowingly unleashes a new menace onto the unsuspecting populace of New Marais—the Ice Soldiers!

Once the second mortar cannon is scrap metal, continue to the rear of the mansion. There are three Militia trailers parked back here, which make for excellent cover from the third mortar position. Hang off the southernmost trailer to get a perfect vantage point to snipe the mortar operator with a bolt attack.

The Militia should be thinned out at this point, so make sure that third mortar cannon is out of commission and then return to the shack. Cole has no problems getting the door open this time.

CHILLING CONSEQUENCES

Back on the surface, Kuo has returned to consciousness, but Bertrand's experiments have left her weakened and barely able to walk. The Militia is now embroiled in a battle with the released Ice Soldiers, so they hardly notice that Zeke has pulled up to the plantation in time for a speedy getaway.

Defend Kuo as she slowly makes her way to Zeke's truck. Fortunately, most of the Militia is too busy with the Ice Soldiers to notice her. However, a few Militia members still open fire on Cole. Take out the soldiers who are foolish enough to try to fight a battle on two fronts as Kuo makes her exit. Once she gets to the truck, the trio makes their escape.

REWARD: 500 XP

POWERING UP ASCENSION PARISH

Although Zeke and Cole are waiting for Kuo to recover, there's still work to be done. Bertrand has holed up somewhere in Ascension Parish, but Cole can't risk heading there until the power has been restored.

Zeke suggests Cole start with the transformer near the canal. The Militia has isolated it from rest of the impoverished Ascension Parish. Their only hope is for Cole to bridge the circuit from one transformer to the next.

TESLA TRANSFORMER TETHER

Approach the transformer and press **R1** to draw energy from it to generate a Tesla Missile. Guide it through the air to the blinking circle on the screen where the Ascension Parish transformer is located.

TESLA MISSILES

The high-speed, flying energy projectiles are critical to reactivating transformers. However, they also serve an offensive purpose, as well.

Their energy level is so high that it electrocutes enemies that are just near its flight path. Plow through groups of Militia to send them into fits of spasms.

Juicing up the transformer is only the first step. There's no time to lose, as the Militia is sure to try to shut it down once they realize what Cole's done.

A TRIO OF TRANSFORMER TARGETS

Follow the waypoint on the mini-map to the Ascension Parish transformer and press **R1** to activate it. Zeke immediately warns Cole that a large Militia force is en route and that Cole needs to defend the transformer until it's online.

STRAIGHT FROM THE TAP

While the transformer charges up, it automatically replenishes Cole's energy without him needing to manually drain it—provided he's standing close enough. It doesn't supply Cole as quickly as his normal Electric Drain, so avoid wasting high energy attacks like grenades. Cole can always manually drain as needed to stay alive and fighting.

Be prepared to deal with Militia armed with rocket launchers, grenades, and rifles. Once the transformer is fully charged, it discharges a wave of electricity to neutralize all Militia in the immediate vicinity.

ONE IS THE LONELIEST NUMBER

Although this transformer is online, the neighborhood's power grid is still down. Until it's restored, Cole is vulnerable without any electrical sources nearby to drain. The transformer is the only source Cole can tap nearby to replenish his health and energy.

Fire another Tesla Missile from here at the next transformer located at the base of a water tower as indicated by the on-screen marker. Use the rooftops to avoid open conflict with the Militia since Cole is without any nearby electricity to drain.

Activate and defend it from yet another massive Militia assault until it's back online, then fire off a Tesla Missile at the last transformer.

Activate it and prepare to defend against the last major wave of Militia. Once it's fully operational, power is restored throughout Ascension Parish.

REWARD: 500 XP

SIDE MISSIONS UNLOCKED

Choppers vs. Monsters, Police Parade (Good), The Hunt (Evil)

THE SACRIFICE

After restoring the power in the Ascension Parish district, Zeke calls in over the two-way radio with some important news: the Militia has kidnapped a girl in broad daylight! Rescuing her would definitely improve Cole's reputation with the masses, so he'd better hurry to save her.

Head to the white waypoint marker located in the southeast of New Marais to begin "The Sacrifice."

RESCUE THE SACRIFICE

Walk along the pier toward the deep swamp. Before long, two of the Corrupted attack Cole, while a woman's cries for help can be heard in the distance. Continue along the pier toward the waypoint marker on Cole's map, battling any Corrupted that try to prevent Cole from freeing their midnight snack.

DAMSEL IN DISTRESS

At the end of the dock, Cole finds a woman tied and dangling from a large altar. Once Cole has taken care of all of the Corrupted in the area, fire a bolt at each of the victim's wrist shackles to get her down.

After being freed, the intended victim reveals a disturbing fact—the Militia has been sacrificing citizens to the swamp to keep something big and terrifying at bay. Luckily, her Uncle LaRoche just might have the necessary resources at his disposal to help.

As Cole follows the woman back to the mainland, a small group of Corrupted pounces on the duo. Dispatch them quickly with the Amp and continue following the woman.

THE ROAD TO LAROCHE

Back in the city proper, the Militia appears, and they are none too pleased to find that Cole has freed their sacrifice. Quickly zap the biggest threat, the rocket launcher-wielding Militia soldier on the roof, and continue following the woman.

Once Cole and his escort reach the tree line, a large group of Corrupted emerges from the swamp, hell-bent on reclaiming their fast food. However, once they see Cole, the Corrupted are happy to go for someone with a little more meat on their bones. Try leading them away from Cole's charge so she doesn't get caught in the crossfire.

BACK ALLEY BRUTALITY

When this newest batch of assailants is defeated, follow the woman into a narrow alleyway to the left. Another large group of Corrupted is waiting for Cole. Due to the confined nature of the alleyway, stick to melee attacks when fighting the Corrupted to avoid unwanted collateral damage.

Take the right fork at the end of the alley. At the next juncture, a single Corrupted lies in wait. Before Cole can reach it, a Militia rocket flies into view and scores a direct hit on the creature. If the Corrupted survives the explosion, quickly fire a few bolts to put it out of its misery.

RAISING THE REBELS

At the next juncture, take a left toward several of LaRoche's men lying injured on the ground. Hold **R1** to lock onto each injured victim, then hold △ to Pulse Heal and save them from the brink of death. LaRoche's men are so grateful that they join Cole in escorting the young lady back to LaRoche.

LaRoche holds court in nearby Leo Park. Upon exiting the alleyway, turn left. A small group of Militia members is located nearby, so use Cole's new allies to assist in their quick demise. Continue with the woman to the large lion statue at the end of the street, where Cole finally meets the man leading the local rebellion.

LaRoche and his niece are relieved to see one another, but their reunion quickly turns sour over a dispute on the morality of offering up sacrifices to the swamp monsters. The argument is short-lived, however, as the ground begins to rumble and the mother of all swamp monsters appears. The Devourer!

BOSS The Devourer

This armored monstrosity is not happy with Cole for running off with its midnight snack, and it shows its gratitude by hurling a barrage of toxic spitballs in Cole's direction. Stay inside the circle of Leo Park and take cover behind the lion statue to avoid the Devourer's snot rockets.

SWAMP MOUTH

The Devourer is covered head to toe in armor, and its only weak spot is located at its mouth. When it performs its projectile attack, the big monster's armor slides out of the way and exposes the flesh there.

After firing a few toxic blasts, the Devourer opens its mouth, attempting to ensnare Cole with its tongue. If Cole gets caught in this slippery situation, aim at the Devourer's uvula and fire off bolts with **R1** to give the monster a sore throat it is not likely to forget.

TONGUE TWISTER

Avoid becoming ensnared by the Devourer's tongue. When Cole gets reeled all the way into the monster's mouth, the Devourer chomps down hard, either killing Cole outright or leaving him a single hit away from death.

Be patient and continue this pattern. Eventually, the Devourer goes down for good. LaRoche calls in to express his gratitude, offering to help Cole more in the near future. From now on, if Cole heals any injured rebels he encounters, they arise to help fight the enemy.

Stay in front of the Devourer while keeping a good bit of distance between it and Cole. Wait until the beast's armor retracts to expose its head, and fire a stream of bolts and grenades into its mouth.

REWARD: 500 XP

SIDE MISSIONS UNLOCKED

In the Name of Science, Firing Squad (Good), King of the Hill (Evil)

Zeke informs Cole that Kuo is awake and wants to speak to him. She sulks in St. Charles Cemetery while waiting for Cole to arrive. She's clearly struggling to come to grips with her new abilities.

Cole knows better than anyone how she feels. Both were unwilling victims of mad science who were turned into outcasts. Cole convinces her that she has the power to make Bertrand pay, but only if she learns control.

TRAINING AMONG TOMBSTONES

Exercising her powers, Kuo demonstrates her ability to fly, and Cole must struggle to keep up. Follow the waypoints to Kuo's location as she explains Wolfe's theory of combining Conduits' powers.

Noticing a Militia patrol in the cemetery, Cole and Kuo decide to experiment with mixing their powers. Kuo flies over and engulfs the off-guard Militiamen in a cloud of frigid water vapor. She prompts Cole to shoot the ice cloud to encase them in ice. This earns Cole Good Karma and 1 XP (Cold Shoulder).

CRUSHED ICE

Frozen foes no longer pose a threat and can be left behind on the battlefield. However, Cole can always return to their frigid forms and smash them apart for extra XP later.

Moving toward the next pair of Militia, Kuo launches them through the air for Cole to finish off as he sees fit. Having gotten quite a workout from their powers, Kuo reveals that she's discovered references in Wolfe's notes to a Blast Core hidden in the cemetery. However, the clues to its location are vague and cryptic.

GRAVE #1

GRAVE #2

GRAVE #3

Kuo hands Cole a photo of a grave where they should start their search. Hold **R1** to bring up the photo for a reminder at any time. The grave they seek is located in the northwest corner of the cemetery. Graves can be found inside the flashing circle on the mini-map. Uncover the grave furthest right with the Kinetic Pulse and press **R1** to pick up the clue within.

GRAVE ROBBERS

It seems Bertrand also has an interest in the Blast Core, based on the number of Militia who suddenly make an appearance among the tombstones. Fortunately for Kuo and Cole, they're preoccupied with the Corrupted roaming the cemetery. Feel free to let them scuffle among themselves while resuming the search.

The next sarcophagus is adjacent to an interior gate along the west wall of the cemetery. Pick up the clue inside for a photo. Cole only now begins to notice the number of exposed body bags littering the cemetery. Kuo explains that a more lethal version of the plague that struck Empire City has worked its way down the coast into New Marais. The local population has been decimated, leaving the living with more bodies than places to put them.

There's little time to mourn the dead, and the last clue is located in a crypt in the far south of the cemetery. The Militia and Ice Soldiers are embroiled in an intense battle there. However, once the Ice Soldiers depart, the Militia soldiers don't let Kuo and Cole's presence go unnoticed.

The crypt is located in the center of a clearing. At one end of the crypt is a vault. Attempt to access it by pressing **R1** when standing before it. Before Cole can access the contents, a Ravager Hive Lord bursts from the ground. Unlike regular Ravagers, this one is capable of summoning its own minions.

BOSS Ravager Hive Lord

The Ravager Hive Lord sprouts bulbous stalks from the ground that eventually hatch to release small broodlings—Spikers. They spit their own weaker version of their master's acidic projectiles. Fortunately, they can either be destroyed before hatching or dispatched with a swift melee attack once hatched.

BATTLE NOT ON HOLY GROUND

Rather than risk being cornered by the Spikers amid the labyrinth of graves, take the fight to the streets. Parked cars thrown with Kinetic Pulse devastate the Hive Lord's health and clear large tracts of unhatched Spikers.

After destroying the Ravager Hive Lord and its Spiker spawn, return to the vault and open it to find a Blast Core.

REWARD: 500 XP

SIDE MISSIONS UNLOCKED

Good Deed (Good), Revenge (Evil), Life Insurance

GOOD GETS BETTER

Cole finds Zeke on a rooftop, surveilling Fort Phillipe across the street. Zeke is keeping an eye out for the machine Bertrand used on Kuo, suspecting it's destined for the heavily fortified installation.

▌▌▌ SOARING HIGHER, SHOOTING SHARPER

With Zeke staking out the fort, Cole takes this opportunity to use the Blast Core. Some time later, he awakens with improved Static Thrusters that allow him to float further and longer. Try it out by crossing the street without touching the ground.

DRIVE-IN CAR HOP

Cole can also now perform supercharged jumps when standing on a car by drawing energy from the vehicle. Clamber onto the nearest car and try it out to send Cole soaring skyward.

FOCUS, GRASSHOPPER

In addition to the other flashy abilities, Cole can now focus his concentration and zoom in on his targets. Hold up on the d-pad to enter Precision Mode and fire a few bolts to test out this enhanced focus.

TIME IS ENERGY

While Cole is in Precision Mode, time slows down to allow him to pick off his targets with ease. But don't dawdle, because Cole's Power Cores steadily drain as long as he's zoomed in.

ULTRA DRAIN

Completing this mission unlocks Ultra Drain for purchase from the Powers screen. It allows Cole to dramatically increase the rate at which he drains electricity, allowing him to get back to the fight much faster.

REWARD: 500 XP

SIDE MISSIONS UNLOCKED

Enemy Surveillance 1, Enemy Surveillance 2, Overcharge 2, Grave Danger

STORIES OF THE PAST

Nix radios Cole to meet her for a surprise. Meet her on the pier in the southeast section of the main island. Once Cole arrives, she begins to reminisce about growing up in New Marais.

Surrounded by thieves and crazies, she spent her childhood in poverty. Her mother was the only stable part of her life. To show Cole what happened to change everything, Nix says they need a boat.

COMMANDEER A BOAT

Nix directs Cole to secure a Militia boat. One is docked behind the dilapidated mansion in the southeast area of the main island. Forge a path past the Militia's turrets to the end of the pier with Nix's help—the waypoint marks the boat's location on the mini-map.

NOT IN KANSAS ANYMORE

When Cole arrives at the property, Militia patrolling the grounds and stationed both on the deck and atop the second floor balconies are quick to open fire. A well-aimed Ionic Vortex makes short work of them.

ISLAND HOPPING

Nix pilots their newly acquired boat through the swampy marsh until a pair of watchtowers comes into view. Use a Precision Bolt to eliminate the two Militiamen armed with rocket launchers that flank the boat.

THE LITTLE ENGINE THAT COULD

The boat is fully fueled, allowing Cole to drain as much power as he needs while he and Nix explore the swamps. Replenish his energy early and often.

Nix can't go any further until the defenders have been neutralized, so she instructs Cole to disembark. Make it onto dry land and pay attention to the enemy markers on the mini-map to avoid being flanked. Secure the area near the turrets to ensure they aren't used against Cole.

POOL PARTY

Use the environment to Cole's advantage by using Cole's blast to knock the Militia into the water. Fire a bolt into the highly conductive fluid to send electricity arcing throughout, which swiftly neutralizes large groups of waterlogged enemies with a quick Enviro Kill.

Continue southwest across the small islands and clear out all Militia en route. As Cole proceeds deeper, Corrupted emerge from the fog and engage the Militia in combat. They provide a well-timed distraction and make Cole's job much easier. Feel free to bypass enemies locked in battle and heed Nix's call to return to the boat while they're preoccupied.

BOARDING PARTIES

Back on the boat, Nix and Cole are subject to attacks by Swamp Monsters striking from beneath the murky waters. They leap suddenly out of the surrounding water to land on the boat's deck.

CLEARING THE DECK

At this range, melee attacks are most effective when mixed with blasts. These buy breathing room and time for Cole to drain the boat and restore his energy. The blasts can even knock the Corrupted near the railing overboard and back into the water.

Cole and Nix soon arrive at the string of islands located directly south of the main island. Cole must once more disembark to handle the Militia stationed there.

But as Cole draws closer to the shack on the first island, he discovers that an unknown assailant has already massacred the Militia soldiers. Before Cole has the time to make sense of the situation, Nix spots something moving into the distance of the next island. Head toward the waypoint there, where a Ravager Hive Lord soon ambushes Cole.

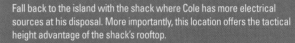

SHACK SALVATION

Fall back to the island with the shack where Cole has more electrical sources at his disposal. More importantly, this location offers the tactical height advantage of the shack's rooftop.

NIX'S ORIGIN REVEALED

Once the Hive Lord has fallen, hop back aboard Nix's boat. The two sail until they reach a crater in the swamps identical to the one created by the Ray Sphere explosion that granted Cole his powers.

With a pained voice, she describes how she saw Bertrand gather the outcasts of society that no one would miss—the homeless, hookers, and swamp dwellers. There in the swamp, he activated the Ray Sphere and wiped them all out.

Nix survived thanks to her Conduit gene but lost her entire family. Considering how powerful her abilities were at the edge of the blast… how powerful must Bertrand be?

REWARD: 500 XP

TRANSFERRING POWER

Nix's guided tour has given Cole a lot to think about, but there's time for reflection later. Zeke has big news and is having everyone join him on a rooftop overlooking Smut Triangle.

Zeke is happy to confirm the arrival of Bertrand's device at Fort Phillipe. Unfortunately, that also means that security has been stepped up in the entire facility. The only hope of penetrating the defensive perimeter is if they can recruit LaRoche's rebels to back them up. However, Kuo and Nix disagree both about what to do with the machine once they have it and how to go about getting it.

Kuo suggests they earn the loyalty of the rebels by supporting them with medical supplies. Zeke volunteers that he's made a map of the Militia patrols so they can set up an ambush and secure antibiotics. Healthy, strong allies are sure to give the Militia a run for its money.

Nix disagrees and argues that strengthening the rebels is counter-intuitive. An angry, weakened force is more easily manipulated and dependent on them. Stirring them up is as simple as Nix disguising herself as a member of the Militia and then going on a rampage.

RECRUITING REBELS

Cole must choose between Kuo and Nix's competing plans. To earn Good Karma and provide medical supplies to the rebels, continue to "Hearts and Minds" (on the next page). To earn Evil Karma and violently trick the rebels into joining Cole, continue to "Fooling the Rebels" (on p. 75).

Kuo has been thoroughly trained by the NSA in asset recruitment and propaganda. She knows the best way to get LaRoche's rebels to commit to supporting Cole's cause is by winning them over with acts of compassion.

The desperate and hungry refugees who make up the bulk of LaRoche's supporters could be easily recruited after earning their favor with some medical supplies. Kuo asks Cole to meet with her at the north end of Fort Phillipe.

AMBULANCE CHASERS

Cole radios Kuo to determine where they can acquire the supplies. However, Kuo has already put her plan in motion. She's commandeered an ambulance from inside the fort that she sends crashing through the gates.

She hurriedly tells Cole to hop on top and protect the ambulance during the getaway. Watch the mini-map for enemies and keep them from destroying the ambulance. The ambulance's current condition is indicated in the upper-right corner of the screen.

BUMPER-TO-BUMPER TRAFFIC

Even though Kuo's getaway route winds through various narrow alleys and side streets, she can't seem to shake her Militia pursuers. Don't be turned into a sitting duck when trucks try to box her in. Use Cole's blasts and Kinetic Pulses to quickly sweep obstacles from her path.

As the ambulance crosses the canal into Ville Cochon, Cole finds the way blocked by Militia engaged in a fierce firefight with a Devourer. They don't

last long against the heavily armored Corrupted, leaving Cole to finish the job. Wait for its armor to retract, then exploit its weakpoint to slay the lumbering beast.

SIGNED, SEALED, AND DELIVERED

Kuo finally brings the ambulance to a stop at LaRoche's secret headquarters. Expecting the medical supplies to earn them a hero's welcome, the celebration gets cut short. It soon becomes apparent the Militia managed to tail them to their destination and has the area surrounded.

REPO MEN

Note the marked Militia targets, indicated by red stars on the mini-map, and fend off their onslaught. Use grenades to clear large groups of them as they gather around tight corners. Use Precision Mode to eliminate the Militia on the rooftops that pepper Cole and the rebels from above. Takedown the minigunners post-haste when they show up before they can unleash their bullet barrages.

When all the gunfire has ceased, LaRoche begrudgingly gives his thanks for their help while lamenting the loss of their secret base. Despite the setback, he's convinced to lend his support to Cole in taking Fort Phillipe.

REWARD: 500 XP

FOOLING THE REBELS

Nix knows that people can always be counted on to be afraid. And when faced with the horror of their mortality, the weak bend to the wills of the strong. LaRoche's rebels are a wasted force under their soft leader—they're a ragtag bunch of loose cannons. Fortunately, the qualifications for being a diversion aren't very high.

Nix suggests they turn Fort Phillipe's heavy-duty artillery on the rebels to send them into a panic. Desperate for proactive leadership in the face of the apparent Militia aggression, LaRoche's men are sure to flock to Cole's side.

CUTTING MILITIA COMMS

Nix departs to acquire a Militia disguise to instigate a massacre of LaRoche's rebels. Meanwhile, Cole contacts Zeke to obtain the locations of all the Militia's communications arrays. He intends to cut them off from the main line and co-opt their public address system. Both arrays are marked on the mini-map with waypoints.

Take the Grindwire over the courtyard to bypass the Militia, who are now alerted to Cole's presence. Drop down and use Cole's blast to clear the walkway ahead of all resistance, knocking Militia helplessly over the railings. Then, lob a grenade at the last communications station.

FEMME FATALE

Once the Militia's communications are cut off from headquarters, take control of Nix as she mans the heavy artillery turret. Hold **L1** to zoom and press **R1** to fire at the propane tanks marked by waypoints on the mini-map.

Start with the far north waypoint at the edge of the fort's perimeter. Use Static Thrusters to drift over to the parapet bearing a massive cannon. The communications station is located with striking distance below on the walkway.

The resulting explosions quickly draw the attention of LaRoche's rebels. They respond in full force, opening fire on Nix's position. The Turret Status is shown in the upper right-hand corner of the screen. The red stars on the mini-map indicate Nix's targets. Take them out before they take her out.

FRIEND AND FOE ALIKE

As Nix decimates the responding rebels, Cole hijacks the communications system to broadcast belligerent propaganda in the name of the Militia. After several waves of rebels have fallen, it's time for Cole to swoop in and bask in the adulation of a savior.

Turn Cole's aggression toward the Militia trucks arriving on the scene. Red stars on the mini-map mark their location but beware the minigunners mixed in with the Militia regulars. With the coast clear, destroy the cannon marked on the mini-map from the ground in a single blow by launching a car at it with Cole's Kinetic Pulse.

PICKUP PICK-UP

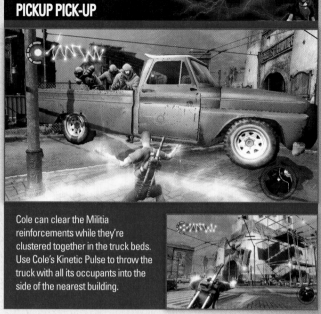

Cole can clear the Militia reinforcements while they're clustered together in the truck beds. Use Cole's Kinetic Pulse to throw the truck with all its occupants into the side of the nearest building.

BOTTLENECK BLOODBATH

With the reinforcements neutralized, the remaining Militia stationed at the fort flood out of the main gate. Panicked and with no apparent leadership left standing, they rush out to mount their own futile counter-attack against Cole.

Decimate them as they are trapped in the bottleneck of the fort's main entrance. Once Cole has vanquished the last of them, LaRoche contacts Cole to thank him and to propose an alliance against the Militia's sudden aggressive change in tactics.

STORM THE FORT

The time to strike at Fort Phillipe is now. The Militia forces are weakened, and Cole has the backing of LaRoche's assembled rebels. LaRoche tasks Kuo and Cole with taking out the turrets so his men can safely breach the fort's walls and secure the device. Kuo wants to see it destroyed after the suffering it caused her, but Nix joins them, eager to use it to swap powers.

▌▌▌▌ TAKE THE NORTH GATE

The debate has to wait until they actually have the machine. Cole and Kuo need to start the attack from the north, then sweep through the courtyard. Meet Kuo at the waypoint, and then proceed to the next one marking the turret just inside the gate.

OVER THE TOP ACTION

Heavily shielded from full-frontal assaults, this turret easily suppresses attackers at the gate chokepoint. Cole has a better angle of attack from above. Climb the light pole and scale the fort's walls to attack the turret gunner from above.

Wait for Kuo to fire an ice cloud, and then freeze the gunner in his tracks. Drop down and disable the turret to allow LaRoche's rebels to enter.

TURRET TASK TRIFECTA

There are three additional turrets marked on the mini-map. Let LaRoche's rebels keep the Militia occupied in the courtyards, and stay above the fray.

Employ Ionic Vortices to clear the turrets of nearby defenders. Once Cole has disabled all the turrets, Kuo begins the search for the device.

THEIR BACKS TO THE SEA

Easily take out the center turret by scaling the outer wall and attacking the unsuspecting Militia from behind.

RESTORE FORT POWER

The Militia has caught on to the rebels' super-powered assistance and cut the power to the fort. The closest transformer is in the construction yard outside the fort walls.

Leave the fort to harness the transformer's power for a Tesla Missile. Guide the Tesla Missile straight through the front gate and take a hard right. The target transformer indicated by the flashing circle is just ahead, beyond an archway.

Move to the newly energized transformer and fire a Tesla Missile from there under the bridge ahead and across the length of the fort to reach the next transformer atop the northernmost cannon parapet.

Take the Grindwire ahead and speed over the tops of the battling forces. Bridge the gap between Grindwires with Static Thrusters and arrive at the final transformer to activate it and bring back the power.

The fort's Militiamen are on their last legs, and eliminating their artillery is sure to seal the deal. Disable the mortar emplacements marked on the minimap. With that done, Kuo announces the power transfer device is secure.

PICK A PARTNER

Cole and his compatriots assemble at the machine. The Blast Core powering it sits in the center. Cole is eager to use it to increase his powers but has a difficult choice to make: which Conduit does he exchange powers with? Press **L2** to choose Nix or **R2** to choose Kuo.

REVERSE COURSE

Choosing Kuo while possessing a Good Karma level neither increases nor decreases Cole's Karma. However, choosing Nix resets his Karma ranking to Thug. Conversely, choosing Nix while possessing Evil Karma has no effect, but choosing Kuo resets his Karma ranking to Guardian.

FOR GOOD

Kuo reluctantly tells Cole that if he is determined to use the dreaded contraption, she prefers he choose her. Realizing how difficult a decision this is for Kuo, Cole assures her that she's making the right choice.

FOR ILL

Cole realizes that Nix's offensive capabilities and powers make a powerful addition to his own. With her abilities to bolster his, Cole is all the more prepared to defeat The Beast in combat.

In his weakened state, Cole almost lets Bertrand escape from the fort via helicopter. Before passing out, he barely musters enough energy to chuck a grenade with pinpoint accuracy, sending the helicopter spiraling down.

THE POWERS OF TEAMWORK

Cole's decision in this mission dramatically increases the number of powers available for purchase. Depending on his Karma level and the partner he chose, Cole has several additional selections to choose from.

Choosing Nix gives access to the Ionic Drain. Additionally, Firebird Strike and Napalm Grenade become available at the Outlaw rank. At the Infamous rank, Cole can acquire the Nightmare Blast, Hellfire Rocket, and Spikers.

Choosing Kuo gives access to the Ionic Freeze. In addition, Ice Launch and Ice Grenade are made available at the Champion rank. At the Hero rank, he can acquire the Shatter Blast, Freeze Rocket, and Ice Shield.

For details on these powers, reference the Powers section in the beginning of this guide (pg. 20).

A NEW FORCE FOR GOOD

Night falls and Cole awakens with a new ability derived from Kuo's powers. Head to the red stars on the mini-map where Militia targets wait, unaware they are about to be guinea pigs for Cole's new power.

Cole now posses the Ionic Freeze—an alternate Ionic ability. It consumes an Ionic Charge to swiftly unleash a series of ice spikes. As they spring forth from the ground, any enemies they strike are instantly frozen. Cole earns 1 XP (Cold Shoulder) for every opponent neutralized in this manner.

As an added bonus, Cole can use his Kinetic Pulse to rip loose these massive icicles and hurl them at any enemies left standing.

A NEW MENACE FOR EVIL

Night falls and Cole awakens with a new ability derived from Nix's powers. Head to the red stars on the mini-map where Militia targets wait, unaware they are about to be guinea pigs for Cole's new power.

Cole now posses the Ionic Drain—an alternate Ionic ability. Similar to the Bio Leech, it drains the life force out of every person within a specific radius around Cole. There is no limit to the number of people Cole can sap in this manner, provided they are within range.

REWARD: 500 XP

JOSEPH BERTRAND THE 3RD

Cole regains consciousness hours later and rushes to the site of the helicopter crash. Surprisingly, Bertrand is nowhere to be found despite the severely mangled wreckage. Perplexed at the absence of Bertrand's corpse, Cole's attention is drawn to the street behind him, where a cloud of smoke enshrouds the clock tower turnaround.

INVESTIGATE THE DISTURBANCE

Direct Cole to the pulsing waypoint on the mini-map to investigate. As he approaches, the ground shudders with great force, and a towering, multi-story Corrupted unlike any other previously encountered appears.

BOSS **Corrupted Behemoth**

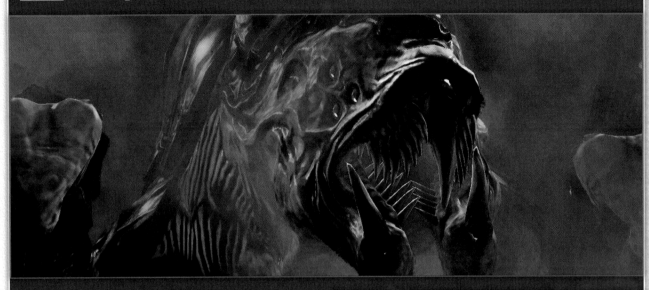

This gargantuan Corrupted nearly defies description. Without remorse or hesitation, it tears down the street and demolishes buildings, cars, and anything else standing in its way.

From its gaping mouth, the creature lobs acidic projectiles that are more devastating variants of the Ravager's attack. The titanic beast also spews an acidic spray when as it exhales to blow back cars, pedestrians, and even Cole. When its gaping maw is at its widest, Cole can attack the glowing purple gullet in its throat.

STAYING SERPENTINE

Dodge, weave, and stay on the move when the creature launches its acid blobs. Their splash damage radius is large—just one can send Cole reeling and drop his health to turn the screen black and white.

When its chest cavity opens, expect it to deploy a barrage of Spikers. In addition, multiple lashing tendrils emerge, which snatch helpless bystanders right off the streets. Fortunately, this also exposes the creature's glowing organs within.

Those standing too near the thrashing terror can fall victim to powerful ground strikes from its legs. Tentacles penetrate underground to burst forth through the concrete and summon Swamp Monsters to preoccupy the few brave enough to attempt a counter-attack. This also exposes additional glowing weakpoints in its joints for Cole to target.

FIRE AND FORGET

The behemoth quickly follows up each ground pound with another barrage of spewed projectiles. Dodge first, then fire a string of bolts at its joint while on the move to avoid being stunned by the downpour of acid.

Before the smoke clears, Cole discovers the truth about Bertrand's Ray Sphere experimentation: this disgusting beast is Bertrand. Unfortunately, he manages to escape via jet boat across the water to Flood Town before Cole can lay hands upon him.

REWARD: 500 XP

POWERING UP FLOOD TOWN

Bertrand has wisely retreated to the devastated, partially submerged island that comprises New Marais to the north. Since the flood, its western region has been abandoned because it lacks basic utilities like gas or electricity. If Cole plans on pursuing Bertrand there, he must bring the power grid back online.

▐▐▐ BRIDGE ON THE RIVER NEW MARAIS

From the transformer, fire a Tesla Missile and use it to power the transformer atop the bridge connecting the islands. Exit the alley to the street and climb the utility pole by the water. Its Grindwire takes Cole straight to the top of the bridge. Pressing **R1** to activate the transformer lowers the bridge and grants access to Flood Town.

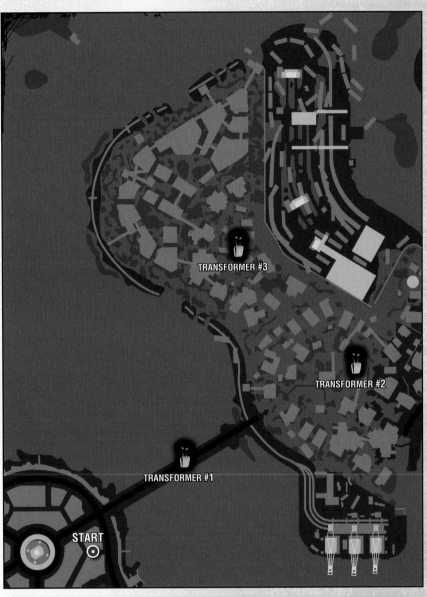

HEART OF DARKNESS

Press **R1** again to fire a Tesla Missile and guide it straight ahead to the next transformer inside Flood Town itself.

Before Cole can reach the other end of the bridge, a pair of Ice Soldiers arrives and attempts to turn him back. According to Zeke, they were South African mercenaries hired by Bertrand and went mad since Cole unintentionally freed them.

Since then, they've run wild through Flood Town, engaging in unprovoked violence. In addition to their superhuman ice jumping ability, both Ice Soldiers here are armed with assault rifles, and one can generate a shield of ice.

After disposing of the outmatched border guards, continue across the bridge and on to the transformer marked on the mini-map.

POWERLESS TO RESIST

Without an active power grid to drain and surrounded by water, Cole should avoid the clusters of Ice Soldiers between him and the transformer. Keep an eye on the mini-map for them and stay out of their line of sight.

Activate the transformer and defend it as it comes up to full power, as indicated by the meter at the bottom of the screen.

While the meter fills, Ice Soldiers drawn to the massive buildup of electricity beset Cole from all sides. Take cover behind the generator and drain it as needed to keep Cole alive.

SHOCKING SURROUNDINGS

Don't fall victim to tunnel vision as the Ice Soldiers surround Cole. Hold them at bay by firing non-stop bolts into the water as Cole spins in place to temporarily stun them and buy precious time. If any manage to make it onto Cole's rooftop, send them packing with a blast to the face.

Once the meter fills, the transformer discharges and completely pacifies the area around it. Deploy another Tesla Missile toward the next transformer in the northwest.

DOING THE ROUNDS

Before initializing each of the remaining Flood Town transformers, take the time to use Cole's Tesla Missile to eliminate all the Ice Soldiers standing between it and him. This clears the way for Cole when he journeys to activate it.

After Cole has defended the position long enough for it to power on, LaRoche reveals the Ice Soldiers have seized control of Flood Town as part of an intensive search.

Another transformer is the target of Cole's Tesla Missile to the north. Go to activate it and defend it against the final Ice Soldier wave. Finally, the power is restored to the huddled masses eking out an existence in the ruins of Flood Town.

DUCK AND COVER

The last transformer is elevated, so the Ice Soldiers attack from even higher positions. Fortunately, the water is to Cole's back so he can take cover behind the transformer. Only expose Cole when necessary to blast off Ice Soldiers who make it onto the platform.

THE DUNBAR BEAM

Zeke rings Cole to see if he knows about LaRoche's medical center. He claims to have a cure for the plague, and the people have been flocking to it. Zeke is volunteering and thinks Cole should, too. However, Cole arrives to discover there is no cure. All LaRoche has managed to do is try to ease the pain of the afflicted. Despite this, LaRoche is desperate for help in combating the Corrupted that have begun attacking the plague victims making the journey. Zeke has hastily rigged an array of floodlights he refers to as Dunbar Beams as a defensive measure.

TRIAL BY FIRE

As Zeke wraps up the explanation, a motion sensor is tripped in the distance. Cole is dispatched to investigate the alarm, marked by the waypoint on the mini-map.

Zeke has mounted a spotlight onto the roof nearby. Press **R1** to use the spotlight. Focus the beam by holding **L1** and pressing **R1**.

Zeke has modified the light to emit a specific wavelength of UV radiation that causes the Corrupted to turn to dust and burst. Aim the beam at the Swamp Monsters, which are slowly trudging through Flood Town as they converge upon the plague-stricken.

SHARE THE SPOTLIGHT

Avoid targeting lone Swamp Monsters and instead focus on the clusters that gather around civilians to take out several at once.

MAKING THE ROUNDS

After Cole is finished fending off the wave of Corrupted here, Zeke calls Cole's attention to the north, where another band of plague victims is under attack.

Use the spotlight marked on the mini-map to destroy the Ravagers that attack both from ground level and nearby rooftops.

Head back south again at Zeke's prompting and another Dunbar Beam. Fend off the Swamp Monsters darting between the debris to keep the bystanders alive.

Return to the north to same location Cole faced the Ravagers, now swarming with both Swamp Monsters and numerous Ravagers.

Now Cole is directed to two different spotlights to the south. By the time Cole gets there, the Corrupted are too numerous to hold back.

Protect as many of the plague victims as possible at each Dunbar Beam before Zeke calls in to insist Cole move on. As more sirens go off, the battle appears lost, and Zeke tells Cole to fall back to where they first met at the clinic.

COMMON ENEMIES

Utilize the Dunbar Beam there and continue to defend the area against the seemingly endless siege. The tide is suddenly turned by the arrival of new, deadlier Ice Soldiers, who arrive to battle the Corrupted.

However, when the dust settles, these Ice Heavies declare they're uninterested in anyone's gratitude. They only want LaRoche's Blast Core.

TOPPLING IVORY TOWERS

Cole needs to return to the clinic and defeat the two Ice Heavies raising a ruckus there. They summon pillars of ice and target Cole with freezing ice beams from this vantage point.

Attack from the base of their columns to negate the tactical advantage. Move between cover to avoid their freezing ice beams.

Once Cole puts both on ice, LaRoche offers his thanks and—more importantly—promises the Blast Core to Cole…but only after one more favor.

REWARD: 500 XP

LaRoche radios to Cole with a plea for help. The downtrodden residents of Flood Town—already stricken by plague in huge numbers—can barely breathe through the heavy smoke polluting the air.

It seems the Ice Soldiers lit fire to the wells in an attempt to smoke out the residents while searching for the Blast Core. Only Cole has the constitution to get close enough to the wells and snuff out the flames.

EXTINGUISH THE FIRES

Approach the waypoint marked on the map and use Cole's Kinetic Pulse to lift the well cap. Click **R3** while raising the well cap to switch which side of Cole the well cap is on. Release **R2** to drop it on top of the well and put out the fire.

Unfortunately, there's only one well cap on hand, so Cole must put out three additional fires at the far ends of Flood Town. Use the Kinetic Pulse to launch it and cover the distance quickly.

IN TOO DEEP

Try to land the well cap in sight, or risk it winding up in an inaccessible body of water. If it's in too deep a pond for Cole to reach, he can use his blast to knock it back onto dry land. Alternately, try landing directly on top of it and using the Kinetic Pulse to levitate and launch it.

WHERE THERE'S SMOKE...

In addition to the marker on the mini-map, a plume of smoke rising into the air can identify the well cap's location.

ARMED AND DANGEROUS

Arriving at the northwest wells, Cole finds himself face-to-face with a new breed of Ice Soldier—one that demonstrates ice powers far beyond what Cole has previously witnessed.

BOSS Crusher

The Crusher lands powerful blows with his ice-encased arms that create a ring of ice spikes around him. From a distance, he summons waves of ice spikes out of the ground and hurls large ice boulders through the air that explode on impact. Be mindful of nearby electrical sources, as the Crusher's attacks inflict massive amounts of damage.

Maintain a high elevation and back away from the edge when the Crusher launches its ice boulders. Most, if not all, get caught on the lip of the roof and shatter harmlessly.

Bolts are useless against the Crusher, but his other attacks still work fine. Ideally, make sure Cole is fully charged and rely on Precision Mode to land Precise Head Shots that significantly deplete the Crusher's health bar.

Once he's defeated the Crusher, Cole can put out the well fire without interference.

Three Ice Soldiers guard the south well. Blast them back into the water with ease and electrocute them by firing bolts into the natural conductor.

The east well sits just outside the walls of the rail yard, where the Ice Soldiers and Militia are locked in an epic battle. Feel free to ignore the fracas unless forced to engage them and finish the mission for LaRoche.

LaRoche thanks Cole and tells him that he's given Zeke the promised Blast Core. Meet Zeke in an abandoned train car by the rail yard to pick it up.

REWARD: 500 XP

Cole meets with Zeke at a train car that he's converted into a jury-rigged command center. Kuo is there with him to share that she discovered another of Wolfe's journals and deciphered its contents.

Based on the new information she's discovered, it seems Wolfe constructed the RFI as a cure to the plague that consumed Empire City before spreading like wildfire down the coast. He was burdened by guilt after the stunning discovery that the plague was caused by radiation poisoning from the Ray Field technology he helped the First Sons create.

TESTING THE RFI

LaRoche made good on their deal, and Zeke now has another Blast Core for Cole. He's determined now more than ever to get the RFI working to stop the oncoming catastrophe. Just as haunted as Wolfe was by his part in the origin of the epidemic, Cole absorbs the Blast Core and loses consciousness.

When he awakens, Cole attempts to activate the RFI, but to no avail. More Blast Cores must be found, and time is of the essence.

ZERO HOUR, 9 A.M.

Despite this setback, Cole is reinvigorated by the latest influx of Ray Field energy. His arsenal now includes the ability to fire concentrated electric rockets. Press ⬤ while aiming to launch a powerful electric charge. Cole's rocket travels with a direct trajectory to land with pinpoint accuracy on its targets.

QUICKER COMBOS

Once purchased, Quicker Combos decreases the number of successive strikes necessary for Cole to execute both Finisher and Ultra Attacks.

REWARD: 500 XP

RAIL YARD INTEL

Kuo contacts Cole with an urgent call to meet by the freight car that serves as their makeshift Flood Town headquarters. Enter the marker and activate the mission to begin. According to Kuo's intel, raids by the Ice Soldiers have been ramping up steadily in the train yard. Whatever they're looking for must have something to do with Bertrand's secret visits to the area. Zeke is perplexed as to why an elitist like Bertrand would dirty his boots in such a filthy place.

Any hopes Cole has of ambushing Bertrand are dashed when he's told Bertrand's visits are completely random. Nix insists she knows the reason Bertrand has been making the trek to the area, but she complains that her information falls on deaf ears in her attempts to tell Kuo.

BEAST MASTER

Nix is convinced that Bertrand is the one controlling the Swamp Monsters. She claims by simply walking with them long enough, he can bring them under his influence. Kuo compares it to a bear bonding with cubs.

Nix claims she's even performed the feat successfully, only to have her personal monster die to protect her from a Militia attack when she tried to escape. Despite her doubts about Nix's story, Kuo supports a mission to photograph and expose Bertrand's secret army of Corrupted. Nix, however, wants to turn Bertrand's tactics against him and raise an army to call her own.

PICTURE IMPERFECT FAMILY

The choice Cole makes between these two options can push his Karma significantly in either direction. To side with Kuo and earn Good Karma, continue to "Exposing Bertrand" (pg. 93). To turn Bertrand's horrific minions against him and earn Evil Karma, continue to "Nix's New Family" (below).

NIX'S NEW FAMILY

Travel to the red marker on a rooftop in the northwest region of Flood Town. Ignore Kuo's attempts to dissuade Cole, and activate the mission marker.

Despite her wild nature, Nix has certainly taken the time to do her research for this mission. She's timed the operation to be executed during the lookouts' shift change, while Bertrand's men are away from the watchtowers and vulnerable. Follow her lead into the rail yard by following the waypoint on the mini-map.

LAYING OUT THE LOOKOUTS

Nix leads Cole to a position just outside of the train yard, where the Militia forces are spread thin. Climb the building immediately ahead and clear the rooftops of Militia using Cole's blasts.

Watch out for Militia rocket launchers as Cole fights through the guards. Focus Cole's attacks on the Militia ensnared in Nix's tendrils to efficiently eliminate the opposition.

Cole must defeat all of the guards before he and Nix can penetrate the train yard itself. The guards are marked on the mini-map with red stars.

CUTTING THE POWER TO SPITE THEIR BASES

Unfortunately, Cole and Nix didn't strike fast enough. Word has made its way back to the main Militia forces in the yard. In response to Cole's infiltration, they've shut off all power in the area.

Cole needs to get to the nearest transformer. It's in the northwest and marked by a waypoint on the mini-map. Use it to launch a Tesla Missile at the next transformer in the rail yard, marked by the pulsing circle and positioned directly east.

TOPPING OFF

Before venturing into the unpowered rail yard, replenish Cole's energy from the transformer. This is the last opportunity he gets until the power is back online.

Immediately sprint to the transformer while dodging incoming rockets fired by Militia. Press **R1** to activate it, then launch a Tesla Missile at the three guard towers to the south.

WATCH NIX'S BACK

Zeke reports that elsewhere in Flood Town, the Ice Soldiers haven't failed to notice the loss of power in the rail yard. For them, this is the perfect opportunity to attack the heart of Bertrand's operation in the area. There's no time to retreat, though, because Nix has now reached a boxcar containing several of the creatures.

THE ICEMEN COMETH

While Nix attempts to turn the Swamp Monsters to her side, Cole needs to defend her from the incoming Ice Soldier strike force. Don't forget to keep an eye on the boxcar status, shown in the upper right corner of the screen.

With the power out, the only weapon at Cole's disposal to fend off the Ice Soldier assault is his Tesla Missile. Guide it through the ever-increasing waves of rocket launcher Ice Soldiers and Ice Heavies that attack Nix's boxcar. The familiar pulsing circles indicate their positions.

In due time, Nix successfully converts the Swamp Monsters to her cause. She tells Cole to guide a Tesla Missile to the last transformer directly to the south. Rush there while avoiding the numerous stretches of water and activate it to unleash Nix's newfound pets.

SPLITTING HEADS, NOT RAILS

With the legion of monsters at their side, Nix and Cole have a distinct tactical advantage over the remaining Ice Soldiers and Ice Heavies. Show them the folly of their choice to interfere by decimating their forces.

Once the dust has settled, Nix decides that she wants to spend some quality time with her new family… so much for raising an army to fight Bertrand.

REWARD: 500 XP

EXPOSING BERTRAND

Kuo leads Cole to the edge of the rail yard. With Zeke's specially modified camera in hand, Cole can document Bertrand's secret Corrupted army he's kept covered up.

They need to build a strong case against Bertrand to turn public support against him and his Militia. They can't settle for a handful of photos when what they need is hard, convincing evidence.

BAYSIDE BREAK-IN

Kuo has discovered a blind spot in the rail yard's defensive perimeter. Follow the waypoints as they appear on the mini-map to the west end of the Gas Works district of the north island.

The only way in is by island hopping across the small bay to the east end of the rail yard. Climb the utility pole by the water, and leap off. It provides enough starting height for Cole's Static Thrusters to let him coast to dry land.

Climb along the partially submerged train car that bridges the island to the edge of the rail yard. Cole disembarks to come face to face with Bertrand's civilian captives imprisoned in a train car.

SHOOTING BERTRAND'S SECRETS

Take out Cole's camera and aim it by holding **R2**. Wait for the viewfinder to turn green before pressing **R1** to take the photo.

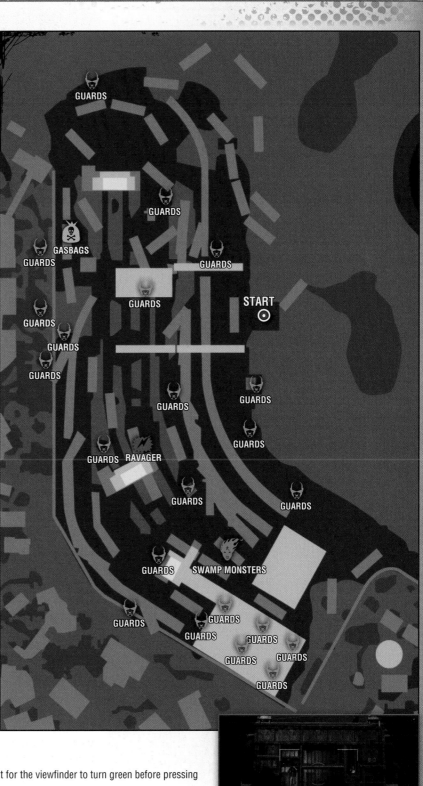

GUARDS

GUARDS

GASBAGS

GUARDS

GUARDS

GUARDS

GUARDS

START

GUARDS

GUARDS

GUARDS

GUARDS

GUARDS

RAVAGER

GUARDS

GUARDS

SWAMP MONSTERS

GUARDS

GUARDS

GUARDS

GUARDS

GUARDS

GUARDS

GUARDS

Falsely imprisoned humans are a good start, but Cole still needs to find where Bertrand is keeping his secret Corrupted army. Kuo directs Cole to three train cars, marked by waypoints on the mini-map.

The rail yard is heavily guarded, and Cole can't risk alerting the Militia to his presence before he has all the evidence his group needs. Avoid combat by climbing high above the Militia squads indicated on the mini-map. Kuo warns him if he starts to get too close—getting caught results in instant mission failure.

CABLE HOOKUP

Although unpowered, the Grindwires connecting the towering, lopsided utility poles are Cole's best bet. They put him out of sight of the nearest Militia watchtower and cross nearly the full length of the rail yard.

As Cole wraps up the last photo, Kuo calls him with an urgent bulletin. Bertrand has been spotted making one of his unannounced rail yard visits. Climb to the roof of the warehouse, marked by the pulsing circle on the mini-map.

READY FOR HIS CLOSE-UP

Kuo wants Cole to snap a picture of Bertrand's nefarious deeds. Position Cole on the south side of the roof and peer through the skylight there. Cole sees Bertrand conversing with someone in a room along the far side of the warehouse.

Cole can only look on in horror as Bertrand demonstrates his ability to transform normal human beings into warped, savage Corrupted. Once the transmutation is complete, take another picture of the aftermath.

It takes no time at all before the photos and video go viral. Televisions across New Marais light up with the damning evidence, destroying Bertrand's reputation in one fell swoop.

Flask in hand, Bertrand ponders his new status as pariah when he notices Cole through the skylight. Consumed by outrage and revenge, he starts to morph into his monstrous form but quickly vanishes from sight.

EMERGENCY EVACUATION

There's no time for Cole to combat the hordes of Militia now alerted. He needs to rescue Bertrand's prisoners, who await their own terrifying transformations, while the rebel assault has the Militia distracted.

Investigate the waypoints on the mini-map that mark the train car captives in sequence from south to north. Climb the roof of each to reach the electronic controls for the gate. Press **R1** repeatedly to break the mechanism with Cole's Amp.

After Cole finishes freeing the second car of caged civilians, Nix makes an unexpected appearance. She explains that she executed her proposed plan without Cole's assistance and has the new minions to prove it.

She brushes off Cole's protests and makes a hasty exit. Fortunately, her new family sticks around to fight it out with the Militia. Let them take the heat off of Cole, and return to rescuing the last civilians.

Upon arriving at the northernmost train car, Cole finds it guarded by a vigilant Devourer. By now, the Militia have noticed his incursion into their territory and are converging on his location, as well.

FEW AND FAR BETWEEN

Make a mental note of the limited number of nearby electrical sources—they're critical to beating the Devourer—but be prepared to venture farther away to heal and recharge Cole.

Take cover behind or atop train cars to avoid the devastating damage inflicted by the Devourer's bulbous, exploding projectiles. Wait for it to retract its armor and lash out with its prehensile tongue. Rockets are Cole's best bet here—keep firing for as long as the Devourer leaves itself exposed, and deal with recharging later.

Once the Devourer has fallen, free the last train car of civilians. The Militia is finished in New Marais and the captives are free, but Bertrand is still at large. Exit the rail yard while the remaining Militia continue to attack in vain.

REWARD: 500 XP

THE BEAST DRAWS NEAR

ESCORT THE NUKE

Zeke pulls up to Cole in a big rig he purloined from the Militia. He says it's time for a joyride to celebrate the benefits of his espionage. Zeke tells Cole to use his blast to shake loose the panels covering the back of the big rig to see what he's talking about.

The panels fall back to reveal a shocking sight—a nuclear warhead. It seems that Ray Field technology alone wasn't enough for Bertrand. He also forced Wolfe to assemble this nuclear device as a fail-safe in the event that a Ray Field experiment went wrong.

to assemble this nuclear device as a fail-safe in the event that a Ray Field experiment went wrong.

Zeke reassures Cole that the people of New Marais are safe from nuclear fallout, provided that they detonate the nuke far enough away.

A BRIDGE TOO FAR

Catch a lift on the big rig and clear the path of Militia forces dispatched to reclaim their nuke. Several Militia pickup trucks loaded with troops attempt to block off the street. Riflemen open fire from balconies flanking the thoroughfare to back them.

Although the group is past the initial wave of Militia resistance, Zeke needs the path cleared so he can cross the bridge. At that moment, Militia gunboats draw alongside the bridge and bombard it with artillery shells.

TWO BIRDS, ONE CAR

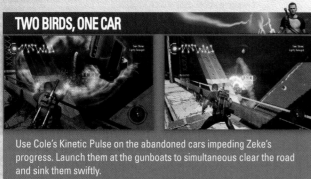

Use Cole's Kinetic Pulse on the abandoned cars impeding Zeke's progress. Launch them at the gunboats to simultaneous clear the road and sink them swiftly.

Midway across the bridge, Cole and Zeke find the Militia locked in battle with a Ravager. Keep the nuke secure by neutralizing the whole lot of them while they're distracted.

Upon arriving at the other side of the bridge in Flood Town, Cole passes by numerous Ice Soldiers battling a horde of Corrupted.

LAUNCH THE NUKE

Zeke finally reaches his destination and parks the big rig by the cranes at the Flood Town docks. From here, they can launch it at The Beast.

Cole needs to climb the nearest crane marked by the waypoint to reach the binoculars wired into the missile's targeting system. Press **R1** to use the mounted binoculars and hold **R1** to acquire a targeting lock on The Beast.

ONE SHOT AT REDEMPTION

However, just as Cole is about to get a lock, a contingent of Ice Soldiers swarms the dockyard. Cole only gets one shot at taking The Beast down with this nuke, and he can't afford to waste it. Eliminate all the Ice Soldiers before firing the nuke.

Once Cole has neutralized all the Ice Soldiers, return to the binoculars and hold **R1** while aimed at The Beast to paint the target. The nuke launches and lands right on target, producing a concussive shock wave that knocks Cole off his feet.

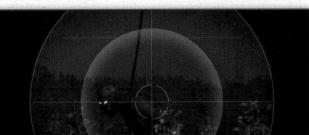

LEAVE NO MAN BEHIND

After getting back on his feet, Cole needs to find Zeke. Cole soon finds his friend pinned under a car by the gas pumps to the north. Use Cole's Kinetic Pulse to lift the car and free Zeke.

Zeke is in rough shape and needs Cole to clear the way back to the truck. Hold **R1** by each of the toppled light riggings to lift it up for Zeke to pass under. As Cole gets his friend to safety, the unimaginable happens—The Beast rears its terrifying head once more and seems to absorb the intense radiation of the nuke.

REWARD: 500 XP

Zeke managed to track the irradiated Beast as it dragged itself back to the Gas Works, but lost track of it amid the pipes and plants. Cole needs to bring the power back online to the Gas Works if he is to have any chance of finding The Beast, much less taking it down.

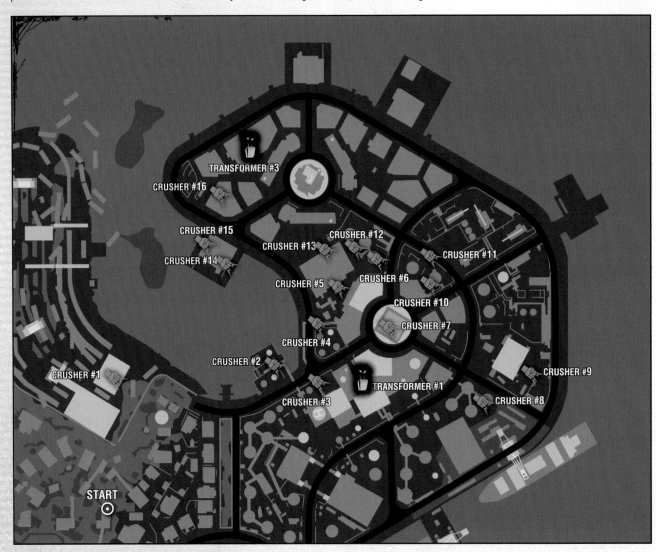

SPARKING TRANSFORMERS

Press **R1** to fire a Tesla Missile from the transformer marked by the waypoint on the mini-map. First, use it to take out the three marked Crushers. With the path clear, guide the Tesla Missile to the target offline transformer.

Activate and defend it from the Ice Soldiers that converge on Cole's position as it powers up. The transformer reaches critical mass and eliminates all aggressors around it.

FROZEN FIEFDOM

Located in the heart of the Ice Soldiers' operations, the transformer is surrounded frozen constructs. Defend it from the alerted Ice Soldier reinforcements until it comes online.

Use this transformer to clear out the six marked Crusher targets with a Tesla Missile, then navigate it to the transformer atop a storage tower.

Activate and defend this transformer. When the discharge clears the remaining threats, fire another Tesla Missile to take down the seven marked Crushers ahead before flying it to the last transformer.

CAGED COLE

Cole finally arrives at the last transformer, only to discover it's a trap. Metal gates fall into place along every side, trapping Cole in a Faraday cage that dissipates his electrical powers.

Bertrand reveals his presence to smugly concede he can only stop The Beast with Cole's help. Proposing an alliance, he says they can be heroes together. He reacts to Cole's skepticism with utter contempt and leaves his men with orders to execute Cole.

LEAD SALAD DIET

Cole needs to survive inside this death trap until help arrives. Dodge repeatedly and take cover behind the wood crates and the transformer while it lasts.

Cole's calls to Nix for help go unanswered. Luckily, Zeke shows up with guns blazing to save the day in the nick of time.

REWARD: 500 XP

Issue #0

Insider's Guide to New Marais

Retaking New Marais

User-Generated Content

NSA Intel

Extras

Zeke contacts Cole after discovering the location of another Blast Core while undercover. He directs Cole to a warehouse in the Gas Works where the Militia stashed a Blast Core. Zeke's sources say it's hidden inside a crate bearing the Militia logo.

Once the gas has a chance to disperse, Cole can drop back in and check out the safe's contents. Unfortunately, this one contains nothing.

■■■WAREHOUSE CLEARANCE

Enter the warehouse and break open the Militia crate next to the bungalow office. Cole discovers it conceals a safe, but the safe only contains property deeds for three other warehouses inside it.

There's only one warehouse left to search, and the Militia have locked it down tight. The safe is located at the far end of the warehouse, toward the water and left of the entrance.

After checking out the properties listed on the deeds, Cole finds a safe on the catwalk in the next warehouse marked on the mini-map. However, this one contains only four Blast Shards.

The safe in the last warehouse is at the end of the blue shipping container in the center of the floor. But before Cole has a chance to open it, the entire warehouse is locked down and filled with poisonous gas. Cole needs to act fast to avoid asphyxiation by blasting a hole in the warehouse walls or ceiling's skylights to escape outside.

Walk up to the safe and press **R1** to attempt to open it. Before Cole has a chance to see what it contains, an Ice Titan rushes onto the scene and decimates the Militia forces.

BOSS Ice Titan

Ice Titans project ice beams from each hand that dwarf those of the previously encountered Ice Heavies. They also channel their sub-zero fields to generate massive ice boulders. These massive projectiles bounce and fly erratically along the ground at Cole.

Cole launches himself through the air and onto the Titan, wedging his Amp into a chink in the ice armor. Press ⬤ repeatedly to pry open the ice armor and expose the weakpoint. Cole can then unleash his bolts and rockets at the exposed face for massive damage.

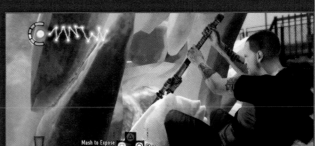

Mash to Expose Weakpoint!   Step

EVERYTHING MUST GO

Conserve Cole's energy by using the various heavy objects around the warehouse to defeat the Ice Titan. Cole's Kinetic Pulse wastes little electricity and turns everything around him into a long-range projectile.

Bolts are insufficient to penetrate the Titan's ice armor. Use Cole's other attacks to destroy its arms and bring it to its knees, but act quickly. Cole must capitalize on its weakened state before it can regenerate the lost limb. During this window of vulnerability, get close to its chest and press **R1**.

BERTRAND'S MASTER PLAN

After defeating the Ice Titan, Cole is finally free to check the last safe. There, he finds the Blast Core along with Bertrand's briefcase containing a revelatory array of documents.

Cole discovers Bertrand created the Ice Soldiers for more than just seizing control of New Marais. The scope of his ambition was international—he sought to create and sell Conduits on the open market to the highest bidder.

Among the business papers were invoices showing sales all over the world. Bertrand was kicking off a new arms race, one where countries would wage war using people of mass destruction.

But why? The money seems irrelevant when Bertrand gives so much away publicly to charitable causes. And his money buys him all the respect he could need. The only explanation left is pure ego… a sick desire to save the world from what he perceives as evil.

REWARD: 500 XP

EASY GOING

Zeke and Cole take a much-deserved break from the exhausting campaign they have been waging against the Militia. Kicking back and watching TV with a few beers in hand, the two drift off into slumber.

Cole awakes to groggily absorb his newest Blast Core acquisition. He's knocked unconscious to the ground, while Zeke continues to sleep completely undisturbed.

THE LIGHTNING TETHER

Cole wakes up hours later to find he now has a new way to navigate New Marais. He can channel his electrical energy out of his hands into a whip-like extension that uses electromagnetic energy to latch onto surfaces.

Cole can now zip through the air with ease using the Lightning Tether. Hold **L1** then press **R2** to lash out with the tether and pull Cole toward the target. It's the most effective way of covering ground short of Grindwires.

REWARD: 500 XP

Zeke contacts Cole to share the rumors that Bertrand is loading some heavy-duty freight down at the harbor. Based on the documents Cole discovered in Bertrand's suitcase, it's likely they're his mass-produced Ice Conduits.

EMBARGO ENFORCEMENT

Cole arrives at the harbor to find Bertrand's cargo ships still docked. To ensure his Conduits delivery never makes it to their destination, Cole needs to prevent the ship from departing.

Head to the fore of the ship where the marker on the mini-map indicates the location of its anchor winch. Before Cole has a chance to disable the mechanism, Ice Soldiers and Ice Heavies converge from all sides. Eliminate them all, then press **R1** near the anchor winches. This overloads the circuitry and strands the boat.

Immediately head to the other large cargo ship in Bertrand's fleet. Unfortunately, even more Ice Soldiers and Ice Heavies are already waiting for Cole, both on the ship and by the cranes.

CONTAINING THE SITUATION

Dish out an Ionic Vortex by the cranes to clear the field. While Cole's enemies are stunned, board the boat. Strategically use the cargo containers as cover and pick off the Ice Soldiers as they navigate around the metal obstacles. Blast those near the rail into the water.

The Ice Titan standing guard at the fore of the boat is far less threatening now that Cole has rockets at his disposal. Bombard the Ice Titan with rockets until out of electricity, then drain the nearest source.

Repeat the process until presented with the opportunity to expose the Ice Titan's weakpoint, then finish it off. Finally, approach the vessel's anchor winch and press **R1** to disable it.

GHOSTS OF EMPIRE CITY

With Bertrand's shipping brought to a standstill, a strangely suited figure from Cole's past makes an unexpected appearance. It is none other than John White—the NSA agent who infiltrated the First Sons in Empire City.

When Cole reacquired the Ray Sphere from the First Sons back in Empire City, John was consumed by a maelstrom of Ray Field energy and presumed dead. He then touches Cole on the forehead and grants him a new ability. Cole now share's John's ability to sense the plague inside of people.

Press **L3** to send out Cole's pulse. In addition to detecting electrical sources, it also gives Cole a glimpse into nearby citizens' internal anatomy. Those infected by the plague display a red glow in their abdominal cavity.

John instructs Cole to meet him at a nearby plague ward. He doubts the government has the resources to stop the plague. He firmly believes he and Cole are the last hope of those suffering from the plague.

▌▌▌THE DEAD AND THE DYING

Head to the plague ward marked by the waypoint on the mini-map. While Cole explores the interior of the warehouse where the plague victims lay dying, John points out one woman in particular.

DYING TO MEET COLE

If Cole takes too long to make it to the plague ward, a countdown timer appears on-screen. When it runs out, Cole fails the mission.

TOUCHING LIVES

There are a number of incapacitated plague victims in the ward. Feel free to pick up Good Karma and XP by Pulse Healing them all.

This patient is located immediately to Cole's left when he enters the ward. In addition to the red glow of plague, she also possesses a golden light visible within. Lock on and attempt to Pulse Heal her per John's instructions.

Despite his best efforts, Cole is powerless to save the woman. This comes as no surprise to John, who assigned this impossible task to prove a point—Cole doesn't have the power to save the sick.

A COSTLY CURE

John makes no distinction between the doomed plague victims and the dead. However, the woman he pointed out to Cole is different from the other infected—she possesses the Conduit gene. Because of this, John has the ability to save her but only at a great cost.

Without elaborating further, John releases a wave of energy resembling the original Ray Sphere explosion that gave Cole his powers. Realizing that John is The Beast, Cole blacks out. When he regains consciousness, he finds the medical ward a smoking ruin.

In the midst of the death and destruction, Cole is shocked to see the woman he could not heal on her feet again. She offers a brief thanks before demonstrating an amazing new ability—flight.

REWARD: 500 XP

Bertrand arrives at the helipad to find it deserted except for Cole. He concedes to Cole that he's trying to scare people into realizing that Conduits are abominations. His ultimate goal is quite simply the complete and utter genocide of demons like Cole and himself.

Bertrand rants that Conduits are not divine, but are instead monsters made by science and the devil. In the thrall of his own vitriolic self-loathing, he transforms once more into a towering abomination. Zeke instructs Cole to hitch a ride on the back of his truck to lure the transformed Bertrand out into the open for an ambush.

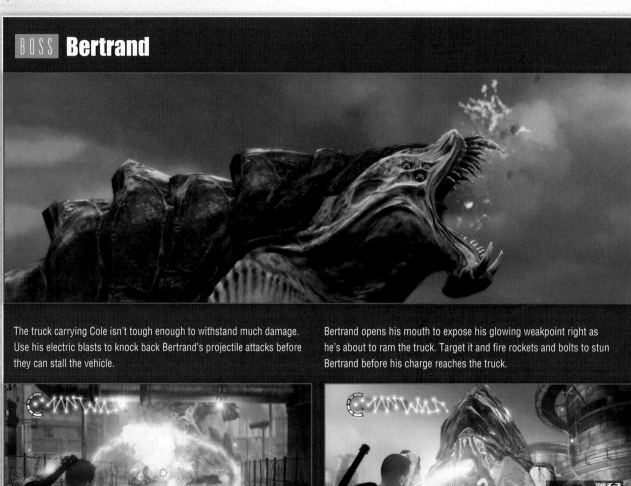

BOSS Bertrand

The truck carrying Cole isn't tough enough to withstand much damage. Use his electric blasts to knock back Bertrand's projectile attacks before they can stall the vehicle.

Bertrand opens his mouth to expose his glowing weakpoint right as he's about to ram the truck. Target it and fire rockets and bolts to stun Bertrand before his charge reaches the truck.

BLINDING BERTRAND

Once Bertrand arrives at the ambush point, the Dunbar Beams surrounding him light up to halt the destructive rampage. Immobilized by the beams but still a threat, Bertrand exhales a noxious acid breath that clears his immediate area.

Dodge his projectiles and wait for him to strike the ground with his legs. Target and destroy the vulnerable, glowing purple joints. When both have been obliterated, Cole hitches a ride on the skid of LaRoche's helicopter.

A MULTITUDE OF MISSILES

While dangling, Cole needs to once again defend the helo against Bertrand's attacks as it lures him to the next ambush location.

Upon arriving, LaRoche's men unleash a missile barrage. Unfortunately, one of the missiles lodges between the armored plates on Bertrand's back without detonating. Cole needs to set it off with a well-placed bolt.

Having expended their missiles at this ambush point, the helicopter moves onto the next ambush area with Cole still in tow. Continue to draw Bertrand's single-minded interest to the final phase of the plan.

FINISH THE JOB

With Bertrand on the ropes, the rebel's hopes are pinned on their last salvo of missiles. Once again, a dud wedged in Bertrand's scales fails to explode requiring Cole's manual ignition.

Although severely weakened, Bertrand still has some fight left in him. Cole needs to take out the glowing weakpoints at his legs and chest to finally bring Bertrand's reign of terror to an end.

REWARD: **500 XP**

Zeke thinks their quest might finally be coming to an end. He's tracked down the location of another Blast Core somewhere in the Gas Works, and it should be the last one needed to power the RFI. Meet Zeke near the dock on 3rd Street on the eastern shore of this island. Despite closing in on his goal, Cole can't help but notice Zeke is in bad shape. Using the new ability John granted him, Cole can see for himself that Zeke is now one of the many afflicted by the plague.

CLAIM THE CORE

Cole is in luck, because the forces of nature seem to have lined up to his cause. A torrential lightning storm system passes over New Marais just as Cole mounts his assault. Defeat all the Ice Soldiers marked on the mini-map here before continuing Cole's search.

EYE OF THE STORM

While the storm rages overhead, Cole can restore his health and electricity by draining straight from the storm clouds overhead at any time.

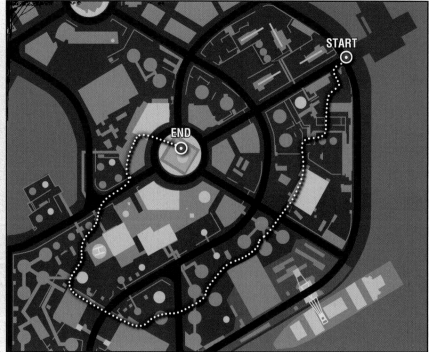

FEARFUL LEADER

Cole arrives at the next waypoint just as the Ice General is fleeing, forcing Cole to give chase. Follow the waypoint identifying the fleeing commander's location.

VANISHING INTO THIN AIR

Cole can also track the Ice General via the ice trail he leaves behind. It only appears for a short time before evaporating into vapor.

The chase eventually leads Cole deep into the heart of the territory that the Ice Soldiers have carved out for themselves in the Gas Works. Scale the ice tower at its center and climb to its peak.

John once again makes psychic contact with Cole to suggest they join forces. He apologizes for his actions as The Beast in Empire City, attributing his aggression to the strain of willing himself back into existence.

He explains that the Ray Field tore him apart at the atomic level. It took all his willpower to slowly pull himself back together, finally regaining physical form. It was his rebirth Cole witnessed at the Empire City pier, with rampant destruction an unintended consequence of returning from beyond the grave.

PASSING GAS VALVES

To extract the Blast Core the Ice Soldiers have encased in this ice tower, Cole needs to thaw its frozen shell. He must open three gas valves to fuel the tower's defrosting flame.

The photo found at the top of the tower shows the first gas valve location. It can be found on the northwest side of the tower and one level up. Press **R1** by the valve to activate it and obtain the location of the next valve.

The second valve is located at the southeast end of the same floor. Before Cole can activate it, he must deal with the Crusher that arrives to stop Cole.

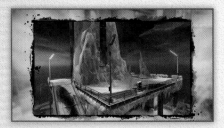

The final valve is located on the topmost platform. Upon releasing it, the top of the tower ignites and begins to melt the ice. This towering inferno doesn't go unnoticed and mere moments later Ice Soldiers and Ice Heavies show up in full force.

Drop to the ground floor as Cole battles it out with the Ice Soldiers. The Blast Core launched clear of the tower and landed on the ground to the northeast. Once Cole is close enough, its location is marked with a waypoint on the mini-map. Head to it and press **R1** to pick it up.

REWARD: 500 XP

THE FINAL PIECE

As Cole prepares to absorb what he expects to be the last Blast Core, Zeke waxes philosophical. He thinks there are two kinds of people: people who don't like what happens to them but deal with it anyway, and then there are guys like Cole. With that in mind, Cole absorbs the Blast Core and passes out.

Awakening later, Cole discovers he has a new devastating Ionic Power at his disposal. Cole can now use his collected Ionic Charges on an Ionic Storm. This devastating force of nature draws thousands of gigawatts of energy from the sky and brings it crashing down on his enemies.

IONIC STORM

The Ionic Storm summons a tightly clustered cylinder of electricity to strike the ground before Cole. The cascading carnage devastates the target area, even dealing splash damage to enemies on its periphery.

Try this new ability out by pressing down on the d-pad to expend an Ionic Charge to fire an Ionic Storm. Follow the on-screen objectives and deploy it down a street with plenty of parked cars to complete the mission.

REWARD: 500 XP

Kuo, Zeke, Nix, and Cole convene for a rooftop meeting before Cole activates the RFI. The nervousness is already palpable when Nix arrives, still distraught from the slaughter of her adopted Corrupted family by The Beast.

Before proceeding, Cole reveals the identity of The Beast as John White. He repeats what John told him—that his apparent acts of mass murder were actually curing those with the Conduit gene afflicted by the plague. He confesses that John asked for his help, but Nix insists on revenge for the family she lost. Cole isn't in the mood to debate and stops wasting time. Grasping the RFI, he focuses his energy and begins to charge it.

Cole, Kuo, and Nix fall to the ground as it powers up, writhing in agony. Remaining cool under pressure, Zeke knocks the RFI loose from Cole's hands with the Amp.

THE FINAL DECISION

Thanks to Zeke's quick response, the trio are no worse for wear, though they now know the terrible cost of the RFI cure—the lives of Conduits everywhere, not just The Beast.

Cole has a difficult decision to make: spare the Conduits at the cost of countless plague victims, or sacrifice the Conduits to cure the plague?

GO FIND YOURSELF

Cole can only complete the mission by choosing the option associated with his current Karma level. To be able to choose otherwise, he must first abandon the mission and shift his Karma level to the other end of the spectrum by completing Side Missions and Karma Opportunities. Once he has reached the required level, return to the rooftop, and the other choice becomes available.

Cole knows the right choice is to save Zeke's life and those of the countless victims of the plague, even if that means sacrificing not just himself but Conduits everywhere.

Kuo is dumbfounded by Cole's decision and makes an ill-advised attempt to snatch the RFI from Zeke. Foiled, she warns them about the consequence of this decision before teleporting away in a cloud of ice.

Zeke has looked the RFI over and finds that it's still not fully charged. Unfortunately, he accidentally damaged its power regulator when he struck it with the Amp. Any attempt by Cole to charge it further is sure to burn the entire device out.

ALL ABOARD

Cole, Nix, and Zeke are gathered at the top of St. Ignatius Cathedral. Zeke has managed to cobble together a charging station there that can trickle power to the RFI at a controlled rate to prevent overload. He's tasked LaRoche's men with setting up several other similar substations throughout the city. Each one charges the RFI incrementally until it reaches full power.

Nix extracts the RFI once it's charged here and departs to the next station. Descend from the church back to street level and follow Nix's waypoint on the mini-map to the shore where LaRoche is waiting.

LaRoche has assembled a small fleet of boats to the north to take them to the next substation on the north island. The rebels onboard are armed with rocket launchers and attempt to slow The Beast's steady journey to the densely populated south island. Rockets cut through air, leaving telltale wisps of exhaust behind.

Nix is soon close enough to teleport directly to the substation but reappears at the feet of The Beast. Unfortunately, there's no time to for her to reach the substation before The Beast's attention falls upon her. She has barely enough time to teleport away before The Beast pummels the ground with his attacks.

GETAWAY STRAIGHTAWAYS

With the substation destroyed, the plan begins to fall apart. LaRoche's men valiantly fight to the bitter end, bombarding The Beast with rockets even as their boats sink into the bay.

Don't let the rebels' sacrifices be in vain, and use the time they've bought Cole to get back to shore. Use Cole's Lightning Tether to zip back from boat to boat.

THAT FIRST STEP IS A DOOZY

Leap from the highest point on the boat before deploying the Lightning Tether. Because of the slight delay before Cole reels himself in, he drops slightly mid-jump, and it's possible to take a fatal plunge into the bay.

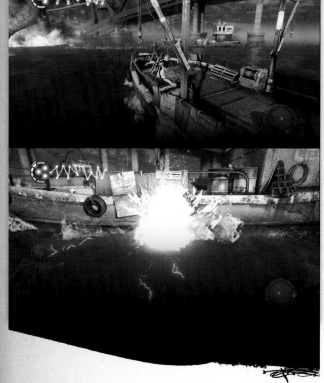

Once back on dry ground, Cole needs to get to the last substation, located on a roof overlooking Smut Triangle in the Red Light District. Nix is already en route, and there's no time to waste—head to the waypoint marking the substation on the mini-map.

RACING THE BEAST

Cole has no time to dawdle. A countdown appears when time is almost up, and Cole must get to Smut Triangle before it finishes or face mission failure.

WATCH NIX'S BACK

Nix is at the substation on top of the Hush Theatre, already in the midst of charging the RFI. It's only a matter of time before The Beast senses its location and attempts to stop them. The Beast's titanic silhouette soon comes into view over the building tops. It all comes down to this.

BOSS The Beast

Dwarfed by The Beast, Cole has his work cut out for him. The Beast relies on his energy-based abilities to attack Cole. He slowly gathers concentrated energy in his hands before hurling it at the ground, where it impacts explosively. Wait until The Beast is about to throw his projectile, then dodge toward it and laterally at the last minute to avoid taking damage.

HOOKED ON THE GOOD STUFF

The substation charges Cole in addition to the RFI. When Cole is close enough, it automatically restores his health and energy—even while he's airborne.

INSUFFICIENT SUCTION

Don't panic when The Beast temporarily suspends gravity in his vicinity. While airborne, use this opportunity to unleash Cole's rockets while The Beast's guard is down.

CRUSHING DEFEAT

The Beast generates a gravitational field that draws Cole in, along with any cars, streetlights, and pedestrians unlucky enough to be too close. Move the analog stick in the opposite direction of The Beast to avoid being sucked into his grasp.

If Cole winds up in the grip of The Beast, tap **R1** repeatedly to blindly unleash his bolts upon The Beast until he releases Cole. Act quickly, because The Beast can easily crush the life out of Cole before he can break free.

After reducing The Beast's health bar almost halfway, another challenger enters the battle…Kuo.

She lost everything in her quest to stop The Beast, and to sacrifice her life is asking too much. She refuses to come to terms with her imminent mortality and appears in Smut Triangle to foil Cole and Nix's plan.

Kuo must have been holding something back in previous fights. Now that her life is on the line, she demonstrates some remarkable offensive capabilities.

She takes a page from the Ice Heavies' tactics and summons a pillar of ice for a more advantageous angle of attack. Additionally, she launches rapid-fire ice blasts from each hand.

HAMMER TIME

It's extremely difficult to land any blows against Kuo while under her ice beam bombardment. Stay out of her line of fire and wait at the ice column's base for her to give up and sink to Cole's level.

When she touches down on the ground, immediately unleash a flurry of blows with Cole's Amp to demolish her health bar. Finisher and Ultra Attacks are especially useful here.

ON ICE FOR NOW

Even after fully depleting her health bar, Cole hasn't heard the last of Kuo. She only temporarily retreats from battle before returning to tag-team Cole with The Beast. Each time Cole empties her health bar, she leaves to lick her wounds briefly but always returns with full health.

Once The Beast's health has been reduced to nothing, Nix tells Cole to deal the finishing blow. Press down on the d-pad to summon an Ionic Storm that brings the full power of the heavens down on The Beast's head.

Nix sees that it isn't enough and teleports directly at The Beast to even the odds. Kuo flies there to stop her, and the combination of the Ionic Storm with their powers —particularly in such close proximity to The Beast's— causes a massive explosion.

Kuo's smoking body is blasted clear, but no trace of Nix remains. This only temporarily stuns The Beast, but it gives Cole the time to retrieve the RFI and take it back to the cathedral's substation.

Head directly to the waypoint on the mini-map and scale the side of the cathedral to reach the top of the substation tower. Cole uses it to fully charge the RFI but isn't quite ready to use it yet.

He hurls himself from the tower toward The Beast as he crosses the threshold onto the cathedral grounds. Unleash every attack Cole has at his disposal to exhaust The Beast's health bar and bring him to his knees.

Kuo limps weakly onto the scene and acknowledges Cole made the right choice. Fearful, she stands by while Cole prepares for the coup de grace. Hold **L1**, **L2**, **R1**, and **R2** simultaneously then release them.

The RFI emits a massive blast of energy that engulfs the whole world. Scores of people from all walks of life and every corner of the globe fall dead, unknowing carriers of the Conduit gene.

These thousands died so that millions could live. In an instant, the plague was stricken from the planet, and Cole is memorialized as a savior.

Alone with his friend for the last time, Zeke sets sail. Despite all the vitriolic rhetoric separating Conduits from humans, he knows that no one had more humanity than Cole MacGrath. As Zeke sails into the unknown, a powerful lightning bolt strikes the boat to illuminate the horizon…

SIDE WITH THE BEAST

Press **R2** to join Kuo and betray humanity by siding with The Beast. Activating the RFI is guaranteed to kill Cole, Kuo, and Nix in the process. But if Wolfe's theoretical cure for the plague fails, who is left with the power to save humanity?

The only way to save even a fraction of those suffering from the plague is to activate their Conduit genes. Cole tells Kuo to make contact with John to act before the plague spreads further. Outraged at Cole's decision, Nix snatches the RFI and flees with it, with Kuo giving chase. Zeke advises Cole to shoot first the next time he sees him before departing.

Keep up with John—now in his Beast form—and press ⊗ when prompted to leap into a sustained hover while within a range of John. Together, they head to St. Ignatius Cathedral in the center of New Marais. The population there is at its most dense and then the purification can begin.

ESCORT JOHN

Kuo and Cole join John at the docks when the power suddenly goes out, thanks to Zeke. Kuo leaves to try bringing the power back online. For the time being, Cole can safely depend on John to supply him with all the power he needs.

GUARDIAN DEVIL

John is depending on Cole to neutralize anyone standing in the way. Eliminate any resistance, or risk being shot out of the sky.

STRAIGHT FROM THE TAP

Cole has an infinite supply of electricity to power his attacks while hovering near John—he steadily replenishes Cole's energy at a fixed rate.

After tearing through the Gas Works district, Cole and John are confronted by the appearance of Nix with RFI in hand. Although it's not fully charged, the RFI is still powerful enough to threaten Cole. He needs to retrieve the RFI at any cost—even if that means killing Nix.

FIGHT #3

FIGHT #2

FIGHT #5

FIGHT #4

FIGHT #1

FIGHT #6

NEUTRALIZE NIX

Chase her down by following her waypoint on the mini-map and climb the gas tower she's waiting on top of. Since the area is powered down, Cole should mind his electricity use carefully or rely on the Amp to attack her.

Cole can only land a few blows before Nix teleports away. Be prepared to run down her new position by locating her waypoint on the mini-map. Zip to her position speedily using the Lightning Tether.

NEIGHBORHOOD WALL-CRAWLER

Direct assaults face the full force of the RFI, which can whittle away Cole's health in no time flat. Instead, scale the sides of buildings to attack Nix from below. This avoids giving her direct line-of-sight to Cole and leaves her unable to attack him with the RFI.

After Cole sufficiently weakens her with a series of withering attacks, Nix flees. Cole can now rejoin John on his rampage. Soon, John steps into the river with Cole in tow.

After the duo crosses to the main island, Kuo manages to restore the power. At the central square of the Red Light District, Nix reappears and uses the RFI to bring John to his knees.

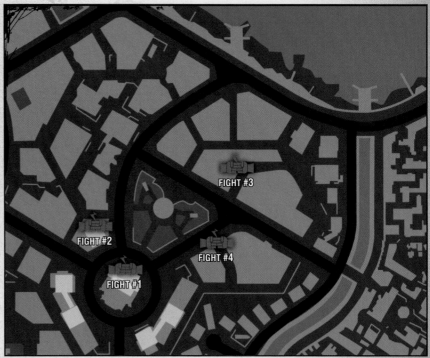

Cole has no choice but to fight her to spare John's life. Chase her down by following the waypoint on the mini-map and start attacking her with everything in Cole's arsenal.

In addition to attacking with the RFI, Nix unleashes her oil-based abilities to lob burning projectiles at Cole as well as slam the ground to produce rippling waves of fire.

Continue to chase her across the rooftops as she flees Cole's blows until bringing her health down to its last shred. Once again, she escapes by the skin of her teeth. Return to John now that he can move again. Steadying himself, he summons a Ray Field that completely wipes out everyone in the square.

OVER THEIR DEAD BODIES

Cole continues with him toward the church. Standing before St. Ignatius Cathedral, they seem moments from accomplishing their goal, when Nix makes a desperate last stand with the RFI.

BOSS Nix

While Kuo guards John, Cole has to climb to the top of the church. There, he must confront Nix once and for all.

KNOCK OFF SHOCK OFF

Knock Nix off the roof with melee attacks. While she lies prone on the ground, unleash Cole's electrical attacks on her.

When she's finally been beaten within an inch of her life, press ▲ to finish her off. The RFI rolls away from her lifeless hands and comes to a stop at Zeke's feet.

Staring at Cole, Zeke steadies his gun and takes a shot. Wounded but unbowed, Cole must now put his friend down for good. Aim at Zeke and press **R1** to put him out of his misery.

BECOMING THE BEAST

With all obstacles to his plan now gone, Cole destroys the RFI with the Amp. John then approaches, weakly confessing his inability to cope with the strain of his powers.

The burden of the responsibility that accompanies them is much too great for him. However, he believes Cole can complete his work. With his last ounce of strength, John transfers his powers into Cole and vanishes. The resulting blast utterly devastates the area for blocks around. New Conduits awaken afterwards with newfound powers, cured of the plague. United under Cole, they leave their old lives behind and learn to master their abilities.

A monumental task lies before them, with millions still infected and doomed to die within weeks. They are proof that some could be saved, with one in a thousand reborn as new Conduits.

Unsurprisingly, the world reacts with fear and violence to Cole's cure. But they are powerless in the face of Cole and his Conduit allies, helpless to stop this next evolutionary jump wherein humanity gives way to Conduits. Cole sought to destroy The Beast...now he is The Beast.

SIDE MISSIONS

A hero's work is never done, and there is no rest for the wicked. Citizens scattered throughout New Marais are in need of help, and it is up to Cole to fulfill their super-powered needs. Completing side missions grants Cole additional XP that is useful for buying new powers and liberates areas of the map from enemy control.

Side missions become available upon completion of the story mission "Karma's a Bitch" (see pg. 43). Additional side missions unlock as Cole progresses through the main story.

The side missions are presented in this chapter by area and they are listed in the order that they are unlocked.

The main island of New Marais is split into western and eastern portions, divided by a canal near the center. Cole only discovers side missions in the west side of New Marais until the story mission "Powering Up Ascension Parish" is completed. Subsequently, the missions on the east side become available.

GOING OVERBOARD

In the southernmost area of New Marais, Cole finds a man who has some valuable information on the Militia. As it so happens, the Militia is keeping a pair of supply ships nearby, and destroying their cache of supplies could put a serious dent in their stranglehold over the city.

After accepting the mission, head down the staircase at the end of the building and continue out onto a pier. Use the small boats at the end of the pier as stepping-stones to cross over to the marshland.

Continue toward the shack located at the end of this landmass. Two boats are docked to the right of the shack that holds the Militia supplies.

Several Militia soldiers are stationed on the first boat. This makes a frontal assault potential suicide. Instead, Cole can use the shack to an advantage. Head to the left side of the shack to shield Cole from the Militia attacks and climb up to the roof.

Now Cole has a significant height advantage over the Militia soldiers. Toss a few grenades onto the deck of the ship to take out the soldiers and destroy some of the supply crates.

Once Cole has defeated the soldiers, hop onto the deck of the first ship and destroy any remaining Militia supplies. Make liberal use of Cole's Blast **L1**+✕ and Kinetic Pulse **L2** to knock supply crates and barrels off of the boat.

KEEP YOUR EYE ON THE SUPPLIES

There are a total of 22 supply items that Cole needs to remove in order to complete the mission. These items include crates, barrels, and a truck. All of these targets are marked with the Militia symbol.

Hop over to the second boat to deal with the next stash after all 12 supply items have been removed from the first boat. Jump from the bow of the first boat and use Cole's Static Thrusters **R1** to float over to the second one, or take advantage of the small boat floating in the water nearby to help Cole make it over.

Once Cole has made it to the boat, a squad of Militia soldiers starts attacking from the marshland. This is the perfect opportunity to use the Militia's supplies against them! Hold **L2** to use Kinetic Lift and pick up the Militia truck or supply crates to hurl them at the soldiers.

If Cole is running out of juice while he is out at sea, use the portable generators located on the deck of each ship to recharge. Remove any remaining supply items until all 22 of them are sunk.

REWARD: 100 XP

OVERCHARGE——NEW MARAIS

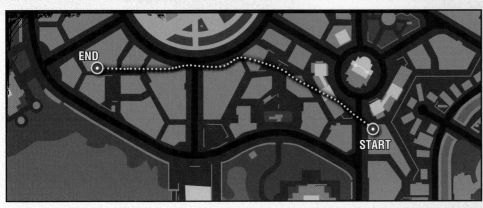

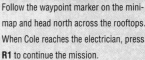

Follow the waypoint marker on the mini-map and head north across the rooftops. When Cole reaches the electrician, press **R1** to continue the mission.

"Going Overboard" is the marker for Cole's first overcharge mission. It is located two blocks to the north of where Cole began the mission. Activate the mission marker to receive a call from Zeke. He wants Cole to meet an electrician friend who has defected from the Militia.

The electrician has rigged a nearby transformer to imbue Cole with an "overcharge" of electricity, automatically frying any Militia soldiers who happen to get in Cole's path. Jump on top of the nearby transformer to get Cole all charged up, and hold ⬤ to see Cole's next destination, marked by a telltale lightning strike.

FLOAT LIKE A BUTTERFLY

Cole cannot touch the ground for very long while he is overcharged, or he loses the extra electrical buildup and fails the mission. Cole's glow changes to a deeper shade of red the closer he comes to losing his charge. Be sure to stay on grindable objects and make liberal use of the Static Thrusters to keep Cole from becoming grounded.

Leap onto the Grindwire in front of the transformer.

Continue to the top of the next building, leap off the Grindwire, and float to the top-left corner of the roof to land on the next Grindwire.

At the end of this grind, leap to the top-right corner of the next building and continue grinding.

Ignore the Militia soldiers on the next rooftop. Cole's super-charged body should make quick work of them. Leap off the Grindwire and float to the left to the next grind line.

Cruise along this double-long wire until Cole reaches the next building. Jump off the Grindwire and float between the two chimneystacks on the next building.

It is a long way down, but Cole should continue floating to the final Grindwire.

At the end of the line, leap off the wire and grab the Vertical Launch Pole conveniently placed on the wall dead ahead.

Let the pole carry Cole up to the roof, where a squad of Militia soldiers is waiting.

Land on the transformer to disperse Cole's overcharge, kill the Militia soldiers, and complete the mission!

REWARD: 100 XP

Head to the mission marker located in the northwest corner of New Marais, in front of the Pier 12 building. Zeke wants some intel on people and objects around New Marais, so he has rigged up a special camera for Cole—one that won't blow up the second Cole gets his lightning-infused mitts on it.

SHUTTERBUG

Becoming an expert photographer is a fairly straightforward affair. Hold L2 to look through the viewfinder and follow the on-screen prompts to center the shot. When the camera reticule turns green, press ⊗ to take the shot!

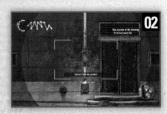

The first picture on Cole's list calls for a shot of a Vertical Grind Pole. Nearby Vertical Grind Poles are marked on Cole's minimap, so head to any of the marked waypoints and take the picture.

Zeke also wants a picture of a mugging in progress. It is very important that Cole isn't spotted; otherwise the photo opportunity is ruined. Send Cole to the rooftops and proceed toward the blue mugging icon that appears on the minimap.

With Cole perched within view of the mugging, look through the camera and take a shot of the crime.

MUG SHOTS

When Cole has successfully photographed the mugging, he is free to jump down and defeat the Militia soldiers for some extra Good Karma.

For the last shot, Zeke needs a picture of an abduction in progress. Like the mugging photo, Cole cannot be spotted while taking the picture. Head up to the rooftops again and send Cole toward the blue abduction icon on the minimap.

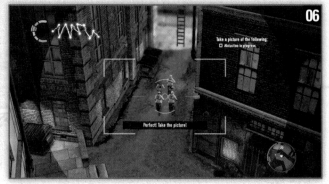

Get the Militia captors and their prisoners centered in the viewfinder, then snap the final picture for Zeke's scrapbook.

REWARD: 100 XP

NEW MARAIS TEA PARTY

Cole finds the contact for his next mission in the back alleys of the northwestern area of New Marais. The Militia has a few supply boats in the area, and it's up to Cole to trash their stash. After the mission begins, head north from the mission contact to the dock where the supply boats are located. The rooftops are too far away from the boats to launch a long-range assault, so this task requires a more direct approach.

Run up the dock toward the first boat and use the guardrails to give Cole some cover. Lob grenades onto the deck of the first boat to clear out the Militia and their supplies and use the nearby light poles to keep Cole charged up.

With the Militia soldiers on the first boat defeated, hop onto the boat and destroy any remaining supplies. Run around the right side of the boat's bridge to keep some cover between Cole and the second boat.

Continue using grenades to clear out the Militia soldiers stationed on the second boat. Cole should be able to pick off any stragglers with a few well-placed bolts.

When the coast is clear, hop over to the second boat. Dispose of any remaining Militia supplies to complete the mission.

REWARD: 100 XP

THE SIDEKICK

When Cole makes his way to the helipad located in the northwest area of New Marais, he meets a peculiar man in a tinfoil hat.

This upstanding and mentally disturbed citizen wants to team up with Cole! Just give him a chance and maybe he can help…

Before the tinfoil hat man can finish his sidekick application, The Corrupted ambush Cole's location and send Cole's would-be accomplice to a terrible death.

The rest of this mission is fairly straightforward. Stick to the helipad area and allow The Corrupted to come to Cole. Use basic melee combos and finishing moves to quickly dispatch the monsters and complete the mission.

REWARD: 100 XP

Underneath a neon "GIRLS" sign in the northern-center area of New Marais, a man waits for Cole with some intel on the Militia. A group of soldiers is patrolling the northern coast, casually bombarding New Marais with mortar fire. Accept the mission and head north to track down the boat.

Make a beeline for the concrete dividers. Duck behind them using ⊙, and fire an arc of grenades into the ship. It is important to keep Cole moving because the Militia cannons can quickly target his position. Use the plentiful supply of nearby power sources to keep Cole juiced up, then continue the rain of grenades until the ship is sunk.

Militia soldiers are patrolling a very small section of the northern coast. Wooden pillars dot the coastline and concrete dividers line the nearby road.

ALTERNATE STRATEGY

For a faster (but slightly riskier) method to sink the Militia boat, simply turn to the road. Use Kinetic Pulse **L2** to lift up a nearby vehicle and toss it at the boat. The resulting explosion kills a majority of the Militia soldiers on the first impact. Land two or three more direct hits to sink the boat for good.

REWARD: 100 XP

POLE POSITION

The wooden poles out in the water seem like the ideal vantage point for Cole's assault because of their close proximity to the Militia ship. The unfortunate truth is that the poles are the worst place to stage an attack. Militia gunners are surprisingly accurate. They can hit Cole with explosives before he can get more than a few shots off, knocking him into the surrounding water and killing him.

MASQUERADE

 01

 02

 03

 04

The starting point for this mission lies between the Yes We CanCan Cabaret and the St. Ignatius Cathedral. Upon activating the mission marker, Cole takes a call from Zeke about some disguised Militia soldiers hiding out in the nearby park. Follow the waypoint on Cole's minimap to the park in front of the Yes We CanCan Cabaret to uncover a disturbing sight. The Militia soldiers have disguised themselves as human statues!

Launch an attack at any of the nefarious street performers to break the Militia's cover. Once provoked, the entire lot of undercover soldiers comes down hard on Cole with flying rocks and melee attacks.

Make liberal use of blast attacks to keep the Militia mob at bay. You can back Cole up to one of the park's entrances, and force the Militia into a tight bottleneck. From here, Cole's grenades and blasts are the most efficient method of wiping out the undercover Militia.

Once the Militia ranks are thinned out a bit, use Cole's melee combos and finishing attacks to take care of any stragglers and complete the mission.

REWARD: 100 XP

FIELD MEDICINE

 01

 02

In the south central area of New Marais, a very sad medic is hanging around outside of a closed Medical Clinic. When Cole talks to him, the medic reveals that the Militia has stolen a huge crate of medical supplies. Being the kind soul that he is, Cole agrees to retrieve them.

Go up to the roof of the Medical Clinic and head east toward the minimap marker. On the roof across the street, several Militia soldiers guard the crate of medical supplies. Stay where you are, and take out the soldiers from a distance.

 03

 04

 05

With the Militia defeated, head over to the medical supply crate and pick it up with Kinetic Pulse **R2**. Aim the crate toward the beam of light in the distance.

Throw the crate toward the beam of light. If the crate missed the mark, just follow the minimap to its location and walk it over to the designated area.

Once Cole has dropped off the medical supplies behind the clinic, return to the medic and give him the good news that the Medical Clinic can reopen.

REWARD: 100 XP, Medical Clinic unlocked

The next mission marker is found on the roof of the Lucky Clover casino. Zeke is sick of the propaganda that Bertrand has been airing all over town, and he wants Cole to help him do something about it.

Good ol' Zeke has found a way to hack the TV network in New Marais, but in order to do it, he needs Cole to drain the electricity out of five satellite dishes in the area.

Locate the first satellite dish on the front of the Bloody Mary building to the left of the Yes We CanCan Cabaret. Use Cole's parkour skills to get near the dish and drain its electricity by pressing **L2**.

The second satellite dish is located on the cabaret, near the roof, underneath the leftmost neon dancing girl sign.

Move to the opposite side of the cabaret roof and look down to the first building on the corner to find the third dish. Float down using Cole's Static Thrusters and drain the juice from the dish.

Stay in the area and head over to the Plex Theater to find the fourth satellite dish.

Seek out the final dish on the building immediately across the park from the cabaret. Climb up the Hotel Marais sign to put Cole within reach of the dish so he can drain it completely.

With all of the satellites down, Zeke is ready to begin his transmission. When Cole makes his way to the huge jumbotron across from the Plex Theater, Zeke flips the switch and begins broadcasting his favorite cartoon—Zeppelin vs. Pterodactyls!

REWARD: 100 XP

TRICK PHOTOGRAPHY

The mission marker for this mission can be found at the southern end of the canal that separates the east and west sides of New Marais. Zeke needs a few pictures of the red light district for his "archives".

Zeke's first request is a picture of Sin Tower, aka the Yes We CanCan Cabaret. Head to the park in front of the building and focus the camera at the two neon dancing girls on the roof to get the shot.

Next, Zeke needs a picture of either the Hush or Plex Theater. The two theaters are located right next to each other, to the right of Sin Tower. Get the façade of either building in Cole's viewfinder and snap another picture.

COLE MACGRATH—ACTION PHOTOGRAPHER

Just when Cole's career as a landscape photographer is taking off, a huge fight erupts between the Militia and a vicious Ravager. Of course, Zeke wants Cole to grab a few snapshots of the action.

OBSERVE AND REPORT

The Militia is preoccupied fighting the Swamp Monsters, but they do not hesitate to fire on Cole if he gets to close or starts attacking. Stick to the rooftops when grabbing the action shots Zeke has requested, and avoid any combat unless it is absolutely necessary.

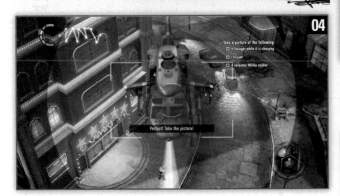

Cole's first assignment as a combat photographer is to grab a still shot of a helicopter. Get up on top of the buildings and put the helicopter in Cole's sights to snag the first photo.

The final shot, which entails capturing the Ravager while it is charging, can be a little tricky to snag. Position Cole to get a good view of the Ravager and keep the camera locked on the monster. Wait for the viewfinder to turn green, then snap the final picture.

AT RISK

If the Ravager photo proves too difficult to take from the roof, Cole can risk his neck by jumping into the fray. Put a few feet of distance between Cole and the Ravager and hit the Ravager with a few bolts to grab its attention. Keep the camera trained on the monster until it charges. Grab the photo and get out of the way quickly!

Next, Cole needs a photo of a fallen Militia soldier. Keep an eye on the Ravager and take a peek at what he is attacking. When the Ravager takes down a soldier, aim the camera at the fallen body and add the macabre scene to Zeke's collection.

Now that all of Zeke's photo requests are fulfilled, Cole can defeat any remaining Militia forces and the Ravager to complete the mission.

REWARD: 100 XP

THOSE WHO TRESPASS AGAINST US

This mission marker lies directly south of the St. Ignatius Cathedral, next to the Finger 15 Club. The concerned citizen informs Cole that those dastardly Militia soldiers have taken over the cathedral and need to be kicked out.

Make haste for the cathedral and climb the nearby scaffolding, or the pillars, to the first level of the cathedral roof.

Several Militia soldiers attempt to attack Cole at once, so stick to hanging off the many handholds nearby and use the environment as cover.

PEEK-A-BOO!

If those pesky Militia soldiers begin strafing around Cole's hiding spots, making it hard for Cole to zap them, press **R3** to switch Cole's firing arm.

With the first level of Militia members pushing up daisies, climb up to the second roof level and repeat the previous tactics to swiftly deal with the Militia menace.

Run all the way to the right on the second roof level of the cathedral and climb up the bell tower. A Militia sniper is camping out at the top, so blast him out of there and claim the bell tower as Cole's own personal sniping position.

The final and largest group of invaders is located here on the highest level of the cathedral. Hide behind the railing of the bell tower and snipe the Militia soldiers using bolts and grenades.

When only two or three Militia soldiers remain, either pick them off from Cole's vantage point or jump down to their level and deliver a beat-down to complete the mission.

REWARD: 100 XP

PAST DECISIONS

A woman waiting for Cole to the southwest of the cathedral offers him a brief reprieve from the day-to-day hustle of a super-powered freak.

Simply activate the mission marker, and the woman thanks Cole for saving her mother back in Empire City. She gives Cole a kiss on the cheek and walks off into the sunset.

NO REGRETS

The outcome of "Past Decisions" can change if there is a save file present from the first *inFAMOUS*. If Cole chose to walk down the evil path in Empire City, the woman surprises Cole with an ambush!

REWARD: 100 XP

MALPRACTICE

A lone medic needs Cole's help in retrieving some medical packages. He is located a short distance to the west of the cathedral Seems the Militia took an ambulance out for a joyride and left four supply boxes scattered around the area.

Walk past the medic into the alley and take a left at the first junction. Two lonely Militia soldiers are guarding the first package, and they are totally unaware of Cole's presence.

Grab the second package. Cole can decide whether to defeat the remaining Militia forces at the mansion, or make a beeline for the third package. Return to the main road, turn left, and continue down the street. The third package is located a few blocks down the road. Cole can grind on the overhead trolley lines to speed up the process.

Quickly dispatch the hapless soldiers, walk up to the package, and press **R1** to pick it up. With the package in hand, it is time to turn Cole's attention to the abandoned car at the end of the alley. The car is set ablaze and begins cruising down the hill toward Cole while a squad of Militia soldiers appears behind it. Use Cole's blast powers to push the car back at the Militia and let them eat the explosion.

Only three Militia soldiers stand in the way of the third package. You can use Cole's height and speed advantage from grinding the trolley lines, or take the fight head-on from the ground to swiftly remove the soldiers and retrieve the medical supplies.

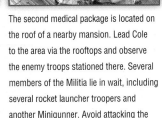

A few Militia soldiers are sure to survive the blast, including a Militia Minigunner, so retreat to the rooftops to avoid a lethal frontal assault. Electrocute the remaining soldiers from Cole's new vantage point. The location of the second package appears on the minimap when these soldiers have been removed from combat.

The second medical package is located on the roof of a nearby mansion. Lead Cole to the area via the rooftops and observe the enemy troops stationed there. Several members of the Militia lie in wait, including several rocket launcher troopers and another Minigunner. Avoid attacking the group head on by leaping and floating to the right side of the mansion.

The final package is located in a parking lot not too far from where Cole began the mission. Follow the waypoint marker on the minimap to the next location. Several Militia soldiers and a Minigunner are waiting there to deal with Cole.

The Minigunner is stationed behind several parked cars, so don't worry about him at first. Focus on taking out the rocket launcher-wielding Militia soldier to the right. Back into one of the side alleys and allow the remaining standard Militia soldiers to walk into an ambush.

With the Militia ranks thinned out a bit, return to the parking lot to deal with the Minigunner. Use Kinetic Pulse to lift any of the nearby cars and toss them at the Minigunner.

The resulting explosion leaves the gunner stunned long enough for Cole to finish the job with a few well-placed bolts or grenades. When the Minigunner and any remaining Militia soldiers are subdued, grab the fourth package.

With the mansion between Cole and the Militia soldiers stationed at the front of the building, climb up to the roof and dispose of the two soldiers stationed here.

Now that all four medical packages are in Cole's hands, return to the medic to complete the mission.

REWARD: 100 XP, Medical Clinic unlocked.

Cole's contact for this mission can be found at the base of Sin Tower. The Militia and a group of Swamp Monsters are locked in battle at the nearby park, and this lady wants Cole to kill them all.

Cole is more than happy to oblige, but he must first head up to the roof of Sin Tower to survey the scene.

In the park, there are a few of The Corrupted and a Ravager locking horns with a Minigunner and some Militia troops. Wait and observe the battle from this vantage point for a minute or two and allow the two groups to thin each other out.

MAKE IT RAIN—DESTRUCTION

While observing the battle from the safety of Cole's perch, keep an eye on the Militia Minigunner and the Ravager. If either of them gets within range of Cole's grenades, lob the destructive force down upon these foes. Soften them up as much as possible before joining the fray.

With their ranks reduced to a comfortable level, leap to the ground and pick off any survivors to complete the mission.

REWARD: 100 XP

To the northeast of the cathedral, a lone police officer requires Cole's assistance. He is holding a Militia soldier prisoner and he is a bit too much for one man to handle. Follow the officer to the Militia prisoner and stand watch while he goes for backup.

Cole now must make a decision, gaining either Good or Evil Karma.

WORDS NEVER HURT ME

If Cole bears the prisoner's acid tongue with a Zen-like patience, the cops eventually arrive and haul the prisoner away, and no one gets hurt.

This prisoner has a bit of a mouth on him and immediately starts talking trash as soon as the cop is gone. Nix calls in over the two-way and brings up an interesting point—this guy is a waste of flesh; what if he escapes to kill again?

STICKS AND STONES

Kill that no-good, trash-talking Militia scum to gain some Evil Karma. When the cops arrive to pick up their prisoner, they are not too happy that Cole fried their prize pig and open fire. Lay waste to the cops and walk away a winner.

REWARD: 100 XP, Good Karma (spare prisoner), Evil Karma (kill prisoner)

TRIAGE

On the far east side of New Marais, a desperate medic needs Cole's help. The Militia is holding six doctors hostage, forcing them to serve only those loyal to their cause. Follow the waypoint marker on the minimap into the plantation lands nearby, where a small group of Militia soldiers is escorting the six doctors.

Before the Militia has a chance to react, use a blast attack to knock the rear group of Militia troops down the hill and separate them from the rest of the group. The doctors instinctively duck down and cover their heads when the first shot is fired.

Pick off the Militia soldiers at the front of the pack, then turn Cole's attention to the enemies knocked down in the first blast. Once all of the Militia forces are down, Cole can claim his reward.

REWARD: 100xp, Medical Clinic unlocked

JAIL BREAK

NO FLYING CARS

Completing this mission permanently locks out the Evil Karma mission "Flying Cars."

The next mission contact is located between the cathedral and Sin Tower. A police officer requests your help in freeing some of his fellow cops, who are about to be executed by the Militia. Follow the officer through the alley to join up with a squad of police who join the cause.

Stay on the outside of the Militia camp and use obstacles like fences and cars to protect Cole from incoming fire. Pick off any Militia soldiers who are not focused on fighting the cops.

With the Militia defeated, climb on top of the trailer housing the captured police and stand near the electrical box located at the front of the trailer. Rapidly press **R1** when prompted to open the cage and release the officers.

REWARD: 100 XP, Good Karma

Now it is Cole's turn to lead the pack. Take a right at the alley where the police officers are waiting, then turn left when Cole hits the streets again. Lead the police to the end of the block, where a squad of Militia soldiers and a Minigunner are guarding a semi-trailer full of cops.

NO JAIL BREAK

Completing this mission permanently locks out the Good Karma mission "Jail Break."

Meet up with Nix on the rooftop located in the central area of New Marais. She's itching to make some noise and wreak havoc. Begin the mission and follow Nix to Sin Tower.

Use ◎ to pan. Use ◻ to zoom. Use ✕ to set/cancel a custom waypoint.

Nix teleports to the top of a nearby smokestack. Pick up a car using Kinetic Pulse and toss the car at Nix.

Next, Nix teleports to the top of the CanCan building. Toss another car her way for a huge explosion.

Nix comes back down to earth and leads Cole to their next destination. Follow her to the canal separating east and west New Marais and observe as she teleports to a tall statue in the middle of the graveyard. Toss another vehicle her way.

There's one more target Nix wants to hit before calling it a day. Follow her north to the coastline, where Nix teleports to an innocent-looking boat in the distance. Grab another car and toss it at Nix to sink the boat.

REWARD: 100 XP, Evil Karma

CHOPPERS VS. MONSTERS

Located on the north side of the canal that separates east and west New Marais, a man frantically waits at the rear of the liquor store with some terrible news. The Militia is tearing it up with the Swamp Monsters again, killing a lot of innocents in their crossfire. Travel to the graveyard to discover a battle that is already in progress.

There is a Militia helicopter and two Ravagers fighting amongst the Swamp Monsters and soldiers, so hang back in the graveyard for a minute or two and let the two groups fight each other. Once the ranks of each army have been thinned out, use Kinetic Pulse to grab a nearby car and destroy the helicopter patrolling the area.

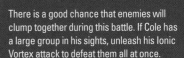

IONIC BREEZE

There is a good chance that enemies will clump together during this battle. If Cole has a large group in his sights, unleash his Ionic Vortex attack to defeat them all at once.

Fighting two Ravagers at once is an Herculean task, even for a guy who shoots lightning out of his hands. Grab the attention of one Ravager and lead it away from the battle area. Defeat the Ravager, then go back and finish off the second one. If there are any Militia soldiers or Corrupted remaining after killing the huge foes, eliminate them to complete the mission.

REWARD: 100 XP

POLICE PARADE

SPOILING THE HUNT

Completing this mission permanently locks out the Evil Karma mission "The Hunt."

Blast the Militia at the rear of the group to separate them from the group at large. Be careful not to kill any of the police officers, since they all need to survive for the mission to be successful.

CIVILIAN MINDED

With a Karmic ranking of Guardian or higher, Cole has an ability called "Civilian Safety." Always active, this power prevents innocents from taking damage from Cole's attacks. With "Civilian Safety," feel free to blast away at the Militia without worrying about accidentally killing any of the cops.

A frantic woman to the north of the cathedral has an important mission for Cole. The Militia is escorting a squad of captured police officers to an execution. Accept the mission and head over to the cathedral to find the Militia and captured police.

With the Militia forces separated, stay on the move and take down the soldiers with well-placed melee combos. Defeat all of the Militia members to complete the mission.

REWARD: 100 XP, Good Karma

NO POLICE PARADE

Completing this mission permanently locks out the Good Karma mission "Police Parade."

TROPHY REQUIREMENT

"The Hunt" is the second of three missions that must be completed to earn "The Cleaner" trophy.

Cole continues his descent into darkness via a mission contact to the north of the cathedral. The contact has located a man who is known for previously leading a Militia death squad. He's currently dressed as a civilian, trying to skip town. Accept the mission and put an end to his days.

LEGEND:
- ① Story Mission
- ① Side Mission
- ① UGC Mission
- ✦ Enemy
- ⚡ Electric Drain
- ◉ Search Area
- ● Medical Clinic
- ◆ Blast Shard
- ● Waypoint

The Hunt

Use ⊙ to pan. Use ⊙ to zoom. Use ⊗ to set/cancel a custom waypoint.

The mission contact gives Cole a picture of the man—a man wearing a black baseball cap, a blue shirt, and a backpack. Travel to the marked area in the cathedral to begin the hunt.

Turn left just as Cole enters the cathedral gates and continue on along the cobblestone path. The man Cole is looking for appears not too far from the entrance. Make the man pay for his crimes by killing him, and complete the mission.

REWARD: 100 XP, Evil Karma

IN THE NAME OF SCIENCE

At Leo Park, a lone scientist waits patiently for Cole to arrive, seeking his help for an important project. He's studying the Swamp Monsters, but he needs some fresh tissue samples. Luckily, a group of the foul creatures has been spotted in the nearby graveyard. Once Cole has accepted the mission, follow the waypoint marker on the minimap to find a group of ghouls feasting on human flesh.

Use Cole's powers to fire on any of The Corrupted to grab the attention of the entire group. Don't engage the creatures yet, because Cole needs to lead the creatures back to Leo Park to let the scientist collect his samples. Make a beeline for Leo Park with The Corrupted in pursuit.

Stand near the statue in the center of Leo Park and use melee attacks to defeat The Corrupted as they enter the area. You can scratch this assignment off the list once 10 Swamp Monsters are knocked out cold.

FINISH HIM!

Spending some experience points to upgrade Cole's melee attacks would be wise for this mission. Finisher and Ultra attacks allow Cole to quickly and efficiently deal with large groups of enemies that tend to get up close and personal.

REWARD: 100 XP, Medical Clinic unlocked

FIRING SQUAD

REMOVING KING OF THE HILL

Completing this mission permanently locks out the Evil Karma mission "King of the Hill."

At the base of the clock tower in the northwest tip of New Marais, a concerned citizen has a new mission for Cole. Militia soldiers are executing civilians on a nearby rooftop! Cole MacGrath is their only hope for survival. Hold ⬤ to see the horror first-hand, as an innocent woman is forced to leap from a nearby roof to her death.

Climb to the top of the building and confront the Militia soldiers. Dish out some ironic justice by using Blast attacks to push the Militia soldiers off of the roof. Be mindful of the hostages; Cole doesn't want to throw them off, as well.

Use bolts or melee attacks to deal with any soldiers who may have escaped Cole's initial blasts. With the Militia defeated, Cole receives thanks from some grateful hostages.

REWARD: 100 XP, Good Karma

KING OF THE HILL

REMOVING FIRING SQUAD

Completing this mission permanently locks out the Good Karma mission "Firing Squad."

At a mission marker in the northwest area of New Marais, between the clock tower and cathedral, Nix calls in with a tidbit of tasty information. LaRoche's men are about to execute some Militia soldiers, and Cole needs to get in on the action. Accept the mission and follow the waypoint to a nearby rooftop.

LEGEND:

① Story Mission
② Side Mission
③ UGC Mission
✖ Enemy
⚡ Electric Drain
⬤ Search Area
✚ Medical Clinic
◆ Blast Shard
⬤ Waypoint

King of the Hill

Use ⬤ to pan. Use ⬤ to zoom. Use ✖ to set/cancel a custom waypoint.

On the roof, LaRoche's men have several Militia soldiers on their knees and gift wrapped for Cole. Walk up behind the Militia soldiers and blast them off the roof.

The Militia don't take very kindly to Cole brutally executing their kin, and they send in an attack helicopter to deliver retribution. Let LaRoche's men fire on the helicopter while Cole heads back down to street level.

Use Kinetic Lift to pick up a nearby car. Wait for the helicopter to hover for a moment, then toss the car their way for a fiery explosion.

REWARD: 100 XP, Evil Karma

01

02

03

04

Between Leo Park and the large water tower on the east side of New Marais, Cole's next side mission contact has some harsh words for Cole. Being a super-powered being, Cole probably doesn't think too much about dying, but this woman sure does, and she's mad about it. Just as her rant ends, a Devourer appears and gobbles her up. Hope her premiums were paid up!

This is a total déjà vu moment because of Cole's first encounter with the massive Devourer. However, this time the beast has brought a group of Swamp Monsters along to make life more difficult. Tackling all of the monsters at once is suicide, so retreat to the rooftops.

The Swamp Monsters also take to the skies in pursuit of Cole. Pick a roof with plenty of room for melee attacks and defeat the Swamp Monsters one-by-one as they arrive.

With the Swamp Monster menace removed, it is time to deal with the Devourer. Head back to ground level and begin pounding bolts and grenades in the Devourer's face. This particular beast has not learned the lesson of its fallen brethren, so stick to the same tactics that you used in the first Devourer encounter to put it down for good.

REWARD: 100 XP

LOSING REVENGE

Completing this mission permanently locks out the Evil Karma mission "Revenge."

01

This mission marker is located in the southeastern area of New Marais. When you accept the mission, Kuo appears to enlist Cole's help dealing with a new Swamp Monster invasion in Ascension Parish. Follow Kuo across the rooftops, where the duo encounters a group of Swamp Monsters and Spikers.

02

Kuo helps out somewhat with her ice blasts, but it's up to Cole to wipe out the majority of the enemies. Stick to melee combos against the Swamp Monsters and Spikers.

PUNT

Spikers can be annoying little critters, but luckily, they're very easy to defeat. Simply stand next to one of the little buggers and press ⊚ to kick them into the rafters!

03

Once the Gas Bags are toast, fire bolts at the Swamp Monsters to get their attention and lure them to Cole's perch. Defeat the monsters as they reach Cole and save the Ravager for last.

04

Ionic Vortex

The Ravager stays focused on Cole during the attack, so don't plan on Kuo acting as a distraction. Dodge the creature's acid blasts and charges, and use grenades and Kinetic Pulse to take it down.

REWARD: 100 XP, Good Karma

REVENGE

Issue #0

Insider's Guide to New Marais

Retaking New Marais

User-Generated Content

NSA Intel

Extras

NO GOOD DEED

Completing this mission permanently locks out the Good Karma mission "Good Deed."

Nix impatiently waits for Cole at a mission marker on the southeast side of New Marais. The Militia has set up some camps near this area, and this girl is itching to bring some chaos into their world. Accept the mission and follow Nix across the rooftops to the first camp.

LEGEND:
- Story Mission
- Side Mission
- UGC Mission
- Enemy
- Electric Drain
- Search Area
- Medical Clinic
- Blast Shard
- Waypoint

Revenge

Use ⊙ to pan. Use ⊙ to zoom. Use ⊗ to set/cancel a custom waypoint.

The first Militia outpost is a bit intimidating. Two Minigunners, a machine gun turret, and Militia soldiers await the dastardly duo. Ride the Grindwire leading to the Militia camp, but drop down to the lower ledge to the left.

Nix keeps the Militia soldiers occupied for now. Hang off the ledge of the roof and wait for Nix to ensnare the Militia in her oily tentacles. Pop out from Cole's cover and ignite the oil with a bolt or two. Repeat this tactic until Nix and Cole have defeated all of the soldiers.

Follow Nix to the next camp, located in the ruins of a burnt-out building. Cole and Nix have the height advantage here, so say hello to the Militia with a Thunder Drop. Focus on taking out the lone Minigunner in the group first, then unleash Cole's powers on the rest of the Militia soldiers.

With the Militia in such a tight place, Cole can use his Ionic Vortex ability to kill nearly all the soldiers at once.

REWARD: 100 XP, Evil Karma

On the east coast of New Marais, Cole faces another overcharge challenge. Accept the mission and follow the minimap marker to locate the first transformer. Hop onto the transformer and hold ⊗ to see Cole's destination, marked by a lighting strike in the distance.

THE GROUND IS LAVA!

Remember: in overcharge missions, Cole cannot touch the ground for very long, or he loses his charge and fails the mission. The aura around Cole gradually changes from white to a deep red hue as he gets closer to losing the overcharge.

FLYING AND GRINDING

At this point in the game, Cole has access to two new abilities: the Car Jump and Improved Static Thrusters. Both of these new abilities make it easier for Cole to keep his feet of the ground and maintain the overcharge.

Perform a Car Leap off of the transformer and immediately press **R1** to activate the new and improved Static Thrusters. Float over to the Grindwire immediately in front of Cole.

At the next building, leap off the Grindwire and float over the building entirely. Land briefly on the corner of the adjacent building.

Jump at the end of the Grindwire, activate the Static Thrusters, and continue floating over the building to the next Grindwire.

Immediately turn to the right, jump forward, and float to the next Grindwire.

Follow the line and leap over the group of Militia soldiers at the next building. The extra energy Cole caries from the overcharge turns the soldiers into crispy critters. Head to the northern most Grindwire attached to the building.

Ride the wire to the end of the line, leap, and float straight to the transformer dead ahead. Cole disperses his overcharge into the transformer and fries all the surrounding Militia soldiers.

REWARD: 100 XP

GRAVE DANGER

The starting point for this mission is located in an alley to the right of the New Marais graveyard. After activating the marker, LaRoche calls Cole and asks for his help in clearing out some Corrupted and Militia soldiers from the area. Meet up with LaRoche's men at the graveyard entrance.

As Cole walks into the graveyard, the minimap lights up with dozens of red dots. Head to the left immediately after entering the graveyard and continue south.

DEATH FROM ABOVE

Militia snipers are peppered all over the rooftops in the graveyard and are Cole's biggest threat during this mission. Look out for the sniper's telltale laser beam zeroing in on Cole. Move Cole away from the threat, or follow the beam to its source and kill the sniper right away.

With LaRoche's men in tow, continue toward the southern end of the graveyard while meticulously defeating any Militia who stand in the way.

A Militia Minigunner waits for Cole at the end of the graveyard. Use the local architecture to Cole's advantage here, staying out of the Minigunner's line of sight while sneaking in grenades and bolt shots.

Now that the southern end of the graveyard is cleared out, turn your attention back to the northern end. Only standard Militia soldiers and a few Swamp Monsters remain, so carefully travel north and wipe them all out.

REWARD: 100 XP

The first of two Enemy Surveillance missions begins on the roof of a building to the northeast of the cathedral. Speak to the man on the roof to learn that a nest of Corrupted has been spotted close to this position. Follow the minimap marker to find a Swamp Monster scout out enjoying an afternoon snack.

Spotting Cole, the Swamp Monster leaps off into the distance. Pursue the Swamp Monster across the rooftops. Use the pulsing white star on the minimap to track the monster's location.

Militia soldiers wielding rocket launchers also spray the rooftops. The soldiers are totally focused on killing the Swamp Monster, so Cole can ignore them and stay focused on tracking his prey.

The Swamp Monster stops running at the southern plantation, where a group of his brethren and a Ravager lie in wait. Avoid the Ravager for now and focus on thinning out the horde of Swamp Monsters.

Once the threat of the Swamp Monsters is removed, turn Cole's attention to taking out the Ravager and completing the mission.

REWARD: 100 XP

ENEMY SURVEILLANCE 2

The second Enemy Surveillance mission starts in the northwestern tip of New Marais, well above the cathedral on the map. Another Swamp Monster is on the prowl in the area, and Cole must track the monster to its lair. Head south from the mission objective and turn right at the first alley to find the monster.

Chase the creature up to the nearby helipad. Continue following the Swamp Monster across the roofs, using the Grindwires to speed Cole along.

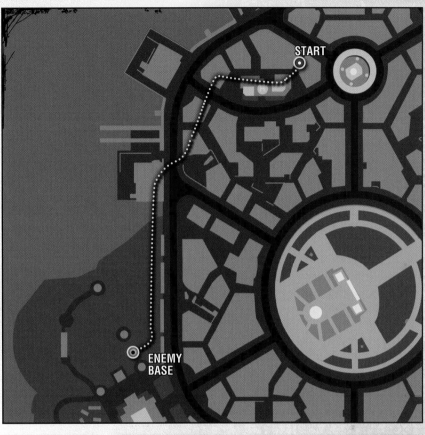

START

ENEMY
BASE

More rocket launcher-wielding Militia soldiers appear along the way. As before, ignore them for now and continue pursuing the Swamp Monster.

Finally, the Swamp Monster lands on the grounds of the plantation on the southwest corner of New Marais and breaks into a full sprint toward its home. Pursue the monster until Cole runs into a family of Swamp Monsters and a Ravager.

NO COUNTRY FOR OLD CONDUITS

There are not a lot of power sources in the area where this battle begins. Lead the Swamp Monsters either toward the nearby plantation mansion, or back to the street where Cole has access to plenty of electrical current to keep him healthy.

As in the last mission, focus on defeating the Swamp Monsters first before Cole turns his attention to the Ravager. Defeat all the enemies to complete the mission.

REWARD: 100 XP

NO THIRD DEGREE

Completing this mission permanently locks out the Evil Karma mission "The Third Degree."

A new opportunity for Cole to gain some Good Karma lies at the south end of the canal. Activate the marker, causing Kuo to appear with some new information. It seems that the Militia is back to their old trick of tying up civilians in the swamp as sacrifices for the monsters.

There are four civilians who must be rescued. All of them are located along the eastern New Marais coast. Follow the waypoint marker to the southernmost victim. Only four Militia soldiers are guarding their sacrifice.

The fourth and final victim is being held captive on the plantation mansion grounds, which are far more fortified than the other sacrificial altars.

FROZEN TAG TEAM

Now would be a good time to hang back and let Kuo jump into the fray first. Wait for her to shoot an ice cloud at a group of enemies, then fire a bolt into the cloud to freeze any enemies caught in the blast. Even larger enemies like the Minigunner cannot resist the freezing cold.

When the area is clear of Militia, approach the strung-up victim and fire a bolt at each of the wrist restraints. Proceed up the coast toward the second victim.

A Militia Minigunner and several standard Militia soldiers are awaiting the duo as they approach the mansion. Utilize Cole and Kuo's arsenal of attacks to dispatch the Militia as they make their way around the back of the mansion.

This day just keeps getting worse! The Militia has set up a machine gun turret on the other side of the mansion. Toss a grenade at the sandbags behind the turret to take out its operator. With most of the Militia cleared out, proceed onto the dock toward the fourth victim.

Another small group of Militia soldiers guards the area. Dispatch them quickly, free the second victim, and continue toward the third.

The same tactics that you have used previously apply to the third victim, with the exception of a Militia soldier stationed on the roof of a nearby shack. Knock him of his perch with a well-placed blast and finish off his friends before freeing the third victim.

Suddenly, a group of Corrupted attacks before Cole can make the rescue. The water surrounding the dock means instant death for Cole if he gets knocked into the drink, so head back to the mansion to give Cole some breathing room. Work on thinning out the Swamp Monsters, then take on the Ravager.

Now that all threats have been dealt with, return to the dock and free the final victim. Follow the minimap marker to reunite with Kuo in the swamp and complete the mission.

REWARD: 100 XP, Good Karma

THE THIRD DEGREE

NO ENDURING FREEDOM

Completing this mission permanently locks out the Good Karma mission "Enduring Freedom."

This mission begins at the cul-de-sac located to the east of Sin Tower. Nix has word that there's a Militia soldier who's been collecting Blast Shards, and tracking him down means a big boost to Cole's energy. Fortunately, Nix knows where his wife hangs out.

DEAD WIVES TELL NO TALES

Be careful when attacking the woman, and only damage her enough to knock her to the ground. If she dies, Cole fails the mission.

Take a look at the picture Nix gives Cole. He's on the hunt for a woman wearing a pink shirt with a gray shoulder bag. Follow the waypoint marker to the nearby park and enter the shaded area on the minimap.

With the location in hand, follow the new waypoint on the minimap. A nondescript package is out in the open, waiting for Cole to snatch it up. Grab the package and claim the Blast Shards.

REWARD: 100 XP, Evil Karma, 5 Blast Shards

Walk around the right side of the statue in the center of the park to find the woman and attack her. When she's knocked to the ground, walk up to her and use the Arc Restrain power on her. Once rendered helpless and captive, the woman gives up the location of her husband's Blast Shard collection.

HEAVY WEAPONS

One of LaRoche's men waits for Cole in the northeastern area of New Marais. His men are pinned down by a Militia helicopter, almost out of ammo, and in desperate need of Cole's help. Accept the mission and follow the rebel to the construction yard in front of the fort.

At the construction site, LaRoche's men are desperately firing rockets at the Militia helicopter but making very little progress in defeating it. Use Kinetic Pulse to lift up a car, toss it at the helicopter, and show these LaRoche boys how it's done.

Focus on the Ravager first. Fire a few shots at the creature to grab its attention, then run a few blocks away. This forces the Ravager to follow and gives Cole some space to work with. Ignore the Devourer for now. Defeat the Ravager, then take to the roofs and return to the construction yard. LaRoche's men are pounding the Devourer with rockets to little effect. It looks like it's up to Cole to finish the job.

Once the helicopter goes down, the Corrupted decide it's a good time to attack, as well. A Ravager and a Devourer appear, looking to ruin everyone's day. Retreat to the rooftops before the Corrupted makes mincemeat out of Cole.

BETWEEN A ROCKET LAUNCHER AND A HARD PLACE

Fighting the Devourer on the ground with LaRoche's men seems like the best tactical option, but this strategy can actually be a huge detriment. The rockets that LaRoche's men fire off don't discriminate between Corrupted and Cole, so be wary about getting caught in the crossfire.

Take advantage of the high ground. Wait for the Devourer to open its mouth, fill it with grenades, and then retreat to avoid its acid spitballs.

Move to another roof if the Devourer gets to a spot where it can repeatedly hit Cole. Keep up with the pattern, and before long the Devourer wishes it never tangled with the Cole and the LaRoche boys!

REWARD: 100 XP

SHIP OF FOOLS

In a small alleyway to the south of the fort, a man waits for Cole with some terrible news. A Militia boat is patrolling the coast, indiscriminately firing grenades into the city. Follow the waypoint marker to the coastline.

The Militia boat is patrolling the waters to the south of the fort. Cole has the height advantage here, and he has a few options to take down the crew. The road behind Cole is full of cars. Use Kinetic Pulse to lift one and walk it over to the concrete guardrail. Fire it at the deck to wipe out several Militia soldiers at once.

To deal with any remaining Militia soldiers, have Cole hide behind the guardrail by pressing ◎ and then hold ✚ to enter Precision Mode. Aim for the head!

Finally, sink the boat to complete the mission.

REWARD: 100 XP

146

DOWN AND OUT IN FLOOD TOWN

Side missions in Flood Town are a dangerous proposition for Cole MacGrath. Pools of water cover nearly every ground surface, so Cole needs to really watch his steps when taking on combat missions in this area. The side missions in Flood Town become available after completing the story mission "Powering up Flood Town."

PRESCRIPTION STRENGTH

At a medical building on the east side of Flood Town, a lone medic waves desperately for Cole's attention. The medic has a crate full of medical supplies that need to be delivered across Flood Town, to the train yard located in the north. Use Kinetic Pulse to lift the crate, then launch it over the water tower toward the light in the distance.

Stick to the ground and underneath the water tower as you continue toward the light. Four Ice Soldiers are waiting to ambush Cole. Allow them to jump down to Cole's position and use the surrounding water as an environmental trap.

Once the Ice Soldiers are history, get to the medical crate and throw it toward the light once more.

The next shot should place Cole in the train yard, where several Ice Soldiers are waiting for him. Beware the Ice Soldiers with rocket launchers on the upper tracks, and defeat all of the enemies in the area before tossing the medical crate again.

If the crate doesn't land within the delivery area on the third try, retrieve it and walk it toward its destination. Once the supplies have been dropped off, follow the waypoint marker to the medic and complete the mission.

REWARD: 100 XP, Medical Clinic unlocked

Cole's next overcharge challenge begins in the southern tip of New Marais, near the shipping cranes. Start the mission and follow the waypoint marker to reach the first transformer.

Leap onto the transformer to imbue Cole with an overcharge, then hold △ to view the lightning strike indicating Cole's destination.

Leap straight up and land on the overhead Grindwire.

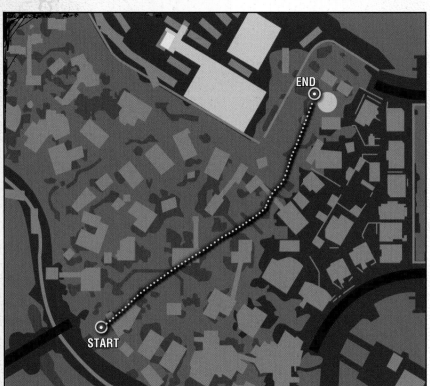

Jump off the end of the first Grindwire and guide Cole to the wire to his right.

Leap over the building at the end of the grind and immediately activate Static Thrusters **R1**. Float over to the Grindwire supported by a telephone pole past the building.

Follow this grind path until it ends, then leap onto the Grindwire leading to the left.

At the end of this line, jump, use Static Thrusters, and guide Cole to the transformer to complete the mission.

REWARD: 100 XP

UNLIKELY ALLIES

TROPHY REQUIREMENT

Unlikely Allies is the first of several missions required to unlock the "Frozen Asset" trophy.

In the southern area of Flood Town, Kuo calls in with some interesting information. She's been contacted by an Ice Soldier who wants to defect! Follow the waypoint marker to meet up with Cole's new Ice Soldier buddy.

This Ice Soldier is different: articulate, well spoken, and forced into his current condition. He wants to lead Cole to a secret cache of Blast Shards! Hop onto the Grindwire to the left of the Ice Soldier and follow him across the rooftops of Flood Town.

At the second rooftop along the Grindwire path, a gaggle of Swamp Monsters ambushes the duo. The Ice Soldier can hold his own in battle, so focus on knocking the Swamp Monsters off the roof and zapping any that happen to fall in the water.

When the Swamp Monsters are defeated, the Ice Soldier continues across the rooftops to the next destination. However, he stops short of their final destination, since he cannot fight and risk breaking his cover by helping Cole against the Ice Soldiers. Jump onto the Grindwire leading into the enemy base.

At the end of the grind, leap onto the roof and start using Blast attacks to knock some of the Ice Soldiers off the platform.

Stay on the roof and take out the Ice Soldiers as they return to attack. When all the Ice Soldiers are defeated, grab the Blast Shard package on the ground.

REWARD: 100 XP, Good Karma, 5 Blast Shards

TROPHY REQUIREMENT

"Assassin's Greed" is the last of three missions that must be completed to earn "The Cleaner" trophy.

On the east side of Flood Town, a man has the opportunity of a lifetime for Cole. He's left a huge collection of Blast Shards lying out in a boat for Cole to pick up. Take a look at the picture the man provides, then hightail it toward the waypoint marker to find the boat.

LEGEND:
- Story Mission
- Side Mission
- UGC Mission
- Enemy
- Electric Drain
- Search Area
- Medical Clinic
- Blast Shard
- Waypoint

Assassin's Greed

Use ⬜ to pan. Use ⬜ to zoom. Use ❌ to set/cancel a custom waypoint.

The Blast Shards were lies! There's nothing on the boat; it is totally empty. Before Cole can think about paying the mission contact his dues, a squad of Ice Soldiers jumps in for an ambush.

Fortunately, Nix has been listening in and rushes to Cole's side. Stay on the boat for now, using Precision shots to quickly wipe out the two Ice Heavies.

Allow the Ice Soldiers to jump onto the boat and defeat them as they land. Blast them into the water and then either electrocute them or finish off the soldiers with well-timed melee attacks.

Eliminate the traitor

With the ambush defeated, it's time to pay the man who sent Cole on this little mission a visit. Follow the waypoint marker to Nix, where she has the man pinned to the ground. Unleash the wrath of MacGrath and put this scam artist six feet under.

REWARD: 100 XP, Evil Karma

EMERGENCY MEASURES

There is a medic located in the middle of Flood Town, next to the rail yard. This individual needs your help retrieving some medical supplies stolen by the Ice Soldiers. Cole must acquire a total of four packages.

The first package is located on a rooftop not too far from Cole's starting position, but an Ice Heavy and several standard Ice Soldiers guard it. Hang back at the house before the package location, and use the two-tiered roof as cover.

Make use of Precision Shot and Cole's more powerful bolt attacks to take them down. When the coast is clear, head over to the roof and pick up the package. Another Ice Soldier squad lies in wait at the next package location. First, destroy the guard tower to the right to kill the pesky rocket-launcher soldier resting inside.

Jumping straight into the group of Ice Soldiers is suicide. Instead, stay on of the adjacent roofs and use the environment to your advantage while taking out the soldiers. Cole's Ionic Powers come in handy to remove a majority of them at once.

Grab the package and proceed to the next waypoint marker. A few Ice Soldiers appear along Cole's path, but none of them is guarding the third package. Ignore the Ice Soldiers for now unless they happen upon Cole's path.

Snatch up the third package to attract the attention of all the Ice Soldiers in the area. Let them come to Cole and dish out some electric justice when they arrive. Defeat them all and continue on to the final package.

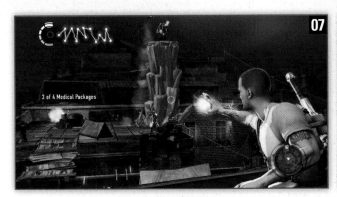

The enemy placement around the final package resembles that of the first—a squad of Ice Soldiers and an Ice Heavy. Hang back and pick them off, or use an Ionic Power to wipe a majority of them out at once. Grab the fourth and final package and make a beeline for the medic.

Ice Soldiers and Ice Heavies are everywhere now, and they're not too happy that Cole has made off with their stolen goods. Ignore them, using Grindwires and Static Thrusters to get Cole to the medic as quickly as possible. Once Cole returns the packages, the Ice Soldier threat is removed and the mission is complete.

REWARD: 100 XP, Medical Clinic Unlocked

ENEMY SURVEILLANCE — FLOOD TOWN

Cole's next mission contact lies on the western tip of Flood Town. This man has seen some Ice Soldiers hanging around, and he thinks Cole should follow one back to their base. Accept the mission and follow the waypoint marker to the Ice Soldier.

There's no point in being subtle. The Ice Soldier sees Cole and immediately takes off from his base. Stay in pursuit and follow the soldier up to the rooftops.

ICE TO MEET YOU

If Cole has access to Kuo's ice powers, the Ice Launch ability can come in mighty handy during this mission. The Ice Soldier has the same ability, so any time he launches himself up to a new level, Cole can follow suit.

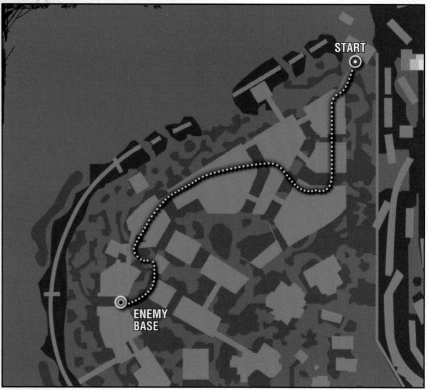

START

ENEMY BASE

Fortunately, the Ice Soldier base only contains six enemies in total. Use Cole's momentum from chasing the Ice Soldier to leap into the center of their base with a Thunder Strike, knocking some of them to the water below.

Use melee attacks on any soldiers still inside the base, and snipe the soldiers that have escaped. Once they are defeated, the mission is complete.

REWARD: 100 XP

DOUBLE WHAMMY

A man waiting in the ruins on the east side of Flood Town has an unusual request. Looks like the Ice Soldiers have captured a group of Militia soldiers at two separate locations, and they need Cole's help. Begin the mission and travel to the small island that is located southeast of Cole's starting location.

At the island, cross over the left bridge and climb the roof of the blue shack. The Ice Soldiers are patrolling just on the other side of this building, but Cole now has the drop on them.

Throw a grenade at the center of the rear group of Ice Soldiers. After it explodes and scatters the troops, drop down from above and quickly finish off the group with melee attacks.

MELEE PAYDAY

By now, Cole should have access to the Ultra Attacks and Ultra Drain abilities. It pays to buy both of these upgrades, since they come in mighty handy when getting up close and personal with enemies. Ultra Attacks kill most enemies in one blow, while Ultra Drain keeps Cole's energy levels topped off.

Now that the first group of Ice Soldiers is feeling the big chill, head north to the next waypoint marker. Keep to the high ground and maintain Cole's height advantage.

The second Ice Soldier group is patrolling with a bit more firepower—three Ice Soldier troops and an Ice Heavy. Before the soldiers notice Cole, enter Precision Mode and fire three quick headshots at the Ice Heavy to take him out of the picture.

The final three Ice Soldiers should be a breeze. Once they're defeated, the Militia soldiers are freed, and another mission is complete.

REWARD: 100 XP

BEST SERVED COLD

A woman waves for Cole's attention on an abandoned rooftop, on the west side of Flood Town. The Militia and Ice Soldiers are locked in an epic battle, but many innocent Flood Town residents are getting caught in the crossfire. Travel north from Cole's starting position to the area where the two groups are waging war.

Hang back when Cole gets near the battle. Both sides are too busy fighting each other to take notice of Cole at this point. Use the distraction of battle as an advantage and take out some of the more advanced troops.

Now it's time to deal with the regular Militia and Ice Soldiers in the area. Many of them can be grouped together at this point in the battle, so jump to the ground and unleash one of Cole's Ionic Powers to kill many of them at once.

The two Ice Heavies in the battle should be the first priority. Zoom in with Precision Mode ✚ and dish out four shots on each enemy to kill them.

PRECISION DRAIN

Precision Mode is a useful tool in Cole's arsenal, but it eats up a lot of energy. Cole uses up energy every second he's aiming, and each shot takes a significant amount of energy. When firing Precision shots, keep Cole near a power source so he can juice up easily and go back to electro-sniping enemies.

Next, Cole should deal with the Militia Minigunner hanging out in the nearby building ruins. Just like with the Ice Heavies, line up the Minigunner with Precision Mode and fry him to a crisp.

All that's left at this point are any remaining stragglers. Return to the roofs if things get too heated, but the remaining foes shouldn't be a huge threat. Destroy them all to claim some experience and free another area of Flood Town from enemy control.

REWARD: 100 XP

Smack dab in the middle of the north side of Flood Town, one of LaRoche's men awaits Cole at the train yard. Three Ice Soldiers are escaping with some intel on LaRoche's men and must be stopped. Cole must be quick on his feet for this mission!

After accepting the mission, immediately run through the warehouse in front of Cole's starting position. The three Ice Soldiers run off in different directions, but for now, concentrate on the soldier running straight ahead.

Next, tackle the Ice Soldier to the right. Get within a few paces and blast him in the back to put him down for good.

Leap up after the Ice Soldier and start firing bolts into his back the second he's in Cole's sights.

Only one more to go. Check out the minimap for the final Ice Soldier's position and make haste toward the marker. Send the Ice Soldier packing with a few well-placed bolts, and call it a day.

REWARD: 100 XP

OVERCHARGE — FLOOD TOWN 2

The second Flood Town overcharge challenge is located right in the middle of the Flood Town area. Accept the mission, and Zeke soon calls in with the location of the first transformer. Follow the waypoint marker and hop on the transformer to fill Cole with an overcharge.

Cole's destination lies under the lightning bolt in the distance. Jump straight up and land on the Grindwire slightly to the left of the transformer.

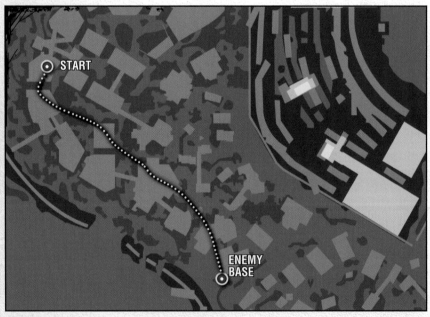

START

ENEMY BASE

Leap over the building at the end of the Grindwire and land on the next one located across the building.

MIGHTY MILITIA

Every rooftop along the path for this mission is chock-full of Militia troops. Cole doesn't have time to deal with them, so speed through as quickly as possible. Cole is mincemeat if he puts a foot on a roof.

03

At the end of the next wire, jump right at the end, immediately activate the Static Thrusters **R1**, and float to the far right corner of the next building. If Cole lands on the building instead of the Grindwire, get airborne ASAP to avoid losing the overcharge.

04

Hit the Grindwire at the end of the building. At the next roof, leap and float to the opposite corner of the building for the next line.

05

Only one more Grindwire left in this line. Jump at the end of Cole's grind and float to the Grindwire running across Cole's path. Turn right after landing on the wire.

06

End of the line, Cole. Once Cole reaches the end of this final Grindwire, jump and float to the transformer to release the overcharge and complete the mission.

REWARD: 100 XP

ICE BREAKER

CHIPPING AWAY REMOVED

Completing this mission permanently locks out the Evil Karma mission "Chipping Away."

01

At a mission marker right outside Zeke's Flood Town hideout, Kuo needs Cole's help. Large groups of Ice Soldiers have been spotted in the area, and it's time to wipe them out. Accept the mission and follow Kuo across the rooftops.

02

After covering a few rooftops, Cole and Kuo are ambushed by a small squad of Ice Soldier troops. Stay on the roof and allow the Ice Soldiers to come to Cole, dealing with them as they arrive.

03

Once Cole has defeated the Ice Soldiers, continue following Kuo to the western coastline. Here, a significantly large squad of Ice Soldiers is waiting for the duo, including an Ice Heavy and a Crusher.

Hang back on the roof and use Precision Aim to take down the Ice Heavy first. Every Ice Soldier is now aware that they are under attack, and the foes begin assaulting Cole and Kuo's position.

04

Fire off one of Cole's Ionic Powers to take out a large percentage of the Ice Soldiers. Kill any remaining basic Ice Soldiers while staying out of the Crusher's way.

05

When the area is mostly clear of Ice Soldiers, begin attacking the Crusher. Stay out in the open and be careful to dodge the charge and ice-tossing attacks. Stay alert and keep Cole charged up to finish the Crusher and complete the mission.

REWARD: 100 XP, Good Karma

ICE BREAKER REMOVAL

Completing this mission permanently locks out the Good Karma mission "Ice Breaker."

Nix's appetite for destruction needs to be sated, so meet up with her at the next mission marker in the center of Flood Town. The Ice Soldiers have been showing off their muscle around the area lately, and it's time to feed them some humble pie.

01

LEGEND:
- Story Mission
- Side Mission
- UGC Mission
- Enemy
- Electric Drain
- Search Area
- Medical Clinic
- Blast Shard
- Waypoint

Chipping Away

Use ⊙ to pan. Use ⊙ to zoom. Use ⊗ to set/cancel a custom waypoint.

02

03

04

Follow Nix to the first Ice Soldier enclave, where two Ice Heavies and a handful of standard Ice Soldiers are waiting. Let Nix keep the regular soldiers busy and focus Cole's efforts on taking down the Ice Heavies.

When the Ice Heavies are defeated, zap any of the Ice Soldiers that are caught standing in the water. Keep an eye out for any enemies trapped in Nix's oil tentacles and blast them, as well. When all of the enemies are defeated, follow Nix to the next destination.

The second Ice Soldier location is a little more fortified, adding a Crusher to the mix. Stay out of the Crusher's way for now and focus on taking out the Ice Heavy first. Take a moment to blast any enemies caught in Nix's tentacles.

TRUST IN BIG OIL

Nix can capture the big Crusher in her oily grasp. Firing on the Crusher while it is captured won't instantly kill the brute, but it does lock it in place for a good long while. Take the time to toss a few rockets at the trapped Crusher to end it quickly.

When Cole and Nix have cleared out a majority of the smaller enemies, combine their efforts on the Crusher to complete the mission.

REWARD: 100 XP, Evil Karma

STAY FROSTY

TROPHY REQUIREMENT

Stay Frosty is the second of four side missions required to unlock the "Frozen Asset" trophy.

Near the Medical Outpost in the western part of Flood Town, Kuo calls in with another mission from Cole's Ice Soldier ally. Activate the mission and follow the waypoint marker to the Ice Soldier's location.

There's something different about the friendly Ice Soldier this time around—he's evolved into an Ice Heavy! The Corrupted are attacking innocent civilians at the train yard, and he wants Cole's help to defeat them. Follow Cole's icy ally across the rooftops to the train yard, where two Ravager Hive Lords and swarms of Scavengers await the dynamic duo!

Immediately take the high ground at a nearby train car and begin blasting away at the Ravager High Lords.

CROSS THE STREAMS

Try to keep the Ice Heavy ally near Cole while fighting the Hive Lords. His beam attack quickly whittles down the health of these vile beasts, making Cole's job a lot easier.

Focus on one Hive Lord at a time and punt away any Scavengers that cross Cole's path. There are plenty of electrical sources to keep Cole juiced up, so be patient while taking down the beasts to complete the mission.

REWARD: 100 XP, Good Karma

From the southernmost Medical Clinic in Flood Town, travel northwest to find this mission marker. Zeke needs a few shots of the damage The Beast has caused in the area. Head south to the loading docks for the first two pictures.

DON'T FORGET THE LENS CAP

Cole's camera is automatically assigned to the **R2** button, overriding powers like Kinetic Pulse or Ice Launch. To put away the camera and reassign a power, simply open up the Quick Swap menu and press **R2** to cycle through the available powers. Just remember to switch back to the camera when it's time to take a picture!

First, Zeke needs a photo of a damaged crane. The cranes are massive, so once Cole enters the loading dock area, simply aim his camera at one of the twisted behemoths and snap the picture.

Zeke also needs a shot of The Beast's footprint. Walk around the gas station on the loading dock to find the footprint. Get the camera out and take a quick snapshot for Zeke's records.

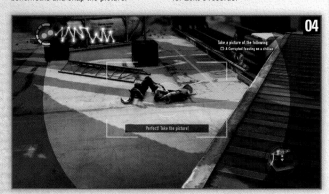

Zeke's next request is a bit more macabre. A Swamp Monster is feasting on a nearby civilian and Zeke wants the shot. Follow the waypoint marker to the corner of the loading dock to find the grisly scene. Take the snap and get ready for the final challenge.

A massive battle between the Ice Soldiers and Corrupted has broken out right behind Cole's location. This is a perfect opportunity for more action shots, according to Zeke.

Grab a good vantage point on some high ground for the first two shots. Cole needs to capture an Ice Soldier mid-air first, so aim the camera into the fight and wait for an Ice Soldier to jump. When the camera reticule flashes green, grab the shot.

For the next shot, simply point the camera at the Ice Heavy while he's on his tower and snap the photo.

For the final shot, Cole needs to capture a Hive Lord Birthing Pod on film, which is trickier than it sounds. Find the Hive Lord burrowing around the area and wait for it to launch a pod attack. Once the pods appear, get close and line them up in the viewfinder for the final shot.

GET THE PICTURE

Be quick about taking the photos in this final challenge. It's game over if the Ice Heavy or Hive Lord is killed in the battle before Cole has the chance to get pictures.

Now that Zeke has a few more additions to his New Marais photo album, it's time for Cole to clean house. Take out all of the remaining enemies to complete the mission.

REWARD: 100 XP

BATTLE BY THE BAY

Fire an occasional rocket at the Crusher to whittle down its health. Stay on the move in case the Crusher or Hive Lord catches Cole's scent and begins attacking him.

To the immediate northeast of the southern Medical Clinic in Flood Town, a desperate man needs Cole's help. The Militia, Ice Soldiers, and Corrupted are going at it again, this time at the loading docks in southern Flood Town. Accept the mission and follow the waypoint marker into the mayhem.

Take a moment to hang out on the roof of the building located on the loading dock and observe the situation. The two biggest threats in the area are an Ice Soldier Crusher and a Ravager Hive Lord. Standard Militia, Ice Soldiers, Swamp Monsters, and Scavengers also litter the area.

When the ranks of all three armies have thinned, choose either the Crusher or Hive Lord to tackle first if either one is still standing. Once the first is defeated, focus on the next, and then defeat any remaining soldiers to complete the mission.

REWARD: 100 XP

Hang back and let the three-way battle thin out the herds, and defeat any wandering soldiers who happen upon Cole's observation point.

ICE TEA PARTY

The starting point for this mission is located in the northern end of the train yard in Flood Town. A concerned citizen informs Cole that the Ice Soldiers have taken over a few supply boats. Looks like a good opportunity for Cole to put a dent in the Ice Soldier's supply line. Accept the mission and head east toward the boats.

Ice Soldiers stationed on a nearby boat patrolling the waters begin littering the area with grenades as soon as Cole is within range. Hang back and take out the few Ice Soldiers guarding the two docked supply ships.

Once it's safe to move in, get on the deck of each of the docked supply ships and blast the Militia-stamped cargo overboard. There are a total of 24 supply boxes that must be thrown over. Toss them all out and claim Cole's reward.

REWARD: 100 XP

BOAT? WHAT BOAT?

Cole can ignore the patrolling Ice Soldier boat. It doesn't contain any of the supplies that must be destroyed to complete the mission. Keep an eye out for incoming grenades and continue tossing supplies overboard.

GEARING UP THE GAS WORKS

The Gas Works district contains some of the most challenging side missions in the game. This is most definitely Ice Soldier turf, and the place is crawling with these fast and deadly conduits. Cole must face down a mad bomber, scores of Ice Soldiers, and his fair share of Titans before he's through with this district. Side missions become available in the Gas Works after completing the story mission "Powering up Gas Works."

PLAYING "HERO"

Meet up with Nix at the mission marker on the north tip of the Gas Works to begin the mission. Nix has a brilliant idea to increase Cole's notoriety in the area. Follow her up to the roof immediately behind the mission marker.

A massive civilian protest is being held on the streets below. Several Militia soldiers surround the protesters, including a Militia Minigunner. Luckily, Cole doesn't have to do most of the work, because Nix's "babies" are going to step in. Press **R1** to unleash the Swamp Monsters into the crowd.

While the Swamp Monsters and Militia soldiers are trading blows, kick back and wait for Nix to call off her pets. Once she gives the signal, Cole is free to kill the Militia soldiers.

Jump into the ruckus using a Thunder Drop. Focus on taking down the Minigunner first, then switch Cole's attention to destroying the basic soldiers. Cole has no reason to protect any of the civilians hanging around the area, so feel free to use Cole's entire arsenal—including Ionic powers—to get the job done.

With the Swamp Monsters gone and the Militia defeated, the civilians rush to Cole's side to give thanks. Little do they know that all of their misery and suffering was engineered by their "savior."

REWARD: 100 XP, Evil Karma

COLD SNAP

01

In the northeast corner of the Gas Works, Cole's latest mission contact has information relating to some Ice Soldiers patrolling the area. Seems the Ice Soldiers have taken to parading their Militia captives around town. Accept the mission and travel east from the starting point.

03

Cole now has the full attention of the remaining Ice Soldiers, but their low numbers make fighting them a breeze. Take down the remaining soldiers and free the Militia soldiers.

02

Move up to high ground before Cole reaches the soldiers and take an inventory of their numbers. Five Ice Soldiers and an Ice Heavy are escorting some captured Militia soldiers. Enter Precision Mode ✚ and quickly take down the Ice Heavy.

04

Cole can't call it a day yet. Once the Ice Soldiers are defeated, two Crushers ambush Cole! Quickly make for the rooftops and fire at one of the Crushers to grab their attention.

REDIRECTED AFFECTIONS

Tag! +1 XP

Crushers tend to favor running away from Cole to hurl huge chunks of ice in his direction. The Redirect Rocket ability is invaluable in combating the Crusher's tactics. If a Crusher jumps away from Cole, fire a rocket at a high angle, then zap the Crusher with a quick bolt to tag it. Keep Cole charged up and fire away to take these fools down in no time.

When both Crushers and Ice Soldiers are defeated, Cole can rest easy once more and claim his reward.

REWARD: 100 XP

OVERCHARGE——GAS WORKS

Cole's next overcharge challenge begins near the helipad in the center of the Gas Works area. Accept the mission and follow the waypoint marker to the first transformer.

After grinding through the silo area, jump at the end of the next Grindwire and float straight ahead to the next grind.

The next grind leads Cole to small rooftop building. Leap over it at the end of the grind to reach the final Grindwire.

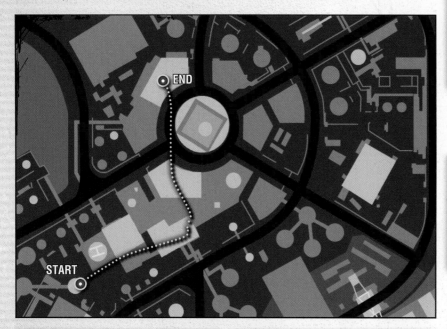

Hold ◎ to focus on the lightning bolt in the distance, marking Cole's destination. Seems like a short trip.

Avoid the Grindwire closest to the transformer, and instead leap onto the second Grindwire to the right of Cole.

Reach the end of this last grind and leap toward the transformer to complete the mission!

REWARD: 100 XP

Follow the Grindwires across the green silos. Take the left Grindwire at each silo to turn toward the destination transformer.

COAST GUARD

One of LaRoche's men is waiting for Cole on the east side of the Gas Works, near the canal separating the area from Flood Town. Accept the mission, and the rebel informs Cole that a pair of Militia gunboats is randomly firing into the mainland. Travel north toward the waypoints that appear.

EXPLOSIVE SITUATIONS

The tall red gas containers make for the perfect vantage point for this mission. Ride any of the surrounding Vertical Launch Poles surrounding the container, but be careful once Cole reaches the top—the containers are full of explosive materials! Leap to the next container if a few Militia grenades land close by.

Yes, the Militia is at it again. The two boats patrolling these waters are filled with Militia soldiers equipped with grenade launchers. Grab a high vantage point and pepper them with rockets and grenades to thin their numbers.

Wipe out the Militia forces and sink the boats to bring an end to the chaos and terror.

REWARD: 100 XP

On the south side of the Gas Works area, Nix has another nefarious scheme. Her "babies" are hungry for some delicious Ice Soldier flesh, and she wants Cole to come along to help feed them.

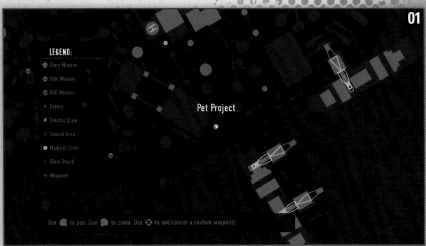

Accept the mission and follow Nix around the corner, where a group of Swamp Monsters and a Devourer wait patiently for their master. Follow the Devourer as it moves into the warehouse area.

The Ice Soldiers are no match for the Devourer's constant barrage of green acid balls. Hang back and let the big baby do most of the dirty work. Take care of any stragglers that manage to make it past the Devourer.

Follow the Devourer a bit farther up the street to confront another batch of Ice Soldiers. Again, let the armored guy handle most of the heavy lifting and focus on clean up.

The final batch of foes is on the other side of a large building, and the Devourer can't follow. Follow Nix across the roof, where two Ice Heavies and a small group of standard Ice Soldiers await.

Let Nix keep the regular soldiers busy while Cole takes out the Ice Heavies first. Once the big guys are dealt with, assist Nix in tracking down the remaining Ice Soldiers and end their short, little lives.

REWARD: 100 XP, Evil Karma

THE GAUNTLET

TROPHY TIME

Completing this mission will unlock the "Dazed and Defused" trophy.

At a mission waypoint in the southern area of the Gas Works district, Zeke relays a call from a madman claiming to be the infamous Blast Shard Bomber. Head to the first mission waypoint, where a Blast Shard bomb awaits.

The bomb explodes before Cole gets a chance to disarm it. On cue, the Blast Shard Bomber appears, taking a moment to goad over Cole's misfortune. This Militia maniac has a bomb strapped to his chest, and he's not afraid to use it!

The Blast Shard Bomber starts making a run for it, setting off a series of bombs in his wake. Give chase to the villain, and avoid falling debris from the explosions.

After passing through a warehouse, the Blast Shard Bomber surrounds himself with hostages for a final confrontation with Cole. Now Cole must make a tough choice—kill the Bomber immediately by detonating the bomb on his chest and injuring the hostages, or risk his life and attempt to disable the bomb first.

CUT THE BLUE WIRE...

As soon as Cole arrives on the scene, the Blast Shard Bomber begins unloading the clip of his machine gun into Cole. Soak up the hits and quickly run within range of Cole's drain ability. Hit **L2** to suck the juice out of the bomb attached to the villain's chest.

With the imminent danger of the bomb removed, blast the Bomber to knock him off his feet and then move in to finish the job with melee attacks. Cole can either kill or Arc Restrain the Bomber without affecting his Karma.

...OR WAS IT THE RED WIRE?

The Blast Shard Bomber has already killed his fair share of civilians, so what are a few more deaths going to matter? Zap the Bomber with any of Cole's attacks until he is dead.

The Bomber may be deceased, but the Blast Shard bomb strapped to his chest is still active. Get out of the area to avoid the explosion.

REWARD: 100 XP, Good Karma (disable the bomb), Evil Karma (detonate the bomb)

It's gotten a little too quiet on the lower-east side of the Gas Works area. Meet up with Nix on the top of a nearby storage tank and get ready to show off Cole's car throwing skills yet again. Begin the mission and follow Nix to the warehouse area.

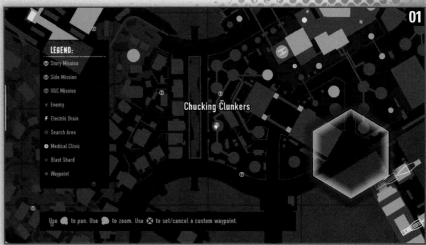

Nix teleports to the top of the catwalk joining two warehouses. Use Kinetic Pulse to grab a passing motorist and hurl it her way for a pretty explosion.

Cole doesn't have to travel very far for the next explosion. Nix appears on the large storage tank behind the warehouse catwalk and beckons Cole to throw another car. Oblige her wishes, and watch as the scaffolding around the storage tank turns to rubble.

Finally, follow Nix to the Industrial Steel building to the north. Nix appears at the top of the building signage, begging for another massive chunk of metal to be tossed her way. Give her one final car and collect the reward.

REWARD: 100 XP

Follow Nix farther up the coastline, where she teleports to the top of a very tall silo. Send another vehicle her way and make some fireworks.

THE BIG CHILL

TROPHY REQUIREMENT

The Big Chill is the third of four side missions required to unlock the "Frozen Asset" trophy.

Near the docked freighter on the south coast of the Gas Works district, Cole's Ice Soldier buddy is ready for another team up.

The Ice Soldier has put on some serious weight since the last time he teamed up with Cole. He has now evolved into a massive Ice Titan, and he is anxious to test out his newfound strength. Follow the Titan to a nearby warehouse and observe as he destroys the walls with massive ice blasts.

A squad of Ice Soldiers greets the heroic pair. Stay behind the Titan and let him deal with the majority of the Ice Soldiers. Take care of any enemies that make it beyond the Titan's massive attacks as he makes his way through the warehouse.

At the exit of the second warehouse, a semi-truck trailer blocks the Titan's path. Two Ice Soldiers are still alive and make a break for it.

Follow the Titan into the warehouse across the street. Continue to let Cole's massive buddy to do the majority of the killing, and hang back to deal with any stragglers.

Chase after the Ice Soldiers to the center of the Gas Works area and take them down to complete the mission.

REWARD: 100 XP

SPECIAL DELIVERY

This mission starts on the roof of a tall structure located to the immediate right of the helipad in the Gas Works area. Activate the mission to receive a call from LaRoche… an Ice Soldier courier is about to deliver an important package at a nearby warehouse, and LaRoche wants it.

From the point where Cole starts the mission, leap and float over to roof of the warehouse marked on Cole's minimap. Walk up to the large skylight and hold ⬤ to observe the delivery. Once the package has been placed, use a grenade on the window to blow it out and begin attacking the Ice Soldiers.

Several Ice Soldiers and a Crusher are placed inside the warehouse, so use the skylights as cover and rain electrical attacks down from above. If the Crusher gets in Cole's sights, drop a few rockets down his throat. Continue clearing out enemies until they are all defeated.

Now, head inside and grab the package to complete the mission.

REWARD: 100 XP

A concerned citizen who is northeast of the helipad in the Gas Works district flags down Cole to assist with a local problem. An Ice Titan and a Devourer are going at it nearby, and many innocent people are caught in the middle. Accept the mission and head east toward the battle.

Stop short of walking straight into the fray and climb the building on Cole's left. Peer down at the Ice Titan and begin raining rockets and grenades down on him.

When the Ice Titan starts throwing ice boulders at Cole, back up on the rooftop and use the electrical sources to recharge. Repeat this pattern until the Titan's arms are destroyed. Hop down and remove his faceplate when the prompt appears, then take down the icy monstrosity for good.

Cole now turns his attention to the Devourer in the vicinity. Fight the monster from above, using the environment as cover. Sticky grenades or rocket attacks inflict good damage on the Devourer when its mouth is open.

Continue the pattern until the Devourer takes a dirt nap. If any Swamp Monster or Ice Soldier grunts remain, take them out to complete the mission.

REWARD: 100 XP

At a mission marker on the east side of the Gas Works, LaRoche contacts Cole with some more Ice Soldier information. Seems the warehouse where Cole retrieved the package back in "Special Delivery" has been overrun again. Follow the waypoint marker to meet up with some of LaRoche's men, then head toward the Ice Soldier base.

After enough Ice Soldiers are down, a vicious Titan appears! LaRoche's men are keeping the Titan occupied for now, so grab some high ground and begin pelting the Titan with rockets.

When Cole and company arrive, more of LaRoche's men are already on the scene and getting ferocious with the Ice Soldiers. Head into the ruckus and defeat all of the Ice Soldiers marked on the minimap.

Blow off the Titan's arms, then rush in to expose its weak point. Retreat and allow LaRoche's men to attack the Titan while it regenerates its limbs, then resume bombarding the beast with explosive attacks.

REWARD: 100 XP

MERCY KILL

TROPHY REQUIREMENT

Mercy Kill is the final side mission required to unlock the "Frozen Asset" trophy.

At the blue mission marker, on the northern coast of the Gas Works district, Kuo meets up with Cole to personally deliver some bad news. The Ice Soldier that defected has officially gone mad from the horrible mutations he has experienced, and it's time to put the boy down. Start the mission and head toward the waypoint marker.

It is a sad scene when Cole arrives. The Ice Soldier (now Titan) is embroiled in a battle with the local police. Cole's former ally begs to be put down, so oblige his request and begin pounding the Titan with rockets.

Once both of the Titan's arms have been blown off, rush in and expose his face. Continue the rocket assault until the Titan goes down for good. Thus ends the tragic saga of the Ice Soldier defector.

REWARD: 100 XP

BIOHAZARD

To the right of the industrial steel building in the northern area of the Gas Works district, a medic is in serious need of Cole's help. Three Ice Soldiers have just escaped with some extremely volatile chemicals and must be stopped before they hurt someone.

Run to the other side of the building to locate the three Ice Soldiers taking off. From here, use Cole's newly acquired Lightning Tether to quickly cover the distance needed to catch up with the soldiers.

Once Cole is in firing range, blast away at one runner at a time. The chemicals they are carrying cause them to explode after only a few hits. Track down the next Ice Soldier and repeat the series of attacks until all three of the foes are put to rest.

NICE SHOOTING, TEX!

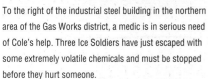

With the right timing and a full energy meter, Cole can take down two of the three runners at the very start of the mission. Use the Lightning Tether to ascend to the top of the building in front of Cole's starting position, and run to the edge toward the Ice Soldiers. Before they have a chance to take off, enter Precision Mode ✛ to slow down time and quickly snipe the runners.

REWARD: 100 XP, Medical Clinic unlocked

OVERCHARGE — GAS WORKS 2

Cole's final overcharge challenge begins at a mission marker in the southeast area of the Gas Works. Start the mission and follow the waypoint marker to the first transformer.

Leap on top of the transformer to imbue Cole with an overcharge, and hold ⊙ to view the destination in the distance.

Jump onto the Grindwire directly in front of Cole, leading to the destination.

Vault over the building at the end of the grind, and land on the next wire that is located straight ahead.

Repeat the process at the next juncture. The new Grindwire turns slightly to the right.

The next jump is much longer. At the end of the Grindwire, leap and immediately activate the Static Thrusters by holding down **R1**. Float straight ahead to the next grind.

This next grind dips down, leading to a telephone pole. When Cole reaches the pole, jump and guide Cole to the wire on the left. Follow this Grindwire to the next building.

Jump at this building, activate Static Thrusters, and guide Cole to the right and land on the Grindwire leading in that direction.

At the end of this last wire, jump and activate the Static Thrusters. Fly straight over the building at the end of the wire and continue floating all the way to the destination transformer.

REWARD: 100 XP

PROUD WARRIOR

Next to the Medical Clinic in the northwest corner of the Gas Works district, Zeke calls in with another little request. He wants to hack the TV network again, and he needs Cole to drain several satellite dishes in the area.

Head east along the coastal road until Cole reaches the first cross street. The satellite is on the tall clock tower building to the left.

Continue down the cross street to the large Industrial Steel building. The next satellite is on the concrete foundation holding up the building sign.

The third satellite can be seen from the Industrial Steel building. Look south, and float or Lightning Tether to the dish and drain it.

Travel east, working around the Industrial Steel building. The fourth satellite is on the chimney of the building directly across the entrance from Industrial Steel.

Jump straight to the east from the fourth satellite to the next roof. The final satellite is on the opposite side of this building. Drain it, and get to the nearest television.

Zeke made a dating video for Cole. Isn't that cute? Sit through Zeke's romantic movie to complete the mission.

REWARD: 100 XP

Zeke has another photography job for Cole that starts on the northwest side of the Gas Works area. Time to snatch up that camera and get to work!

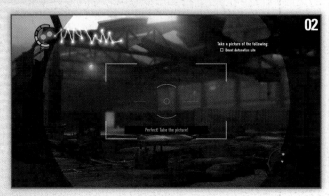

The first shot Zeke needs is of the plague ward that The Beast destroyed. Head south from the mission start location and continue on to the blast site. Get up close to the damage and snap the shot.

Follow the waypoint marker to the Ice Tower. Land on any nearby roof and grab a photo of the tallest building in all of New Marais.

Looks like the Ice Soldiers have gotten wind of Cole's little photo parade. After snapping the second shot, an Ice Titan appears. Of course, Zeke thinks this is a perfect photo opportunity.

Cole needs to grab shots of the Ice Titan shooting Ice Beams and hurling Ice Balls. Fire a few blasts to get the Titan's attention, look through the camera lens, and wait for a counterattack. When the reticule turns green, snap the shot, and then quickly get out of the way!

Zeke's still not done with the Ice Titan, and now he wants a shot of a one-armed Titan. Fire rockets at the Titan until one of its arms falls off, and snap the final shot.

GIVE THE MAN A HAND

It doesn't matter if the Titan is missing one arm or both arms. A picture of either satisfies the requirement.

Now that Zeke's scrapbook is complete, kill the Titan to finish the mission.

REWARD: 100 XP

HIDDEN PACKAGES AND RADIO CONVOYS

Certain Militia members and Ice Soldiers scattered across both islands of New Marais carry valuable information. When defeated outside of an active mission, the corpses of these enemies glow yellow, indicating that they're hiding something. Walk up to the enemy and press **R1** to begin a hidden mission.

RANDOM ENCOUNTER

Enemies holding onto a hidden mission will appear in a certain area but will spawn inside random groups. Patrol the areas indicated in the map before each mission and defeat all enemies in Cole's path until the hidden mission appears.

HIDDEN PACKAGE——CATHEDRAL

01

A Militia soldier stationed on the cathedral grounds holds a picture showing the location of a hidden Blast Shard stash. Patrol the area around the cathedral, defeating any Militia soldiers who cross Cole's path until a glowing yellow corpse appears.

02

Start the mission and hold **R1** to look at the picture of the package location. It looks like the package is hidden in the left belfry of the cathedral. Use the various handholds on the side of the cathedral to climb up the belfry and claim the package.

REWARD: 100 XP, 2 Blast Shards

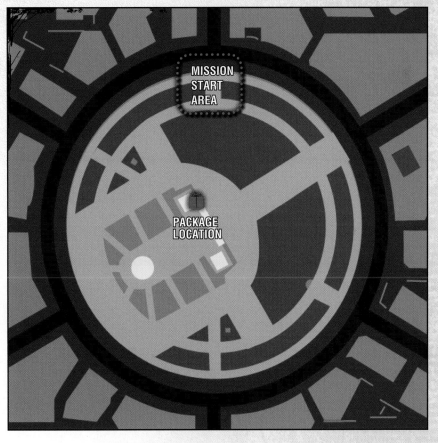

MISSION
START
AREA

PACKAGE
LOCATION

HIDDEN PACKAGE——GRAVEYARD

On or around the bridge that crosses from western New Marais into the eastern graveyard, a pair of patrolling Militia soldiers holds the location of another hidden Blast Shard package. Find them and destroy them.

Grab the picture off of the fallen soldier and hold **R1** to take a peek. Looks like this package is hidden on the top of a water tower on the far, east side of New Marais.

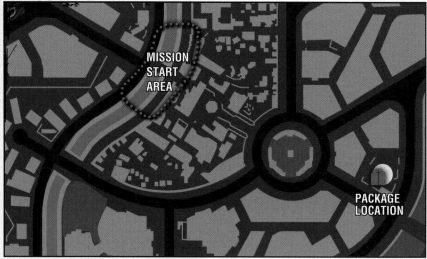

Follow the waypoint to the water tower and climb to the top to grab the package!

REWARD: 100 XP, 2 Blast Shards

CONVOY——LEO PARK

After taking out a group of Militia soldiers near the Medical Clinic in southeast New Marais, Cole hears some interesting chatter over one of their radios. Walk up to the fallen soldier and press **R1** to get the message. A Militia convoy is rolling through Leo Park! Head northeast to Leo Park. Three Militia pickup trucks and a helicopter are passing through and need to be taken down.

Take care of the helicopter first. Fire grenades or rockets at the helicopter, or pull the jalopy trick and hit the whirlybird with a car to take it down in one shot.

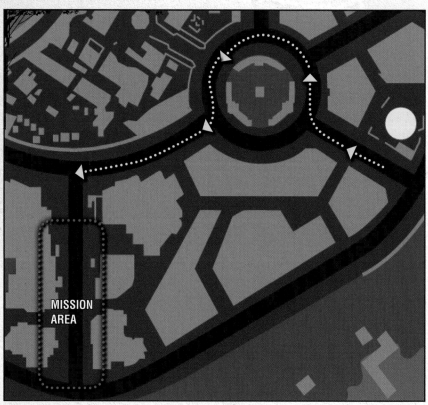

174

Now it's time to take down the Militia trucks. All three need to be destroyed before the mission can be completed. Hit the trucks with two sticky grenades to stop them in their tracks, then swoop in to finish the job. Kill any Militia soldiers who may have survived the explosions, and call it a day.

REWARD: 100 XP

CONVOY—FORT

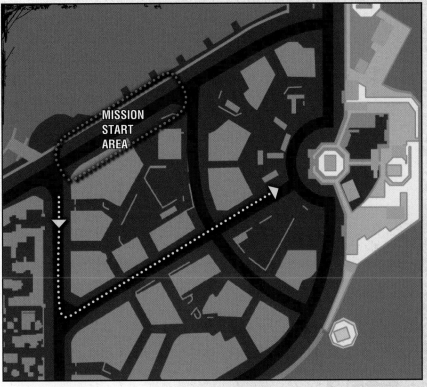

Along the northeastern coast of New Marais, near the Fort, a pair of patrolling Militia soldiers carries word of another convoy passing through New Marais. Defeat the soldiers, and listen to their radio to get the info.

The convoy is heading south along the canal that separates east and west New Marais. Chase after them and prepare for a fight. The convoy only consists of three pickup trucks and a few soldiers on foot.

Take out the truck in the rear and the soldiers guarding it. Grab the truck using Kinetic Pulse and throw it at the next truck in the convoy. The resulting explosion should destroy the second truck and take out a few of the soldiers with it.

Continue taking out the Militia soldiers, and chase down the final truck. Hit it with a few grenades to end this convoy.

REWARD: 100 XP

On the rooftops of the northern area of Flood Town, to the left of the train yard, two Ice Soldiers hold the location of another hidden package. Take them down and grab the photo.

The package is located inside a boxcar in the nearby train yard. Follow the waypoint marker to the general location of the package. Look for the boxcars located next to two explosive tankers, as shown in the picture.

Climb inside the boxcar and snatch up Cole's prize.

REWARD: 100 XP, 2 Blast Shards

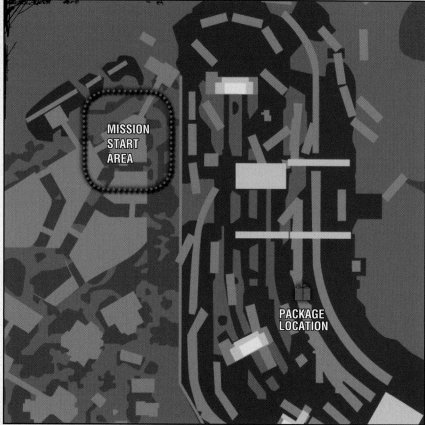

MISSION START AREA

PACKAGE LOCATION

CONVOY——CENTRAL FLOOD TOWN

MISSION START AREA

Two Militia soldiers smack dab in the middle of Flood Town have information on a Militia boat convoy coming around. Take them out, and listen in on their radio to discover the location.

The Militia boats are south along the west coast of Flood Town. Take to the Grindwires and head toward the minimap waypoints.

Get Cole as close to the coast as possible and begin pelting the boats with grenades and rockets. Dodge their rocket fire and stay charged by using the power sources nearby.

Once one of the ships begins to sink, focus Cole's attacks on the remaining boat. The ocean will swallow up any enemies unlucky enough to still be alive when the boat goes down.

REWARD: 100 XPReward: 100 XP, 2 Blast Shards

HIDDEN PACKAGE——TRAIN YARD 2

MISSION START AREA

PACKAGE LOCATION

A group of three Militia soldiers patrolling the center of the rail yard area holds the picture of the next hidden package. Beat them down, and grab the picture.

This package is located on the deck of a large house near the central area of Flood Town. Follow the mission marker to the general package location and look for the large, brown house.

Guide Cole to the building and walk around the side to the porch where the package is located. Drop down and claim the Blast Shards within.

REWARD: 100 XP, 2 Blast Shards

CONVOY—GAS WORKS

On a rooftop in the northern area of the Gas Works, two Ice Soldiers are going to be late for their convoy rendezvous. Take them out, and listen in on their radio call to discover the convoy location. Follow the new minimap markers and continue south toward the convoy.

A squad of Ice Soldiers and a Titan are patrolling the streets. Fire off an Ionic Storm to take care of nearly all the Ice Soldiers at once, then switch Cole's focus to the Titan.

Pelt the Titan with rockets and other high-explosive attacks until both of its arms fall off. Get up close to reveal his weak spot, and then finish the job.

REWARD: 100 XP

MISSION
START
AREA

CONVOY

Mission Complete (100 XP)

0 side missions until next upgrade

Your Karma is unchanged.

Territory Taken: Enemy activity suppressed.

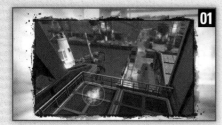

Around the eastern part of the Gas Works, a group of Ice Soldiers holds the key to the final hidden package. Defeat them, and grab the picture.

The last package is located on the control area of a crane near a ship docked on the south side of the Gas Works. Follow the waypoint marker to the general area of the package and begin climbing the tall industrial crane.

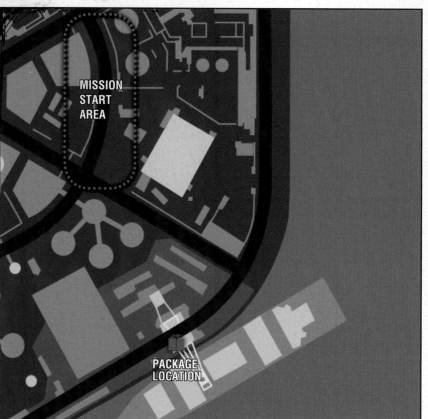

MISSION START AREA

PACKAGE LOCATION

Once on the control area near the top of the crane, head over to the corner and claim the final hidden package.

REWARD: 100 XP, 2 Blast Shards

GETTING STARTED—UGC MENU

Entering the multi-verse of content provided by the UGC system is easy. At any time during the game, press **START** to open the Pause menu and select the User-Generated Content option. The main UGC menu serves as the portal for playing and creating custom missions.

CONNECT TO THE WORLD

To begin downloading or uploading new missions, first select the Connect to UGC Server option. Once connected, new missions will begin downloading automatically based on the defined mission filters. Any missions created in *inFAMOUS 2* can also be uploaded for people across the globe to experience.

COLE' FILTERED

The Mission Filters menu offers a variety of options to decide what UGC missions appear in New Marais.

Mission Filter Options

FILTER	DESCRIPTION
Show	Sets the most basic filter. Options include Featured, Newest, Favorite, Recently Played, or show no UGC missions at all.
With Tag	Defines a specific game type to display. Tags are set by the mission creator from a list of provided descriptors.
Region	Dictates whether UGC missions are pulled from the local regions or worldwide.

MY MISSIONS AND ME

Use the My Mission menu to keep tabs on any missions you create and save. Highlight the mission you wish to work on and press ⊗ to Edit the mission. Alternatively, press ⊚ to Remix the mission. Remixing a mission creates a copy of the entire mission and saves it in a separate slot.

(RE)MIX IT UP

The Remix option is very useful if you wish to experiment with your mission structure. Use this option to experiment with different ideas without destroying the structure of your original mission.

FOLLOW THE RECIPE

The Create Mission from Template option offers some great examples for the budding UGC designer. Representing a multitude of potential mission styles, the templates are a great place to see real-time examples of how the various Core Logic objects work together to create a mission.

Before creating your own mission from scratch, load up one of the templates and just take a look around. Each set of Logic objects comes with a creator comment explaining the function of each set-up. Feel free to experiment with the templates, as well. Try changing some of the Logic around and see what happens!

MADE FROM SCRATCH

The final UGC option, Create Empty Mission, is the kick-off point for when you want to get serious about making a mission. Selecting this option starts a new mission at the location where Cole is standing. The only two objects that appear are the Mission Start and Mission Success Logic Boxes.

STARTING OFF ON THE RIGHT FOOT

You're free to move the Mission Start Logic Box around anywhere in New Marais, but positioning Cole closer to your desired starting area cuts down on any unnecessary set-up time.

⊗ Menu L1/L2 Fly △ Create Object R1 X-Ray View

This circular cursor acts as your Swiss Army knife in the UGC editor. With it, you are able to perform all of the actions required to build a level, including placing objects, moving things around the map, and connecting Logic Boxes together.

CONTROLS

Editor Controls

FUNCTION	CONTROL
Move Cursor/Highlight Radial menu options	Left stick
Move Camera	Right stick
Move Cursor Up/Down	L1/L2
X-Ray View	R1
Open Radial menu/Accept selection	⊗
Create Object	△
Edit highlighted object	▢
Move highlighted object	◎

RADIAL MENU

The Radial menu contains all of the actions you can perform within the editor. Simply press ⊗ at any time to open up the menu. The contents of the menu will change depending on the location of the cursor.

Menu Options (No Object Highlighted)

OPTION	DESCRIPTION
Create Object	Opens the Create menu.
Edit Groups	Opens the Edit Group menu.
Exit	Exits the Mission Editor.
Upload Mission	Adds your mission to the UGC servers.
Save	Saves your work in progress.
Play Mission From Start	Play your mission from the beginning, starting at the Mission Start object.
Play Mission From Here	Starts the current mission from the cursor's current location.

Menu Options (With Object Highlighted)

OPTION	DESCRIPTION
Move	Move currently highlighted object.
Edit Groups	Opens the Edit Group menu.
Delete	Removes the object from the mission.
Edit	Opens the Edit menu for that object.
Duplicate	Allows you to make multiple copies of the same object.

QUICK TIPS

Issue #0

Insider's Guide to New Marais

Retaking New Marais

User-Generated Content

NSA Intel

Extras

KNOW YOUR LIMITS

The gauge on the right side of the screen represents the amount of available memory for a mission. Adding objects and Logic Boxes will increase the gauge. Once it reaches 100%, you cannot place any new objects inside the mission.

ALWAYS LABEL

Always assign a name to an object or Group when possible. Labeling allows you to quickly identify a Timer, Counter, or specific Group of enemies or objects without getting confused during the creation process.

LOGICAL CONNECTIONS

You can quickly add a Splitter, Combiner, or Switch to a Logic chain. Move the cursor over a connection line and press ⊗ to open the Radial menu. From here, select which object to insert into the connection to add it into the mix.

CLONING MADE EASY

There's a very simple method for making multiple copies of the same object. Highlight the object you wish to duplicate and press ⊗ to open the Radial menu. Select Duplicate Object in the lower right corner, and move the newly created copy to its location. Press ◎ to create a new copy of the object, move, and repeat to make as many copies as you wish.

UGC TUTORIAL—TOOLS

The key to designing custom missions in *inFAMOUS 2* lies within the Core Logic objects. When connected together, these items form the skeleton, brains, and heart of any mission. A deep familiarity with how each of the Core Logic objects function and how they relate to one another directly leads to more interesting and complex missions.

LOGIC BASICS

Most of the Core Logic objects operate with simple input/output functionality. The object takes in an input, performs its assigned action, and (depending on the Logic) passes the results through its output jack. This is represented in the UGC Editor via a simple sentence structure. If X happens, then Y occurs. Plugging Core Logic objects together in a chain can create nearly any scenario imaginable.

In the following sections, the functions of some of the more complex Core Logic objects are explained in detail. A complete list of all the tools and their various functions follows.

MONITORS AND VOLUMES

Every string of Logic has to start somewhere, and that's where Monitors and Volumes come in. Both of these Core Logic objects do not have an input jack. They wait for a defined event to occur, and then trigger the Logic Box they are attached to.

▌▌▌ MONITORS

Monitors are the eyes and ears of a Logic string. A monitor waits for a specific event to occur before triggering its output. Setting up a Monitor is fairly simple. Highlight the Monitor with the cursor and press ◎ to open the Edit menu.

The first option in the Monitor's Edit menu is Condition. Conditions represent different states of a specific Group of objects or characters, such as if an enemy has been defeated, if an object has been collected, or if the mission has started.

Next in line is the Combination option, where you can select if the output is triggered when at least one object in a Group has met the Condition, or if the output won't be triggered until the entire specified Group has been triggered.

The final option is called Who/What. Here, you specify which Group of objects the Monitor is observing.

THE ALL-SEEING MONITOR

Feel free to place Monitors anywhere in the game world. They can observe their set Conditions regardless of their proximity to the Group they are assigned to.

EXAMPLE

You're creating a combat mission where the mission success depends on Cole defeating all characters in the Group.

Enemies. Place a Monitor in the world and open the Edit menu. Set the Monitor options to the following:

OPTION	SETTING
Condition	Defeated
Combination	All
Who/What	Enemies

Next, create a Mission Success object and place it near the Monitor. Highlight the Monitor and press △ to create a connection. Move the cursor to the Mission Success object and press ✕ to connect.

When highlighting the Monitor or Mission Success objects, the Logic text should read:

"When all enemies are incapacitated or defeated, the player successfully completes the mission."

 ## VOLUMES

Volumes designate an area of the map and wait for Cole (or a defined Group) to enter or exit its space before triggering its output. They are useful for triggering an event when Cole reaches a specific area of the map.

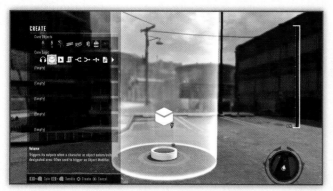

In the Edit menu, you have the option of choosing the shape and size of the Volume. A cylinder shape forms a circle around the object and extends infinitely up into the sky. No matter how far above the object Cole is, the output is triggered when Cole enters the perimeter of the Volume.

Volumes can also be set up in a cube shape. Cubes have a defined height, so these are useful for designating a very specific trigger area.

Additional options include setting the trigger to occur when Cole leaves the Volume and automatically resetting the Volume after it has been triggered.

OBJECT MODIFIER

Mastering the Object Modifier is the absolute key to making interesting and complex UGC missions. With it, you can change add/remove objects from the world, change Cole's health levels, assign orders to enemies, or even alter the laws of physics. Object Modifiers are typically attached to Monitors or Volumes, performing the assigned action once the trigger criteria has been met.

The Object Modifier contains the most options out of all the Core Logic objects, which are detailed below.

 ## OBJECT

This option is used to add or remove a defined Group from the game world. Select the Group using the Who/What option, then select Add to the World or Remove from the World under the Action option.

EXAMPLE

You have a Group called Enemies that you wish to stay hidden until Cole reaches a certain area. First, create a Monitor and set the Condition to Mission Start. Create an Object Modifier with the following properties:

OPTION	SETTING
Modify	Object
Who/What	Enemies
Action	Remove from the World

Connect the Monitor to the Object Modifier to complete the Logic string. Now, when the mission starts, the enemies are removed from the world. Now, try using a Volume and another Object Modifier to add the enemies back to the world!

PHYSICS

Even the laws of physics are no match for the Object Modifier! Give an object some velocity or spin, and even alter the specific gravity.

Probably the most important selection is the Moving Interactions option. This allows you to decide if an object can interact with the environment while it's in motion or if it only obeys the laws of physics you specifically assign to it.

Experiment with the Physics options to create moving targets for Cole or send enemies flying!

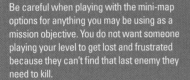

FUN WITH PHYSICS

To create more complicated physics scenarios, take some time to play in the Physics template under the Create Mission from Template menu. Sucker Punch provides some valuable examples on how to set up moving targets.

 # MAP

The Map option is used to change how a Group is represented on the mini-map. You can choose nearly any type of mini-map marker and how the markers appear on the mini-map. Mini-map icons can even be hidden, removing the player's ability to see where hidden enemies may be located.

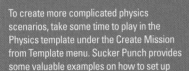

WHERE DID HE GO?

Be careful when playing with the mini-map options for anything you may be using as a mission objective. You do not want someone playing your level to get lost and frustrated because they can't find that last enemy they need to kill.

 # HEALTH

This option allows you to change the percentage of hit points for a Group of characters or Cole. Once triggered, an Object Modifier set to change health can set a character's health anywhere from zero to 100%.

 # COLE'S ENERGY

Want to drain Cole's available energy as soon as he enters an ambush? Then this option in the Object Modifier is for you. Once triggered, Cole's health can be set anywhere between zero and 100%.

 # COLE'S POWERS

With the open nature of *inFAMOUS 2,* a player could enter your mission with any number of powers unlocked. If you want Cole to have a specific ability, or take a power away during a specific part of a mission, the Cole's Powers modifier comes in mighty handy.

Select which Power Type you wish to alter (i.e. Bolts, Blasts, Rockets, etc.), then the specific power. Finally, chose if the power is Enabled or Disabled when the Object Modifier is triggered.

POWER CHALLENGE

Limiting Cole's powers at the start of a mission can be used to increase the challenge of a mission. Using Monitors/Volumes and Object Modifiers to unlock powers after the player meets objectives could make for some interesting missions.

 # DAMAGE RESPONSE

The Damage Response option allows you to affect how much damage one Group takes from another. Use this option to make enemies more difficult to kill, or give Cole a boost when fighting a specific Group.

 # HOSTILITY

A Hostile Group attacks its assigned enemy (or Cole) on sight. Hostility can be set to Hostile or Neutral. Altering Hostility can turn civilians against Cole, or make Swamp Monsters as tame as fluffy kittens.

 # ORDERS

For more slightly more complicated AI combat behavior, the Orders section of the Object Modifier is where you need to go. When triggered, you can set a Group to guard an area, wander around, or openly assault any hostile Groups that get in their sights.

You can also adjust the minimum and maximum range that the AI operates within, and adjust their response to combat.

 # BOMB

The Bomb modifier works just like it sounds. Any bombs placed in a specific Group can be set to detonate or defuse when the Object Modifier is triggered.

 # BREAKABLE

Any destructible objects placed in a Group can be manually destroyed with this modifier.

ACTIVATE

An Object Modifier set to Activate can be used to activate or deactivate any objects within a Group.

COLLECT

When triggered, an Object Modifier set to Collect instantly grabs any collectable objects in a defined Group.

SCRIPT COMMAND

The Object Modifier works fine for adjusting an AI's hostility, but for more complex actions like moving to a specific point or performing an animation, you need to reach for the Script Command Logic.

The Script Command object's most basic use is to get characters from point A to point B. Characters can be told to simply walk to a point, or to lead Cole along a path.

WAYPOINT TO YOUR HEART

Script Commands work best when used in conjunction with the Path Point object. Be sure to assign your Path Points to a different Group than your characters to avoid any confusion.

Characters can also be told to perform a specific animation when the Script Command is triggered. Choose the type of animation to be played, and select how long the characters perform the animation. Use this command to add a little personal flavor to your missions.

PATH POINT

Path Points are used to set a path for AI characters to follow. Create a Path Point, highlight it, and press to extend the path to where you would like the characters to go. Press to end the path, or press ⬤ to set down another Path Point marker and continue extending the path.

Be sure to assign waypoints to their own Group. This makes it much easier to assign characters to specific paths when using the Script Command object.

TIMERS, COUNTERS, AND LOGIC MODIFIERS

Need a time limit for your mission, or want to designate a set number of enemies a player must defeat before moving forward? Then Timers and Counters are for you.

Timers and Counters require a trigger to start, so they are usually connected to a Monitor or Volume, and then routed into another Logic object like a Mission Success, Mission Failure, or an Object Modifier.

COUNTER

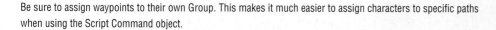

If one of your mission objectives calls for a specific number of collectables to be picked up or hostages to be rescued, then the Counter should be used. Setting up a Counter works exactly like a Timer. Set the count total, and choose if the numbers count up or down. You can also set a caption to be displayed next to the on-screen count.

TIMER

Timers can be set to count up or count down time, and they trigger an output once the count is complete. Use Timers to create pressure on the player to complete a mission quickly, or set up an event to occur at regular intervals.

Captions can also be added to Timers, which display text next to the on-screen display.

LOGIC MODIFIER

The Logic Modifier's core function is to alter a specific Timer or Counter when triggered. Use this object for actions like adding more time after Cole completes an objective or changing the displayed number on a Counter.

DON'T FORGET TO LABEL

The Logic Modifier does not have to be directly attached to the Timer or Counter it is modifying. Instead, it identifies Timers and Counters by their name, so don't forget to add one when placing those objects.

First, select which Timer or Counter you wish to modify, and then select how you would like to change the object's attributes. Link the Logic Modifier to a Monitor or Volume set up with the required criteria to trigger the change.

For quick reference, here is a complete list of the UGC Logic tools available for your use. Combine these tools in interesting ways to help distinguish your mission on the UGC servers.

UGC Core Logic Objects

OBJECT	ICON	EFFECT
Mission Start	!	Designates Cole's starting location for the mission. This Logic is created automatically when a new UGC mission is created and cannot be destroyed.
Mission Success	✓	When triggered, the mission completes successfully. There must always be at least one of these in your mission, but multiple options can be employed to create different success scenarios.
Fail Mission	✗	When this Logic is triggered, the mission fails.
Mission Checkpoint	▶	When triggered, sets its own location as the player's respawn point and triggers any connected output. If Cole dies or fails the mission, he respawns here, and the checkpoint's output is triggered.

Mission Start Options

MODIFIER	DESCRIPTION
Name	Enter the name of the mission.
Caption	Enter flavor text for the mission.
Objective	Describe the overall objective of the mission.
Time	Set how long to display the caption on-screen at mission start.
Primary Tag	Set the gameplay category the mission falls under for when other players search for the mission.
Secondary Tag	Choose a second gameplay category for the mission.
Time of Day	Set the time of day in the game world when the mission is started.

Fail Mission Options

MODIFIER	DESCRIPTION
Caption	Create a message to be displayed on-screen when the mission fails.

OBJECT MODIFIER

The Object Modifier object has the ability to change many attributes within a mission. This is the go-to item when you need to alter something in the mission world.

MODIFY	EFFECT WHEN TRIGGERED
Object	Adds or removes a Group to the world.
Physics	Adjusts the physics for a specific Group.
Map	Adjusts the mini-map icon behavior for a specific Group.
Health	Sets the amount of hit points for Cole or specified Group.
Cole's Energy	Sets Cole's energy level to a certain percentage.
Cole's Powers	Enables or disables any or all of Cole's powers.
Damage Response	Sets how much damage Cole takes from a specific Group, or vice-versa.
Hostility	Defines the hostility or neutrality of a specific Group toward Cole or another Group.
Orders	Triggers a specified Group to perform an action, such as patrol, guard, wander, assault, or idle.
Bomb	Detonates or defuses any bombs in a specified Group.
Breakable	Destroys any breakable objects in a specified Group.
Activate	Activates or deactivates any objects in a specific Group.
Collect	Instantly collects all collectable items placed in a mission.

MONITORS

Monitor Logic waits and observes the world until user-defined criteria is met, and then triggers connected outputs. These objects are most commonly used to activate Object Modifiers.

OBJECT	ICON	DESCRIPTION
Monitor	🎧	Assigns and waits for a defined Condition to be met by a specific Group.
Volume	◈	Sets up a user-defined perimeter and triggers the connected output when Cole or a specific Group exits/enters the perimeter.

Monitor Options

MODIFIER	DESCRIPTION
Condition	Set the Condition of the Group the Monitor is observing. Available choices: Incapacitated, Defeated, Wounded, Arc Restrained, Drained, Healed, Changed Target, Used, Destroyed, Triggered, Collected, Mission Starts.
Combination	Choose between having all or any members of a Group meet the set Condition before the Monitor output is triggered.
Who/What	Select the Group the Monitor is observing.

Volume Options

MODIFIER	DESCRIPTION
Shape	Select between cylindrical and cube-shaped Volume areas. A cylinder's Volume extends into the sky indefinitely, while a cube can be used for a more targeted area.
Scale	Set the overall size of the Volume area.
Length	Adjust the length of the Volume area.
Width	Adjust the width of the Volume area.
Height	Adjust the height of the Volume arwea (cube only).
Who/What	Set the Group that must enter the Volume to trigger its output.
Trigger	Set the output to be triggered when the specified Group exits or enters the Volume.
Auto-Reset	Set the Volume to reset after the output has been triggered.

CHARACTER AND PLAYER BEHAVIOR

These tools can be used to manipulate the actions of AI characters, or even force Cole to move to certain locations.

OBJECT	ICON	DESCRIPTION
Script Command	📜	Used to direct AI characters to move along a specific location, path, or area. This can also be used to prompt AI characters to perform a specific animation or aggressively stun a target.
Path Point	⌂	Sets a defined path for characters to follow.
Player Control Modifier	🎮	Enables or disables player control over Cole. Also defines if enemies are allowed to attack Cole when player control is disabled.

Script Command Options

MODIFIER	DESCRIPTION
Action	Choose the action a Group performs when the object is triggered. Options include: Move to a Point, Move Along Path, Lead to a Point, Lead Player Along Path, Play Animation, Stun.
Who/What	Set a Group to perform the specified action.
Move Speed	Set the target Group to run or walk when the action is triggered.
Who/What	Set the Group or area the target Group moves toward when triggered.
Animation	(Play Animation action only) Choose an animation for the specified Group to perform.
Time	(Play Animation action only) Set how long the specified animation is to be performed.
Reaction	(Stun action only) Set the type of reaction the specified Group has to the stun action.
Strength	(Stun action only) Set the strength of the stun effect.
Damage	(Stun action only) Define the amount of damage the specified Group takes from the stun action.

Path Point Options

MODIFIER	DESCRIPTION
Tag	Change the Group the waypoint is assigned to.

Player Control Modifier Options

MODIFIER	DESCRIPTION
Enable Joystick	Choose to enable or disable player control over Cole when triggered.
Enable Combat	Allow or disallow NPCs to attack Cole when control is removed from the player.

▌▌▌ TIMERS AND COUNTERS

These objects add a time limit or Counter to the mission. These are typically placed in the middle of a Logic string. Timers and Counters can be named individually in order to keep track of multiple objects of the same type.

OBJECT	ICON	DESCRIPTION
Timer	🕐	When triggered, a defined amount of time elapses and then triggers the connected output. Timers can be displayed on-screen, along with a caption.
Counter	⫟⫟⫟	When triggered, the Counter increases or decreases accordingly. When the count reaches 0 or another specified count, the Counter triggers the connected output.
Logic Modifier	◐	Modifies the attributes of a Timer or Counter based on an alternate set of criteria. This Logic can add, reset, or change a Timer or Counter.

Timer Options

MODIFIER	DESCRIPTION
Name	Change the label on the Timer. This option is useful in missions where multiple Timers are used.
Time	Set the length of the Timer.
Repeats	Set the Timer to repeat the countdown, and in turn re-trigger its output.
Display	Have the Timer countdown display on-screen. The Timer can also be set to count down or count up.
Caption	Write a caption to be displayed with the countdown.

Counter Options

MODIFIER	DESCRIPTION
Name	Change the label on the Counter. This option is useful in missions where multiple Counters are used.
Count	Define the number of counts that need to be tracked.
Repeats	Set the Counter to repeat after it is completed.
Display	Set the Counter to decrement or increment the count by 1 each time it is triggered.
Caption	Write a caption to be displayed with the Counter.

Logic Modifier Options

MODIFIER	DESCRIPTION
Modify	Set the Logic Modifier to change a Counter or Timer.
Logic Box	Chose the specific Timer or Counter to modify.
Action	Choose how the specified Timer or Counter is affected when the Logic Modifier is triggered.

▌▌▌ TEXT DISPLAY

Turn to these tools to insert dialogue, display objectives, or display any kind of text-based information.

OBJECT	ICON	DESCRIPTION
Set Objective	★	Specifies an objective for the mission. The text from an objective can be displayed on-screen for a set amount of time, and it is always visible to the player via the Map screen.
Show Brief	📄	Displays a small amount of text on the screen for a specified amount of time or until the player pushes a button. Useful for showing dialogue, explanations, or hints.

Set Objective Options

MODIFIER	DESCRIPTION
Caption	Set the text to be displayed on-screen and on the map when the Set Objective box is triggered.
Time	Set the amount of time the caption is displayed on-screen.

Show Brief Options

MODIFIER	DESCRIPTION
Caption	Insert the text to be displayed on-screen.
Type	Set the text to simply pop up on the screen, or force the player to push a button before the text is removed from the screen.
Time	Define how long the text is displayed on-screen.

▌▌▌ CONNECTIONS

Connection objects allow for chaining multiple Monitors, behaviors, or modifiers into other objects.

OBJECT	ICON	DESCRIPTION
Splitter	⌐<	Allows for one Logic input to trigger multiple connected outputs. Additional settings allow outputs to be triggered one at a time, all at once, or an output chosen at random.
Combiner	>⌐	The opposite of the Splitter. This object allows multiple Logic inputs to connect to a single output.
Switch	⫟	Contains two inputs, A and B. Passes the signal from input A until input B is triggered or vice-versa.
Selector		When triggered, assigns a random object from a specified Group to a special Trigger Group.

Splitter Options

MODIFIER	DESCRIPTION
Trigger Behavior	Define if the attached outputs are triggered all at once, in sequence, at random, or by a defined probability percentage.

Combiner Options

MODIFIER	DESCRIPTION
Combination	Set if all inputs must occur before the output is triggered, or if any of the attached inputs can activate the output on their own.

Switch Options

MODIFIER	DESCRIPTION
On Control Input	Enable or disable the input when the secondary input is triggered.

Selector Options

MODIFIER	DESCRIPTION
Who/What	Define the Group that the Selector pulls its random object from.

Traffic Modifier Options

MODIFIER	DESCRIPTION
Shape	Choose to affect the traffic/pedestrians in the entire game world, or just within a specified Volume.
Traffic	Set the presence of traffic during the mission.
Parked Cars	Set the presence of idle vehicles during the mission.
Civilian Density	Select between low, medium, high, highest, or no presence of civilians during the mission.

Music Options

MODIFIER	DESCRIPTION
Play Music	Select which music track plays when the object is triggered.
Tension	Set the tension of the music from low, medium, high, or dynamic.

Creator Comment Options

MODIFIER	DESCRIPTION
Name	Enter the title of the comment.
Caption	Enter the text for the creator note.

UNIQUE OBJECTS

These objects serve very specific purposes that do not fall into the other categories described above. These tools help make missions more dynamic and personal.

OBJECT	DESCRIPTION
Traffic Modifier	Modifies or removes traffic, parked cars, and civilians for a mission. The settings of this Logic can be applied to a specific Volume or to the entire game world.
Music	When triggered, this Logic changes the in-game music to any specified track.
Creator Comment	Creates a note that can only be viewed while inside the mission editor. Useful for keeping track of complicated Logic strings, labeling areas, or hiding notes for other mission authors.

RESCUE WOLFE'S INTERNS

Wolfe is quite the genius, but he didn't develop all the Ray Sphere technology entirely on his own. A team of hardworking interns assisted with his complex research and made him mediocre coffee.

Unfortunately, maverick Militia members are after them to gain access to Wolfe's hidden research files. These fearless foot soldiers are clothed in experimental armor that protect them from the brunt of Cole's attacks. No longer threatened by his electric abilities, they have tracked the interns down and cornered them in an alley located a short distance from St. Ignatius.

Each intern possesses a personal code, and at least three codes are required to unlock the Ray Sphere files. Cole must escort them to the safety of nearby St. Ignatius if he wants to discover what Wolfe was secretly working on.

ESCORT MISSION

This mission is designed to introduce you to the tools available in UGC. Using the familiar escort mission type as a guide, learn the basics such as placing NPCs (non-playable characters), programming NPC behavior and movement, adding objectives, and setting up the requirements to successfully complete (or fail) a mission, as well as other basic in-game Logic.

GETTING STARTED

THE NAME GAME

When creating a mission from scratch, the only objects to begin with are Mission Start and Mission Success. Right off the bat, highlight Mission Start and press ◉ to bring up its Edit menu. Highlight Name and press ◉ to bring up the keyboard to title this mission.

SAVE EARLY, SAVE OFTEN

Be sure to save frequently while working on a mission. To save, make sure the cursor is not currently highlighting anything and press ⊗ to open the Radial menu. Highlight the disc icon at the bottom and press ⊗ to save your current progress.

▌▌▌▌ CORE OBJECTS

GROUP THERAPY

It's important to have clearly labeled and organized Groups when tackling more complicated missions in UGC. Proper use of Groups mitigates the need for redundant Logic tools.

For this mission, four Groups are needed: Allies, Allies Route, Mavericks, and Mavericks Route. Open up the Radial menu, highlight Edit Groups, and press ⊗ to select it.

In the Edit Group screen, select New Group and press ◎ to create a new Group. Select the Name field and press ◎ to enter a new name to replace the default. Feel free to alter the icon or color to help identify the Group at a glance.

IT'S MADE OF PEOPLE

Now it's time to populate these Groups. At the end of the alley, open up the Radial menu and select Create Object to access the Create menu. Highlight Male Civilian or Female Civilian under Core Objects and press ⊗ to select it. Choose a location in the world and press ⊗ again to place the civilian. Place a total of five civilians for Cole to escort to safety.

Now it's time to place the Mavericks. Before they can be added to the mission, they must first be loaded into the Create menu.

Use the left stick to select an empty row and press ◎ to open up a list of available assets. Scroll until arriving at Militia, then press ⊗ to assign it to the empty row. It is now possible to select Militia from the Create menu.

Select Militia and place them according to the map below. Because the last objects placed belong to the Allies Group, this Militia member is given the same Group assignment. Change the Tag on the Militia soldier to Mavericks before duplicating it and placing additional copies.

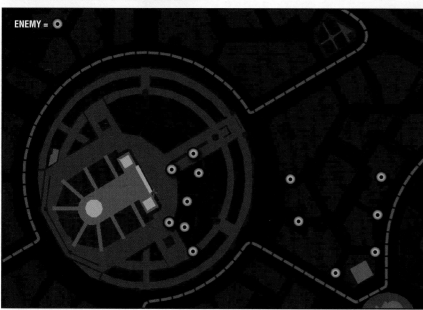

ENEMY = ◎

Now that all the visible elements of the mission are established, it's time to move on to the Logic.

▮▮▮ CORE LOGIC

CHOOSING SIDES

Normally, Militia soldiers focus their hostility exclusive on Cole and ignore civilians. To change this, start by selecting and placing the Monitor Logic in the world.

Open its Edit menu and highlight Condition. Cycle through the options until arriving at Mission Starts. Now whatever output is connected to the Monitor is triggered when the mission begins.

KNOWING FROM THE START

Monitors set to Mission Starts (referred to onwards as Mission Starts Monitors) are extremely useful. When properly connected, they establish the ground rules and Logic that defines the behavior of your mission's elements right from the get-go.

The Mavericks' hostility is the first of several Logic elements that need to trigger at the start of the mission. Rather than placing a new Monitor for each element, use a Splitter to trigger multiple Logic objects from a single Monitor. Select Splitter from the Create menu and place it nearby.

Now, highlight the Monitor and press △ to select its output cable. Move the cursor over to highlight the Splitter and press ⊗ to establish the connection.

To alter the Mavericks' hostility settings, select Object Modifier from the Create menu. Place it near the Splitter and connect the two in the same manner as the Monitor to the Splitter.

Bring up the Object Modifier's Edit menu. Select Modify and cycle through the options until reaching Hostility. Change the first Who/What to Mavericks. Ensure that Hostility is set to Hostile, and then change the second Who/What field to Allies. This causes NPCs in the Mavericks Group to treat those in the Allies Group as enemies.

Place another Mission Starts Monitor nearby, attach a Splitter to it, and attach an Object Modifier to the Splitter. Set it to Modify Damage Response, Who/What to Mavericks, Damage Taken to 50%, and Who/What to Cole. This simulates their armor's resistance to Cole's attacks.

Add and attach another Object Modifier, setting it to Modify Hostility, Who/What to Mavericks, Hostility to Neutral, and Who/What to Cole. This makes the armored Militia fearless in the face of Cole's powers.

ELEMENTARY PATH-OLOGY

Now that the mission is populated, these AI characters need to be directed. From the Create menu, select Path Point under Core Logic. Press ✕ to place it near the starting position of the interns.

Like many elements in UGC, paths are assigned a Group by default. Changing the assignment for a path is as simple as for the interns. Simply bring up the Edit menu and change the Tag to Allies Route.

The Path Point accomplishes very little by itself. Select it and press △ extend the path. Move the left stick to discover a glowing blue line connecting the selected Path Point to the current cursor position. Extend it to the first turn in the alley and press ✕ to place a new, connected Path Point there.

Continue in this manner according to the map below to create Path Points that help guide the AI characters through narrow passages and ensure they reach their destination without getting stuck.

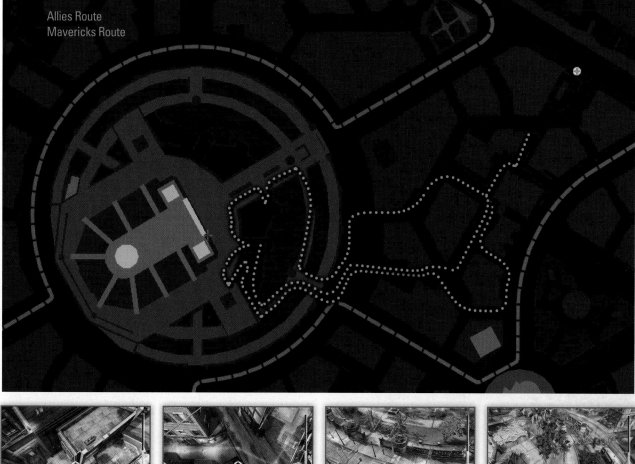

Now it's time to create a new path for the Mavericks. Near their starting position, repeat the process to set a patrol route that snakes through the alleyways. Once finished, change this path's Tag to Mavericks Route.

MARCHING ORDERS

Although the Groups share Tags with the defined paths, the AI characters do not automatically follow paths that happen to share the same Tag. To accomplish this requires both the Script Command and Object Modifier. Begin by selecting Script Command from the Create menu, placing it, and connecting it to the already placed Splitter by St. Ignatius.

Open the Script Command's Edit menu and select Lead Player Along Path under Action. Set Who/What to Allies, Move Speed to Run and Who/What to Allies Route. The first Who/What field determines who moves along the path, and the second determines which path they follow.

NO MAN LEFT BEHIND

Lead Player Along Path is useful to ensure that characters stick to Cole. This Action causes NPCs to move along the assigned path but stop when they get too far from Cole. They then stand in place and beckon to him until he catches up.

Because of their role as aggressors, the Mavericks require slightly more complicated instructions. Select, place, and connect to the Splitter an additional Object Modifier from the Create menu.

Change Modify to Orders, Who/What to Mavericks, Action to Patrol, Who/What to Mavericks Route, and Combat Response to Freely Engage. This commands the Militia to not only move along the correct path, but also to engage in combat when encountering hostiles.

FEAR RESPONSE

Combat Responses are not always aggressive. Changing this setting causes the modified Group to ignore, flee, or even cower before hostiles they encounter.

PLANNING FOR SUCCESS

Now that both Mavericks and Interns know where they're going, it's time to set up the requirements for beating the mission.

Highlight the Mission Success Logic by the Mission Start Logic. Press ◎ to select it for moving and guide it with the left stick to the destination at St. Ignatius where the Allies' path ends. Press **L1** and **L2** to raise or lower it in order to maneuver past buildings or other obstacles.

ON SOLID GROUND

Objects can only be placed on a solid surface. If the cursor is red, then placing the selected object in that position is forbidden.

From the Create menu, select and place the Volume Logic in a position centered upon the endpoint of the Allies' path.

Open the Volume's Edit menu and adjust the shape and dimensions to be large enough for all the interns to fit. Set the Group it detects by changing Who/What to Allies. Change Trigger to On Entry so that it's triggered when the Group enters the area (as opposed to exiting it).

Set Combination to Any so that the output is triggered when any intern enters the area (as opposed to only triggering when all members of the Group are present). Change Auto-Reset to Yes so that the Volume continues to detect the area after the first intern triggers it.

Success in this mission comes when a predetermined minimum number of interns arrive at their destination. Achieve this by placing a Counter and connecting the Volume output to it. Before tweaking the Counter, connect its output to the Mission Success Logic.

Bring up the Counter's Edit menu and name it, if desired. Set the count to 3 and Display to Count Up. Select Caption and press ⊕ to bring up the keyboard and enter "of 5 Interns" into the text field.

Now when each intern enters the area designated by the Volume Logic, the Counter counts up to the set value before triggering its output (Mission Success in this case). When the player successfully escorts the required number of interns to their destination, he or she successfully completes the mission.

FAILURE IS AN OPTION

It's important to include failure conditions for a mission so that players aren't stuck in it forever. In this example, failure is triggered when an insufficient number of interns remain.

Select and place the Mission Failure Logic from the Create menu in the world. Set its Caption to read: "Too many interns were lost, and now the files are locked forever."

Then, place a Monitor and a Counter. Connect the Monitor output to the Counter, and the Counter's output to Mission Failure.

Open the Monitor's Edit menu and set Condition to Incapacitated, Combination to Any, and Who/What to Allies. It now triggers the Counter whenever an intern is incapacitated.

Open the Counter's Edit menu and set the count to 3. Now when three interns are incapacitated, the mission ends in failure due to an insufficient number remaining to reach the destination.

▮▮▮ FINISHING TOUCHES

BRIEFLY SPEAKING

To set up the mission for the player, it's helpful to include dialogue or other on-screen text. The Show Brief Logic was designed just for this purpose. Place and connect a new Mission Starts Monitor, a Splitter, and Show Brief Logic.

Now highlight Show Brief and open the Edit menu. Change Edit Caption to read: "Interns: Those maverick Militia have cornered us in this alley!" Change Type to

Player Controlled so that the player can read the text at his or her leisure.

Place an additional Show Brief and connect the previous Show Brief to it. Set it to read: "They want the encrypted files Wolfe hid at the church. It takes three of our personal codes to decrypt it."

Finally, place a third Show Brief and connect in the same fashion. It should read: "If you escort us there, we'll turn the research over to you."

STAYING OBJECTIVE

Even with context, players who start this mission are adrift and without guidance until given their objectives. This is where the Objective Logic comes in.

This Logic behaves similarly to the Show Brief. The only difference is that it cannot be player-controlled and is displayed at the top of the screen instead of the bottom. Also, it is displayed on the map screen until accomplished.

Place the Objective past the last Show Brief and connect the latter to the former. Now once players have finished reading the introductory speech, they are presented with the objective.

Open the Objective's Edit menu and set the Caption to: "Escort the interns to the church. At least three must survive to decode the files."

THINNING THE HERD

Make testing runs through this mission easier by decreasing the number of random pedestrians who show up. Near the Mission Start position, open the Create menu and place the Traffic Modifier. Then, open its Edit menu and change the population density to None.

80% OF SUCCESS IS SHOWING UP

There are lots of people in New Marais, and Wolfe's interns can easily get lost in the crowd. Open the Create menu and select Object Modifier. Attach it to the same Splitter used for the Script Command Logic.

Open its Edit menu and change Modify to Map, Who/What to Interns, and Display Radar Icon to Waypoint. Now the interns appear as waypoints on the mini-map when in range and as pin icons on the border when farther away. This ensures that players don't lose track of them.

Connect another Object Modifier to the same Splitter. Set Modify to Map, Who/What to Mavericks, and Display Radar Icon to Always. Now Militia positions are always visible to the player.

FEAR OF THE UNKNOWN

Showing enemy positions on the mini-map is a helpful way to track them when testing your mission. Watching their movements on the map can confirm whether or not they are following the orders or path desired. However, feel free to take the waypoints out later to increase the challenge.

▮▮▮ TAKE IT FOR A SPIN

Now that all the basics are in place, it's time for a test drive. Select Play Current Mission from the Pause menu, or select Play Mission From Start from the basic Radial menu.

Having mastered the basics, it's time to up the ante. The next section shows how to take this basic mission and throw in twists and turns to keep players on their toes.

TRAITORS IN THEIR MIDST

Although Cole can trust Wolfe's interns, they are joined in the alleyways by a ragtag assortment of LaRoche's rebels. However, some rebels may turn on Cole if they witness too many of their brothers in arms attacked on his watch. Fortunately, some of the Militia soldiers are sympathetic to the plight of the accused deviants. They may turn on the Ice Soldiers if too many humans are hurt in the crossfire. In addition, there's even a special guest appearance by Zeke—but only for players who play by the rules.

TRUST NO ONE

This sample mission takes the basic escort structure of *Rescue Wolfe's Interns* and adds the possibility of both mid-mission betrayal and unexpected allies. Advanced tools such as Player Control, Selectors, and Switches are used to keep this mission unpredictable for players even after the first playthrough.

UPPING THE ANTE

The groundwork for this mission already exists in *Rescue Wolfe's Interns*. To start working on this advanced version without losing the original, press ⓞ from the mission list to create a duplicate of the mission, which you can edit freely. Be sure to change the Name field of the Mission Start Logic to set it apart from the original in the My Missions list once it's saved.

Before getting too fancy, it's important to build on the strong Logic foundation already present. This means duplicating several assets that figure prominently into this advanced sample mission.

A CASE OF BRIEFS

Start by updating the player's briefing to reflect the new scenario. First, change the first Show Brief to read: "Interns: Those maverick Militia and Ice Soldiers have cornered us in this alley!"

Add an additional Show Brief Logic item to the end of the existing briefing chain. Have it read as follows: "Be careful, I don't know if all these rebels can be trusted."

GATHERING GROUPIES

Before getting to the nuts and bolts of these gameplay additions, it's important to first create all the Groups necessary. The two existing Groups now serve as Parent Groups. When a Logic tool affects the Parent Group, it triggers the same result in all Groups that fall under that Parent Group. Parent Groups can be changed via the Edit Group menu.

Create the following new Groups and set their Parent Group to Allies: Rebels, Sympathizers. Next, make the following Groups and set their Parent Group to Mavericks: Fire, Ice. Finally, create a Group named Interns.

BADDIE BOOM GENERATION

Change the Tag on all the already placed Militia to Fire. Next, open the Create Object menu, navigate to an open row, and load the Ice Soldier asset. Place an Ice Soldier and set its Tag to Ice. Then, open its Radial menu and duplicate it to place an Ice Soldier partner for each existing Militia soldier.

TIPPING THE SCALES

An easy way to scale the difficulty of missions is by tweaking enemy hit points (HP) to make them tougher or easier. However, it can be time-consuming to change each individual enemy's stats after they've been placed.

Instead, set up a Mission Starts Monitor and connect it to an Object Modifier. Set the Object Modifier to Modify Health, change Who/What to the desired Group, and tweak the HP percentage as desired.

SEPARATE, BUT EVIL

The Mavericks get tougher in this version of the mission. Now an Ice Soldier partner joins each Militia member. These unlikely allies have joined forces to prevent anyone from accessing Wolfe's research.

The Ice Soldiers are genetic elitists who refuse to attack Cole and only target his allies. Conversely, the Militia soldiers are still human deep down. Normally, these two factions attack each other on sight. But to team them up, more Logic is necessary.

Find the Splitter connected to the Object Modifier making Mavericks hostile toward Allies. Place and attach three Object Modifiers to the same Splitter making Ice neutral toward Fire, Fire neutral toward Ice, and Ice neutral toward Cole.

COLE'S POSSE

Now it's time to broaden Cole's allies beyond the interns by adding rebels. First change the Tag on the existing civilians to Interns and change the Who/What on the Map Object Modifier from Allies to Interns. Fly to the Volume object at St. Ignatius and change Who/What to Interns so that only they count towards mission success.

Next, open the Create Object menu and place a Male Civilian. Edit its variation to Rebel and Tag to Rebels, then duplicate it to place five to six more.

REBELS AT THE READY

If out of slots to load assets but in need of additional armed NPCs, Rebels fit the bill nicely. They are variations of the Male Civilian that come armed with either pistols or rocket launchers.

Attach and connect two Splitters to the Splitter already present. In each one's Edit menu, change Trigger Behavior to Probability and adjust Probability to 70%. Now when the Splitter they share is triggered, each independently has a 70% chance of occurring.

Change the Tag on several of these rebels to Sympathizers. These are the rebels who may turn upon Cole if too many of their allies fall in battle.

Finally, connect a new Object Modifier to the Splitter dictating the routes. Set it to Modify Orders, Who/What to Allies, Action to Guard, Who/What to Interns, and Combat Response to Freely Engage. Now all of the rebels join Cole in escorting the interns to safety.

THE TIPPING POINT

Place and connect two Object Modifiers to one of these two Splitters. Set the first to Modify Hostility, Who/What to Sympathizers, Hostility to Hostile, and Who/What to Cole. Set the other Object Modifier to Modify Orders, Who/What to Sympathizers, Action to Assault, Who/What to Cole, and Combat Response to Freely Engage.

SHINE ON, YOU CRAZY DIAMOND

When using similar character models for different Groups, it can be hard to tell during testing if a given Group is behaving correctly. To help keep track, change its model to something easily visible that distinguishes them from the other NPCs. The Silver Man variation of the Male Civilian is perfect for this purpose.

Attach three Object Modifiers to the remaining Splitter. Set one to Modify Hostility, Who/What to Ice, Hostility to Hostile, and Who/What to Fire. Do the same for the next Object Modifier, except swap Fire and Ice. Set the last Object Modifier to Modify Orders, Action to Assault, the two Who/What fields to Ice and Fire, and Combat Response to Freely Engage.

‖‖ CHANGING ALLEGIANCES

Every man has his limit, and some of the Militia are veterans who have lost close friends to Ice Soldiers. Seeing normal humans cut down by Ice Soldiers reopens old wounds. If too many of Cole's human allies are killed, they might reach a breaking point and turn on their partners.

Similarly, some of the rebels have their doubts about Cole's heroism. USTV's idea of "fair and balanced coverage" has painted Cole as the greatest menace of all. If too many Ice Soldiers kill their comrades, they may turn on Cole.

CASUALTY COUNT

Place a new Monitor in the world. Set it to detect whenever a member of Allies is incapacitated or defeated. Attach it to a Counter that decreases when triggered and, in turn, triggers its output when reaching the count of 3. Attach a Splitter to this Counter.

Now each time a total of three of Cole's allies are incapacitated, there is a 70% chance the Sympathizers among the Rebels turn on Cole and attack him. There is a separately calculated 70% chance, however, that the Ice Soldiers turn on the Militia and fight among themselves.

▌▌▌▌▌ OPTIONAL ADDITIONS

SIT STILL AND LISTEN

Many players are eager to just get into the action and don't pay attention to instructions. To ensure that players take the time to absorb the opening dialogue and read the objective, it's possible to disable control of Cole temporarily.

Navigate back to the Splitter connecting the Mission Starts Monitor to the Show Brief Logic. Attach a Player Control Modifier to it and set Enable Joystick to No and Enable Combat to No. Now the mission begins with the player having no control over and no combat with Cole.

This is only intended to be a temporary state. To remove the player restrictions, attach a Timer to the Splitter. Open its Edit menu and set the time to 3.0 seconds.

Place and connect an additional Player Control Modifier to the Timer and set Enable Joystick to Yes. Now once the set time has elapsed, the player can control Cole once again. Feel free to adjust the time based on how much text the players have to read before starting.

SOUNDS DANGEROUS

Music is a powerful tool in any medium to align the audience's state of mind with the experience being shown. Place the Music tool anywhere in the world, and it dictates what music the player hears.

Set the mood for the start of the mission by attaching a Music Logic tool to the same Splitter as the Player Control Modifier. Open its Edit menu to choose from a selection of the game's soundtrack. Set the Tension to Dynamic to have it change based on the amount of action going around Cole. Alternately, set it to one of the other three levels based on your preferences.

Music isn't just background noise to the action—it can also be used to inform players. For instance, it can be used as an audio cue so that players know that Sympathizers or Militia have turned on their allies.

Place and connect additional Music objects to the probability Splitters you placed earlier. Choose distinct music selections and tension levels to differentiate between different cues. Now, when the Sympathizers turn on Cole or the Militia turns on the Ice Soldiers, the music switches to reflect the change in circumstances so players can hear it even if they can't see it.

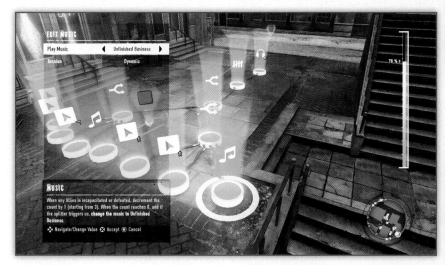

EMERGENCY BACKUP

There's a very real possibility Cole's that none of Cole's rebel backup survives the mission. Fortunately, Zeke comes to Cole's aid in his time of need—provided that players treat Cole's charges with the proper respect.

Some players might decide to betray the rebels and Bio Leech one for their energy. Punish them for exploiting their allies by depriving them of Zeke's assistance.

Open the Create menu and load the Militia Zeke asset. Place him at the entrance to St. Ignatius. Set his Tag to Zeke and Action to Idle.

Place a Mission Starts Monitor before placing and connecting an Object Modifier to it. Set the latter to Modify Object, Who/What to Zeke, and Action to Remove from the World.

Add an additional Monitor and set Condition to Incapacitated, Combination to All, and Who/What to Rebels. Place and connect a Switch to this Monitor. Open the Switch's Edit menu and verify On Control Input is set to disable. This setting prevents the Switch's output from triggering once the second input (connected to the side) is activated.

Place another Monitor and connect it to the side of the Switch. Set its Condition to Drained, Combination to Any, and Who/What to Allies.

Add a Splitter to the world and connect it to the Switch. Place and connect three Object Modifiers to the Splitter. Set the first to Modify Object, Who/What to Zeke, and Action to Add to the World.

Adjust the next to Modify Damage Response, Who/What to Zeke, Damage Taken to 5%, and Who/What to Any Source.

Finally, tweak the last to Modify Orders, Who/What to Zeke, Action to Guard, Who/What to Interns, and Combat Response to Freely Engage.

Now if the player's rebel allies all wind up incapacitated, an extra-tough Militia Zeke blows his cover to come to Cole's aid. However, if a player Bio Leeches one of the interns they're supposed to protect, Militia Zeke never shows, and Cole must keep fighting by himself.

REBEL RESCUE REWARD

Mission success is rated solely on the basis of rescuing the interns. However, a well-designed mission actively provides feedback to players when performing successful actions. Ensure that players feel a sense of accomplishment when effectively guiding their rebel allies to the church.

Create a new Group and name it Success. Open up the Create Object menu and load the Collectibles assets into an empty row. Place one and set its Tag to Success. Then, duplicate it and create a ring of them around the end zone.

Above the end zone, place a new Mission Starts Monitor and connect a new Object Modifier to it. Set the Object Modifier's Modify to Object, Who/What to Success, and Action to Remove from the World. This ensures the ring of collectibles isn't already visible at the church before anyone is rescued.

Duplicate the Volume object in the end zone and stack its doppelganger right on top so their areas overlap. Set the new one to detect Allies, then connect it to a new Splitter. Connect two new Object Modifiers to this Splitter.

Set the first to do the opposite of above: Add Objects in the Success Group to the world. Set the other Object Modifier's Modify to Collect, Who/What to the Success Group, and Action to Collect.

Now when any of Cole's allies enters the end zone, a brilliant flash of purple electric energy signals their successful rescue.

BOSSA NOVA

Ramp up the challenge as players arrive at the church by throwing in a boss fight for good measure. Start by creating a new Group named Boss. Open Create Object and load the Crusher asset into an empty row. Place the Crusher atop the end zone and set its Tag to Boss.

The Crusher should not appear until late in the mission. To ensure this, place a Mission Starts Monitor near the church. Place and attach an Object Modifier to it. Set the Object Modifier to Modify Object, Who/What to Boss, and Action to Remove from the World.

Fly the cursor to the entrance to the church grounds where the Allies Route leads. Place a Volume object from the Create menu. Adjust its size until it covers the entire entrance, then set Who/What to Cole and Auto-Reset to No.

Place and attach an intermediary Splitter to the Volume object. Then add and connect an Object Modifier to the Splitter. Set it to Modify Object, Who/What to Boss, and Action to Add to the World. Now Cole's presence in the entrance triggers the appearance of the Crusher boss—but only once.

Connect another Object Modifier to the Splitter and set it to Modify Hostility, Who/What to Boss, Hostility to Neutral, and Who/What to Fire. This prevents the Crusher from fighting with the Militia in the mission.

▋▋▋ GROUND FLOOR, GOING UP

Now that you've got a feel for UGC with these two versions of a ground-based escort mission, the next section mixes things up. In it, you learn to craft an intense race featuring a narrative, Timers, Checkpoints, rooftop parkour, and alternate paths.

ZEKE'S COMIC CATASTROPHE

From the well-worn pages of the *Thievius Raccoonus* to the collected works of Tolstoy, Zeke loves nothing more than a good book. But above all else, he loves comic books. As his only escape from his apocalyptic surroundings, Zeke has been known to go into spastic fits when he can't get his weekly dose of comics. On this particular week, the Militia cornered Zeke as he was leaving the local New Marais comic shop. The Militia stole his entire supply and scattered the funny books across the rooftops of the Gas Works district. Now Zeke is on the verge of a fatal flip-out, and it's up to Cole to retrieve Zeke's coveted stash of four-color fun.

MASH-UP MISSION

This mission sample expands on some of the core tools available in the UGC editor, using them to mix up gameplay genres to create your own unique mission. *Zeke's Comic Catastrophe* focuses on setting up parkour and collectable item mission objectives to create navigation-based gameplay. This example illustrates how to add branching paths and narration to a mission, along with setting up and manipulating Timers, Counters, and Checkpoints.

▐▌▌ Navigation-based gameplay.

▐▌▌ Using collectibles.

▐▌▌ Setting up Checkpoints.

▐▌▌ Creating alternate paths or endings to a mission.

▐▌▌ Setting up and manipulating Timers.

▐▌▌ Adding narrative flair to a mission.

LOCATION, LOCATION, LOCATION

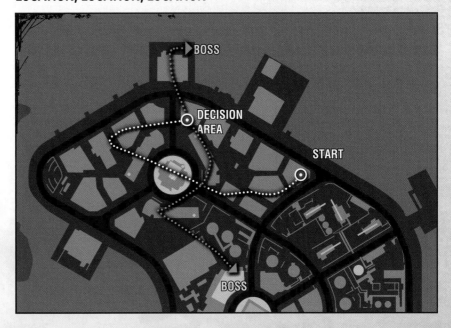

 SETTING UP

As the old saying goes, preparation is the key to success. Before even opening the UGC menu, it helps to have some basic idea of what type of mission you wish to create and where in New Marais that mission takes place.

This mission takes place in the northern area of the Gas Works district. With plenty of rooftop space and Grindwires connecting the various buildings, this area is a fun spot to create a mission with navigation and collectable object challenges. Head to the top of the building marked on the map as Start/End Area and begin building *Zeke's Comic Catastrophe*.

GROUP IT TOGETHER

Groups are an invaluable tool for keeping UGC missions organized and running smoothly. Nearly every tool in the UGC arsenal identifies objects by Group, so the better the objects you are using are broken down, the more control you have over the behavior of the mission. *Zeke's Comic Catastrophe* requires 10 Groups in total. Press ⊗ to open the Radial menu and select Edit Groups in the upper left corner. Next, create the following:

- Comics
- Path 1 Comic
- Path 2 Comic
- Rings 1
- Rings 2
- Rings 3
- Bully
- Bully Boss
- Zeke
- Lord Nerdly

With all of the Groups created, the next step is to load in the objects and characters used in this mission.

LOCK AND LOAD

Open the Radial menu, and select the Create Object option at the very top of the menu. Select the first empty slot on the list and press ◉ to bring up the list of available object Groups. Select Zeke and press ⊗ to load him into the slot.

SO MANY OBJECTS, SO LITTLE SPACE

Aside from the objects included in the Core Objects and Core Logic sets, there are only five empty slots to load objects into. Be careful when selecting what objects you want to use in a level, and make the most out of each set of assets chosen.

Scroll to the next empty slot and open the list of objects. Select the UGC Demo objects and load them in. This set contains two objects used in this mission: the spotlight and rings.

In the next slot, load in the Collectables assets. This contains the comic book objects that Cole must collect for Zeke in this mission.

For the last two slots, load in the Militia and Militia Minigunner assets. These two characters play the role of Zeke's bullies.

PUTTING THE PIECES INTO PLAY

Now that the mission items and Groups are loaded in, it's time to begin putting the objects into place. Press △ to create an object and select Zeke.

Move Zeke in front of the roof's smokestack and press ⊗ to set him in place. With Zeke still highlighted, press ◉ to open the Edit menu and set his Group to Zeke.

Create a new object and select the spotlight from the UGC Demo assets. Move the spotlight on Zeke's left and press ⊗ to set it down.

Finally, open the Edit menu for the spotlight and assign it to the default Group. The spotlight serves as a beacon for players after they have collected all the comics and must return to this location.

LET THE RINGS BE THE GUIDE – PATH 1

The ring objects serve a dual purpose in this mission: to serve as a guide for players, leading them to objectives or fun Grindwire paths, and to add more valuable seconds to the countdown Timer for the mission.

Create a new object and select the ring from the UGC Demo assets. Use the left stick to move the ring over the gap between the current building and the one behind it. Press **R1** to elevate the ring high enough so that Cole has to jump through it, and press ⊗ to lock it into place.

Next, select the ring and press ◎ to open the Edit menu and assign this ring to the Ring 1 Group. Highlight the ring once more and press ⊗ to open the Radial menu. Select Duplicate Object in the lower left corner of the menu.

Move the freshly copied ring over the Grindwire attached to the far right corner of the building and press ◎ to drop a copy in this location. Move farther down the Grindwire and press ◎ again to create another copy.

There is a Grindwire leading up to the Industrial Steel building in the left corner of the next building. Take the new ring over to the Grindwire and create a copy at the beginning of the line. Add two more copies along the path.

Continue over to the Industrial Steel building, where another Grindwire awaits. Add two more rings along this line.

Another grind waits on the opposite side of this building, so add two more rings along the wire.

At the end of this line, turn right, and position the next ring over the gap to the building on the right. The goal here is to have Cole jump through the hoop and land on the adjoining chimney.

Head to the right corner of the next building, where a long Grindwire leads to an open rooftop. Drop three more rings along this line and press ◎ to end the copying process. Pat yourself on the back; the first of three ring paths is complete!

RING AROUND THE ROSEY

As you lay down each ring path, take a second to play through the mission and see if the placement works for you. If a ring is too low, too high, or needs to be shifted a bit to make a jump feel all the more sweeter, take the time to adjust its placement. Fine-tuning a level makes your mission that much more fun for anyone who plays it.

THE BULLY

Create a new object and select the Militia soldier. Move the Militia soldier on the second tier of the building rooftop and press ⊗ to set him down.

Open the Edit menu for the Militia soldier and assign him to the Group called Bully.

On this rooftop, the player is faced with a decision that affects how the rest of the mission progresses. If the player kills the Militia soldier, the player is led along a short path toward a quick boss battle. However, if the player Arc Restrains the soldier instead, they are led along a longer grind path toward a more… interesting boss encounter. Setting up this Logic is covered a little later in the guide.

LET THE RINGS BE THE GUIDE – PATH 2

With the Militia soldier in place, return to the last ring created. Highlight the ring, open the Radial menu, and select Duplicate Object. Move the copy to the Grindwire behind the Militia soldier, leading down to the pier building on the edge of the water.

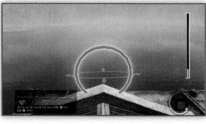

Place the copy in front of the Grindwire and press ⊗. Open the Edit menu for the new ring and change its Group to Rings 2.

Create three more copies along the Grindwire…

…and two more on the roof of the pier building leading the player toward the rear of the building. Now the second ring path is complete!

THE KING OF BULLIES

There's a nice open area at the rear of the pier building that serves as a nice battleground for a boss encounter. Press ⍟ to create a new object and select the Militia Minigunner.

Place the Minigunner near the end of parking lot so he has the drop on Cole when Cole comes through that final ring. Highlight the Minigunner and press ◉ to open his Edit menu, and assign him to the Bully Boss Group.

Return to the rooftop where the Militia soldier is located. It's time to set up the final ring path.

LET THE RINGS BE THE GUIDE – PATH 3

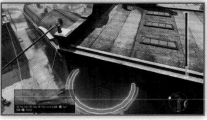

Grab any of the rings already in the world and create a copy. Move the new copy to the Grindwire on the south side of the building and place it on the wire.

Highlight the copy, press ◉ to open the Edit menu, and assign it to the Ring 3 Group. Create another copy of this ring and place two more along the Grindwire.

The next building is a long rooftop leading to a vertical climb at the next building. Hold **R2** and use the left stick to rotate the ring until it is laying flat, and stick it into the building above one of the windows.

At the top of the roof, move the next ring to the Grindwire in the far right corner leading to a long brown building. Place three more rings along this path.

On the roof of the long building, turn right and place two more rings leading the player toward the brick building at the end of the row.

There are two Vertical Grind Poles leading up the side of this building. Rotate the next ring until it's flat, and place one ring at the top of each pole.

Once at the top of the building, turn around and face toward the large smokestack. There is a very long Grindwire here leading to a big, flat rooftop in front of the Ice Tower. Place six rings along this line, three on each segment of the grind.

MEET LORD NERDLY

The rooftop at the end of the long grind shall serve as the lair of Lord Nerdly, king of comics and the true mastermind behind the theft of Zeke's precious funny books.

Open the Create Object menu, and select the Male Civilian from the Core Objects Group at the top. Set the Civilian on the steel grate located on the roof.

Highlight the Male Civilian and press ⓞ to open his Edit menu. Assign him to the Lord Nerdly Group, and change his Variation stat to Upper Class. Finally, highlight the HP Max option and increase it to 400. Lord Nerdly is going to be one tough dude.

COMICS ARE FOR READING

With the placement of Lord Nerdly, it is time to set down Zeke's coveted comic stash. Enter the Create Object menu, and select the Comic Book from the Collectables Group. Place a comic a few feet next to Lord Nerdly.

Highlight the comic, open the Edit menu, and assign this comic to the Path 2 Comic Group. Exit the Edit menu and create a duplicate of the comic.

Move this comic all the way back to the Militia Minigunner and place it close to his location. Assign this comic to the Path 1 Comic Group.

Create another copy, and move it the starting area where Zeke is located. Place the comic in front of the first ring and assign it to the Comics Group.

Create another copy, and move it the starting area where Zeke is located. Place the comic in front of the first ring and assign it to the Comics Group.

Finally, create a copy of the last comic and place nine more along the first ring path you created earlier. Try to keep the comics along the path the player is following, so that they can flow from Grindwire to Grindwire while retrieving Zeke's stash.

Once completed, there should be 12 comics dropped in total: 10 in the Comics Group, and one each in the Path 1 Comic and Path 2 Comic Groups.

KEEPING TABS

When creating objects that are going to be tracked during a mission with a Counter, be sure to keep track of how many have been dropped. The UGC editor does not provide a total count of each object. Keeping pen and paper handy nearby can help you keep track while creating more complicated missions.

With all the objects and actors in place, it's time to start hooking up the Logic.

 ## MAKING THE LOGICAL CONNECTIONS

Zeke's Comic Catastrophe now has a skeleton, but it needs a brain and heart to become a fully functional level. Head back to the first area, where Zeke was placed earlier. This building serves as the start and end point for the mission, and we can begin by establishing the win/loss scenarios.

MISSION START!

All mission Logic has to start somewhere, so for the beginning of *Zeke's Comic Catastrophe*, open the Create Object menu and select the Monitor.

Place the Monitor on the edge of the roof, and press ◉ to open its Edit menu. Set the Condition option to Mission Start. Now, any Logic objects attached to this Monitor trigger their output right when the mission begins.

UNDER PRESSURE

Enter the Create Object menu and create a Timer object. Place the Timer near the Mission Start object and connect the two together. Highlight the Timer and open its Edit menu.

The first highlighted option allows the name of the Timer to be changed. Press ◉ to open up the keyboard and enter "MAIN" to identify the Timer.

THE IMPORTANCE OF LABELS

Take the opportunity to add a name to any object that allows this option. It helps prevent confusion down the road while creating a mission

Next, set the Time to 45 seconds. Leave the Repeat option set to No, and set the Display to Count Down. Finally, highlight the Caption option and enter the phrase "until fatal comic withdrawal."

Finally, create a new object and select the Fail Mission object. Place it near the Timer and connect the Timer to the Fail Mission object. Enter the Edit menu for the Fail Mission object and enter the caption, "Zeke has died from a lack of good comics."

With this Logic, when the mission starts, a 45-second Timer begins counting down. When 45 seconds have passed, the player fails the mission and receives a message about Zeke's death.

RING LOGIC

Forty-five seconds doesn't seem like enough time to gather all of Zeke's comics. This is a perfect opportunity to use all those rings placed in the mission earlier.

Create a Monitor and find a good open spot for it. Open its Edit menu and set its properties to the following:

Ring Logic Monitor

MODIFIER	SETTING
Condition	Triggered
Combination	Any
Who/What	Rings 1

Highlight the Monitor, create two duplicate copies, and place them next to the original. Edit the Who/What modifier of each of the new Monitors to Rings 2 and Rings 3.

Next, create a new object, select the Combiner from the Core Logic section, and place it in front of the three Monitors. Connect each Monitor to the Combiner.

To complete this Logic circuit, create and place a Logic Modifier object in front of the Combiner, and attach the Combiner's output into the Logic Modifier.

MASTER OF TIME

Logic Modifiers allow you to manipulate any Timer or Counter set up in your mission. The Logic Modifier identifies Timers and Counters by their name, so be sure to label any that you set down.

Open the Edit menu for the Logic Modifier and set it up like the following table:

Logic Modifier Settings

MODIFIER	SETTING
Modifier	Timer
Logic Box	MAIN
Action	Add Time
Time	5 seconds

Now, any time Cole passes through a ring, five seconds are added to the countdown clock. Congratulations, all the Logic for the Timer is now set up!

 COMIC COLLECTOR

With the Timer Logic locked in, now it's time to take care of the comic book collectables. Start by creating a new Monitor with the following settings:

Comic Book Monitor Settings

MODIFIER	SETTING
Condition	Collected
Combination	Any
Who/What	Comics

Next, create two duplicates of this Monitor, place them side by side with the first Monitor, and change their Who/What to Path 1 Comic and Path 2 Comic, respectively.

Next, create a Combiner and attach all three Monitors to it. Make sure the setting on the Combiner is set to Any.

Finally, create a Counter with these settings:

Comic Counter Settings

MODIFIER	SETTING
Name	Comics
Count	11
Repeats	No
Display	Count Up
Caption	of 11 comics collected

Link the Combiner to the Counter to complete the Logic circuit for collecting Comics. Any time Cole runs over one of the comic book collectables, the Counter adds one to the total display.

With the Timer, ring, and comic book Logic set up, the last thing to do in this area is set up the Logic for completing the mission.

THE KEYS TO SUCCESS

The criteria for completing this mission are simple: collect 11 comics for Zeke, and return them to Zeke before the Timer expires. The first step is setting up a Volume around Zeke.

Create a new object and select the Volume tool from the Core Logic section. Place the Volume between Zeke and the spotlight created at the start of the mission. Enter the Edit menu for the Volume and change its shape to Cube.

Adjust the size of the cube so that it encapsulates both Zeke and the spotlight. Take a moment to double-check that the Who/What option is set to Cole.

Next, create a new Monitor with the following set up:

Mission Success Monitor Settings

MODIFIER	SETTING
Condition	Collected
Combination	All
Who/What	Comics

Make two duplicates of this Monitor, with the Who/What changed to Path 1 Comic and Path 2 Comic, and place each Monitor next to the first.

Now, here things get a little bit tricky. Depending on what path the players choose later on this mission, they could collect either the Path 1 Comic or the Path 2 Comic. The victory condition has to be set up so Cole collects 11 comics instead of the full 12 that are actually placed in the mission. The Combiner comes in handy to solve this situation.

Create a Combiner and set its Combination setting to Any. Link the Path 1 Comic and Path 2 Comic Monitors into the Combiner.

Next, create a new Combiner with the Combination setting set to All. Link the first Combiner, Comics Monitor, and Volume into the new Combiner.

Finally, create a Mission Success object and link the Combiner's output into it to complete the Logic circuit.

Now, when Cole collects ALL of the regular comics, obtains one of the special comics, and enters the area around Zeke, the mission is successfully completed!

HIDING THE PATH

Move the cursor over to the rooftop where the lone Militia soldier is set up. This location is where the player must make a decision and decide the outcome of the mission. The first thing to do is to hide the special comics and the rings that lead to each boss battle.

Like most actions, start by creating a Monitor with its Condition set to Mission Starts. Next, create a Splitter and attach the Monitor to it.

Enter the Create Object menu and select the Object Modifier from the Core Logic menu. Open the Edit menu for the Object Modifier and create the following settings:

Object Modifier Settings

MODIFIER	SETTING
Modify	Object
Who/What	Rings 2
Action	Remove from the World

Create three more duplicates, and change the Who/What setting on each copy to the Ring 3, Path 1 Comic, and Path 2 Comic. Connect the Splitter to all four Object Modifiers.

When the mission starts, the extra comics and ring paths set up are invisible to the player. Now, it is time to set up the Logic that brings these objects back.

SPLITTING THE PATH

When players reach this part of the mission, they are faced with a choice to either kill or Arc Restrain the Militia solider. Their choice determines which path appears to the boss they encounter at the end.

Let's begin with Path 1, the short path that leads to the Minigunner boss. Create a new Monitor with the following settings:

Path 1 Monitor Settings

MODIFIER	SETTING
Condition	Defeated
Combination	All
Who/What	Bully

Next, add a new Splitter to the world and link it up to the Monitor. Make a new Object Modifier with these settings:

Path 1 Logic Modifier Settings

MODIFIER	SETTING
Modify	Object
Who/What	Rings 2
Action	Add to the World

The player needs to be informed when the new path is opened. Open up the Create Object menu and select the Set Objective object. Enter the Edit menu for the Set Objective object and enter, "New path opened. Defeat the boss to get the last comic!"

Connect the Splitter to the Object Modifier and Set Objective objects to complete the Logic circuit for the first path.

With all this Logic in place, setting up the second path is easy. Highlight each of the four objects you just created and make a single duplicate of each. Hook the objects together exactly like the original Logic circuit.

Only two options need to be changed. Highlight the new Monitor, press ◎ to open the Edit menu, and change the Condition setting to Arc Restrained.

Next, highlight the Object Modifier and set the Who/What setting to Rings 3. With both of these Logic circuits complete, you have now successfully set up the split paths.

KARMIC CREATION

While you cannot create huge Karmic boosts in UGC missions, you can use set-ups like this to add Karmic decisions to your missions. Along with the Arc Restrain option, you can also use the Drain option to force a player to Bio Leech an enemy before continuing.

CHECKPOINT, PLEASE!

The last pieces of Logic that need to be set up in this area are for creating an Objective to inform players that they can make a choice on how to continue, and creating a Checkpoint in case players die while fighting the soldier.

Start by creating a cylinder-shaped Volume object and placing it near the ring leading onto the rooftop. Increase the size of the Volume to cover enough area so that Cole is sure to pass through it when he exits the Grindwire.

Next, create a Splitter and plug the Volume object into it. Follow up by creating a Set Objective object and attaching it to the Splitter. Highlight the Set Objective object, and in its Edit menu, enter the objective text "KILL or ARC RESTRAIN the Bully to continue." Now, players will know what to do when they reach this area.

MISSION DIRECTIVES

The Set Objective object is a great tool for informing players what they need to do next. Any text you enter is displayed on-screen and on the map once the object is triggered, allowing players to check what they need to accomplish at any time.

Enter the Create Object menu again and select the Create Checkpoint object. Connect a cable from the Splitter to the checkpoint. This checkpoint will be triggered as soon as Cole

enters the area. Open the edit menu for the Create Checkpoint object and name it "Decision Time."

Since there is both a Timer and a Counter associated with this mission, these items need to be accounted for if the player dies.

Begin by creating a Monitor with the following settings:

Checkpoint Monitor Settings

MODIFIER	SETTING
Condition	Mission Starts
If	Checkpoint Triggered
Checkpoint	Checkpoint

Attach a Splitter to the new Monitor and place a Logic Modifier near the Splitter with the following settings:

Checkpoint Logic Modifier Settings

MODIFIER	SETTING
Modify	Timer
Logic Box	Main
Action	Set Time
Time	60 seconds

Connect the Splitter to the Logic Modifier so that if players die from this point forward, they restart at the checkpoint with 60 seconds on the clock.

To take care of the comic book collectables, create an Object Modifier and set up the options to look like the following table:

Checkpoint Object Modifier Settings

MODIFIER	SETTING
Modify	Collect
Who/What	Comics
Action	Collect

Connect the Splitter to the Object Modifier to complete the checkpoint Logic circuit. If the player dies, all nine regular comic collectables are instantly added to Cole's count.

The middle portion of the mission is now complete. Let's head over to the Militia Minigunner and set up the first boss battle.

HANGING TOUGH

There are three set-ups that need to be created in this area: making the Minigunner tougher than normal, spawning a comic once he is defeated, and setting an objective for the player once all the comics are collected.

Making the Minigunner harder to defeat is simple. First, create a Monitor with these settings:

Minigunner Monitor Settings

MODIFIER	SETTING
Condition	Change Target
Combination	Any
Who/What	Bully Boss
Who/What	Cole

Then, create an Object Modifier object to look like this:

Minigunner Object Modifier Settings

MODIFIER	SETTING
Modify	Damage Response
Who/What	Bully Boss
Damage Taken	30%
Who/What	Cole

Connect the Monitor to the Object Modifier to complete the circuit. Now when the Minigunner begins attacking Cole, he only takes 30% of the normal damage Cole would normally dish out. Watch out, this comic-stealing Minigunner is one tough cookie!

Getting the Path 1 Comic to spawn when the Minigunner is defeated is a very similar set-up to making the rings spawn. First, create a Monitor set to trigger when the Bully Boss Group has been incapacitated.

Then, make an Object Modifier set to add the Path 1 Comic Group to the world. Link the Monitor and the Object Modifier together to complete the circuit.

The final piece of this puzzle is setting up a final objective after players have collected the last comic book. Create a Monitor with these settings:

Path 1 Conclusion Monitor Settings

MODIFIER	SETTING
Condition	Collected
Combination	All
Who/What	Path 1 Comic

Duplicate the Monitor and change the Who/What setting to the Comics Group. Next, create a Combiner and link both Monitors into it.

Finally, create a Set Objective object. Highlight the object press ◎ to enter its Edit menu. Change the caption to read, "All comics collected! Get back to Zeke before he has a meltdown!"

Connect the Combiner to the Set Objective object to complete the Logic circuit and along with it, the first ending path of the mission.

THE DIABOLICAL LORD NERDLY

Move the cursor all the way to the rooftop where the Male Civilian, aka Lord Nerdly, was placed earlier to set up the final battle. Setting up Lord Nerdly is slightly more complicated than the Militia Minigunner, because Civilians are not automatically hostile toward Cole. With a bit of manipulation via the Script Command object, this otherwise meek background character can become a mighty foe.

Begin by creating a cylinder-shaped Volume object and place it in front of Lord Nerdly. Increase the size of the Volume so that Cole is guaranteed to hit it when he comes flying off the Grindwire.

There are several Logic outputs that need to be triggered when Cole enters this Volume, so create and place a Splitter near the Volume and connect the two together.

Let's make Lord Nerdly super tough. Much like with the Minigunner earlier, create an Object Modifier with the following settings:

Lord Nerdly Object Modifier 1 Settings

MODIFIER	SETTING
Modify	Damage Response
Who/What	Lord Nerdly
Damage Taken	20%
Who/What	Cole

Connect the Object Modifier to the Splitter so that when Cole enters the Volume, Lord Nerdly becomes super tough and only takes 20% of normal damage from Cole's attacks.

Next, Lord Nerdly needs to become aggressive toward Cole. Create a duplicate of the previous Object Modifier and change the settings to the following:

Lord Nerdly Object Modifier 2 Settings

MODIFIER	SETTING
Modify	Hostility
Who/What	Lord Nerdly
Hostility	Hostile
Who/What	Cole

Plug the Splitter into the new Object Modifier. Now when Cole enters the Volume, Lord Nerdly becomes super tough and begins attacking Cole.

The Logic circuits needed to spawn the final comic and objective after Lord Nerdly is defeated are exactly the same as the ones used for the Minigunner boss. Copy over the objects from the Minigunner boss area, but this time, change any reference to Path 1 Comic to Path 2 Comic.

TAKE IT FOR A RIDE

All the basic components of *Zeke's Comic Catastrophe* are now in place! Open the Radial menu and select the Play Mission From Start option in the lower right corner. Run through the mission a few times and make sure all of the Logic is working correctly. If something seems off, run through the guide again and check that all the Logic components are set up in the proper order, making any necessary adjustments.

Once you feel confident that the mission is playable, open the Radial menu again and select Upload Mission in the lower left corner to share your mission with the world!

 ## ADDING SOME FLAIR

With the basic structure of the mission complete, there are many Logic objects you can add on to make the mission more unique and interesting.

LORD NERDLY'S TIRADE

A great villain deserves a great introduction, so let's give Lord Nerdly a few lines of dialogue using the Show Brief and Player Control Modifier Logic objects. Return to the Logic board created to make Lord Nerdly hostile toward Cole.

Enter the Create Object menu and select the Player Control Modifier object from the Core Logic menu. Set the Enable Joystick and Enable Combat options to No. Connect the Splitter to the Player Control Modifier. This Logic freezes Cole in place and prevents Lord Nerdly from attacking him once Cole enters the Volume.

Now the Lord Nerdly has Cole's undivided attention, it's time to give him a voice. Open the Object menu, select the Show Brief object, and connect it to the final slot on the Splitter. Open the Edit menu for the Show Brief object, set the Type to Player Controlled, and write the caption: "LORD NERDLY: It is I, LORD NERDLY, who took Zeke's Comics!"

MAY I ASK WHO'S SPEAKING?

The Show Brief tool only displays the text you put into it. If you're creating dialogue for specific characters, put their name in all caps before the script so that the player knows for sure who is speaking.

Create a duplicate of the Show Brief object and connect it in-line after the brief you just created. Now write the caption: "LORD NERDLY: I now possess the only copy of the ultra-rare holograph cover variant of THE AMAZING ARACHNID in all of New Marais!"

Copy one more Show Brief object, connect it to the second one, and add the final line: "LORD NERDLY: You can have this comic when you pry it from my cold, dead hands!" Finally, create a duplicate of the Player Control Modifier and change the Joystick Enabled option to Yes. Connect this new object at the end of the final brief.

With the Logic set complete, the player is treated to a short little cutscene before Lord Nerdly attacks! Use these tools to experiment with adding dialogue in other areas of the mission. Try making Zeke tell the player why he needs his comics at the start of the mission, or add a death cry for the Militia Minigunner when he is defeated!

COMIC COLLECTING MADE EASY

If you find that the comic book collectables are too hard to spot while blazing through the mission, there's an easy way to make them show up on the mini-map.

Return to the starting area of the mission, and go to the Logic board with the Monitor set-up to start the Timer when the mission begins. Move the cursor over the wire connecting the Monitor to  the Timer and press ⊗ to open the Radial menu. Select the Insert Splitter option to automatically add a Splitter object between the Monitor and Timer.

Create an Object Modifier and give it the following settings:

Comic Book Waypoint Object Modifier Settings

MODIFIER	SETTING
Modify	Map
Who/What	Comics
Display Radar Icon	Waypoint

Connect one of the Splitter connections to the Object Modifier, and now all collectables in the Comics Group appear as waypoint markers on the mini-map.

Use this same technique to make mini-map icons for the special comics, enemies, Zeke, the rings, or anything else you want to make sure that players can find in your missions.

NSA Intel

The NSA has compiled a thorough dossier on every aspect of New Marais for its agents in the field. It covers all potential hostile forces an undercover asset might encounter, dissecting enemy equipment and tactics.

Additionally, NSA researchers have assembled a suggested training regimen based around various cutting-edge tactics to sharpen agents' skills. The top priority for any agents sent into New Marais, however, is acquiring both the encrypted dead drop communications from Dr. Wolfe and the Rayacite shards scattered after his lab's elplosion.

Of course, for those agents looking to further their career with flashy accolades first and foremost, a definitive list of trophies and their requirements is included, as well.

From the mean streets of Empire City to the water-logged alleys of New Marais, Cole just can't seem to go anywhere without someone—or thing—trying to cut his life short. Cole must contend with zealot-minded Militia thugs, horribly mutated Swamp Monsters, and super-powered mercenaries, all looking to take a piece of New Marais for themselves. This list provides a more detailed look at the adversaries that Cole faces on his quest to kill The Beast.

NEW MARAIS POLICE

The NMPD has seen better days. Ever since a massive flood submerged New Marais a few years back, the police have faced difficult times in restoring order to their fair city. Subjugated by the Militia and hard-pressed under Bertrand's boot heel, the police are grateful for any help they can get to restore law and order.

The police are more than willing to join Cole during battles… assuming he walks the path of Good Karma. When Cole treads down the dark road of Evil Karma, the NMPD attack Cole on sight.

ATTACKS

Police officers in New Marais are equipped to deal with the harsh realities of New Marais. While their handguns won't give much trouble when fought on their own, in a group, the officer's hail of gunfire can cut Cole down with haste. A select few members of the police carry hand grenades, and some have been seen carrying rocket launchers.

WEAKNESS

Should Cole find himself on the wrong side of the law, the NMPD officers do not pose much of a threat. They fall easily to simple Alpha Bolts and Alpha Blasts, and a well-placed grenade can wipe out a group of them in one elplosive blast.

THE MILITIA

Bertrand's Militia is dedicated to the "purification" of New Marais. Disenfranchised by the world for various reasons, they have joined up with Bertrand's cause to create a world free from jubilation, decadence, and Conduits.

▶ MILITIA SOLDIER

The basic Militia solider forms the core of Bertrand's forces. They patrol the streets of New Marais in search of unclean individuals to be "cleansed" from the land. Along with basic patrols and missions, the Militia also serve as Bertrand's personal guards—and a constant thorn in Cole's side.

ATTACKS

The Militia's greatest strengths stem from their sheer numbers and their weapons. The basic Militia soldier comes equipped with one of several standard weapon load-outs. Assault rifles, shotguns, grenade launchers, rocket-propelled grenades, sniper rifles, and even riot shields can be found amongst the Militia's armaments.

Militia soldiers work in groups, supporting each other during a firefight. Soldiers equipped with heavy weapons tend to stay at the rear of the pack, in order to bombard Cole with elplosive ordnance, while those carrying rifles and shotguns move in to perforate Cole with a hail of bullets.

WEAKNESS

Bertrand's Militia may possess superior firepower and numbers, but they do not hold up well to Cole's electrical attacks. Most soldiers fall easily to a few well-placed bolts and are highly susceptible to Cole's Blast attacks. Melee attacks quickly dispatch Militia soldiers, as well; Finisher and Ultra attacks can drop them in one blow.

Cole needs to keep his distance from Militia soldiers carrying assault rifles and shotguns, finishing them off with long-range attacks. On the flip side, getting up close and personal is the best tactic when dealing with grenade launchers and RPGs. These soldiers do not fire when there's a chance they could be caught in the elplosion. For soldiers carrying a riot shield, use a Blast attack to knock the shield from their hands, and then move in for the kill.

▶ MILITIA MINIGUNNER

Bertrand only chooses the meanest and biggest members of the Militia to wield the mighty mini-gun. These hulking brutes are used as the heavy muscle for important Militia operations. They possess a hearty constitution, and they won't go down without a considerable fight.

ATTACKS

The Militia Minigunner can be a formidable foe early on in Cole's adventure. Upon spotting Cole, the Minigunner revs up his weapon and begins spitting a constant stream of bullets. His strength allows him to aim the gun quickly, tracking Cole across the battlefield. A backpack full of bullets ensures that the Militia Minigunner does not run out of ammo to send Cole's way.

WEAKNESS

Defeating the Militia Minigunner requires swift feet and a lightning-fast trigger finger—and luckily, Cole is in possession of both. Use the environment to take cover and stay out of the Minigunner's line of sight. The Minigunner is forced to remain stationary while firing his weapon, so Cole's best option is flanking the brute. Grenades and headshots offer the quickest path to taking the Minigunner down. If Cole finds himself face-to-face with the Minigunner, melee attacks leave the marksman stunned and unable to fire.

A dirty little secret amongst the population of New Marais, The Corrupted have been terrorizing the populace for some time. No one knows where they came from or what they want, other than to feast on the flesh of humans. The Militia members offer human sacrifices to keep the creatures at bay, but how long until these inhuman monsters are unsatisfied with these meager offerings and invade the city for a more substantial feast?

▶ SWAMP MONSTER

These grotesque monsters serve as the grunts of the Corrupted army. Long, razor-sharp claws protrude from their arms, while their legs have mutated to a point that allows them to spring several stories in the air. They crave the taste of human flesh, and they stop at nothing to acquire a meal.

ATTACKS

Swamp Monsters are strong and speedy foes. They prefer to swoop in on Cole in packs and slice at him with their razor-sharp claws. These freaks are also incredibly strong and can knock Cole off of his feet in one blow. Their mutated legs give them plenty of footing and make them highly resistant to Blast attacks.

WEAKNESS

When it comes to dealing with Swamp Monsters, the Amp is the best tool for the job. Melee attacks keep the Swamp Monsters stunned and prevent them from retaliating. Make liberal use of Finisher and Ultra attacks, once they are available, and Cole can take down multiple freaks with one blow.

▶ GASBAG

These Corrupted foot soldiers are bred for only one purpose—to self-destruct so that their brothers may feast on their victims.

ATTACKS

The Gasbag is eltremely fast and charges at Cole on-sight. It relentlessly pursues Cole until it is close enough to capture him in its elplosive blast.

WEAKNESS

While swift and deadly, the Gasbag's one-track mind serves as its disadvantage. When a Gasbag approaches, begin walking backwards while keeping aim on the creature, and fire Blasts to keep it at bay. Once the Gasbag is at a safe distance, a few electrical bolts fired by Cole's hands ensure that the creature meets a premature end. Gasbags can be used to a tactical advantage, as well—any enemies caught in their death rattles suffer massive damage.

▶ RAVAGER

The four-legged Ravager is one the most dangerous and resilient creatures Cole must face in New Marais. Armored, fast, and deadly at both long and short-range, Cole must use all of his skill to take these creatures down. Bolts bounce harmlessly off it, requiring Cole to use his other attacks to pierce its defenses.

RAVAGER HIVE LORD

A more elite variant of the Ravager, Hive Lords possess all of their skills with an eltra ability. Hive Lords can give birth to dozens of acid-spitting Spikers.

ATTACKS

Ravagers have been gifted with a multitude of deadly mutations. Their brute strength allows them to charge straight at Cole, knocking away any cars or people that may get in the way. At long-range, they spit streams of acid that can burn through flesh. Ravagers can also bury themselves into the earth and tunnel underground to reach Cole wherever he may be hiding. Even the rooftops are not safe, because the Ravager can dig up through steel and concrete to reach Cole.

WEAKNESS

The Ravager's heavy armor plating prevents Bolt and Blast attacks from harming it, so explosive attacks are the best way to confront these foes. Grenades and rockets make quick work of the creature. In a pinch, use Kinetic Pulse to throw electrically charged objects (cars are always best) into the Ravager's path.

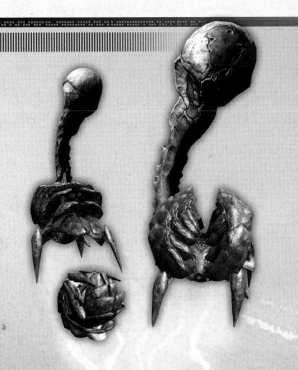

▶ SPIKERS

Birthed from pods created by the Ravager Hive Lord, Spikers serve as a pesky annoyance to Cole in battle.

ATTACKS

An individual Spiker doesn't have much going for it in the offense department. It rolls around the battlefield, waiting for the right moment to uncurl and unleash its acid spit attack. In large groups, however, Spikers can quickly overwhelm Cole with an unwanted acid bath.

WEAKNESS

Spikers are the weakest enemy Cole encounters in New Marais. Simply get one of the little bugs underfoot, and press ◎ to kick the Spiker into the rafters.

DEVOURER

Out of all The Corrupted, the heavily armored Devourer poses the greatest challenge to Cole. Its massive weight allows the Devourer to stomp through anything it its path. Bolts, grenades, and rockets bounce off its thick hide.

ATTACKS

The Devourer has only a few, but deadly, tools at its disposal. Large acid globs spew forth from its gaping maw, and its grasping tongue reels in fleeing victims to feed its massive hunger.

WEAKNESS

This abomination only has one weakness, its mouth. When the Devourer opens its mouth to launch an attack, fire as many bolts, grenades, or rockets as Cole can summon to give the beast a nasty case of indigestion.

THE ICE GANG

Rumored to have originated as South African mercenaries, the Ice Gang are soldiers imbued with power beyond their imagination. Forced to become Conduits by unnatural means, these deadly soldiers are slowly going insane from the mutation process. The Ice Gang seeks control of the Flood Town and Gas Works districts of New Marais.

ICE SOLDIER

The basic Ice Soldier is a formidable foe for Cole MacGrath. They can leap many stories in the air on pillars of ice, and they can form shields of the frosty stuff at will. The Ice Soldiers' speed makes them more deadly than the Militia, because they can perform hit-and-run attacks on Cole.

ATTACKS

While the Ice Soldiers may possess some super-human abilities, they still rely on guns to attack their foes. Ice Soldiers can be spotted with similar armaments as the Militia: rifles, shotguns, and rocket launchers can be counted amongst their numbers.

WEAKNESS

Ice Soldiers wear better armor than the Militia, but they still fall to the same tactics. By the time Cole must face these villains, he has many more powers at his disposal. The trick is getting them in Cole's sights, since their speed makes it difficult to get a bead on them.

▶ ICE HEAVY

Ice Heavies stand as the next mutation in an Ice Soldier's life. They wear heavy armor and have more offensive capabilities than their soldier brethren, but at the expense of mobility.

ATTACKS

An Ice Heavy prefers to remain stationary while attacking. He forms a huge pillar of ice underneath his feet to gain a height advantage. From his self-created vantage point, the Ice Heavy focuses deadly beams of ice on Cole, tracking Cole anywhere within his line of sight for a full 360 degrees.

WEAKNESS

The Ice Heavy's weakness is his tendency to stay in one position for a long period of time. Destroy the ice pillar under his feet, and the Ice Heavy comes tumbling back down to earth. This leaves him open to melee attacks or high explosives from long-range. If Cole can't get up close and personal, enter Precision Mode and land a few quick headshots to quickly bring the Ice Heavy to an end.

▶ CRUSHER

Representing the third phase of Ice Gang mutation, the Crusher is a swift and strong foe. Ditching the bulky armor of the Ice Heavy, a Crusher forms its own armor of thick ice formations. Bolts have no effect on this foe, so unleash the rest of Cole's arsenal to bring it down.

ATTACKS

The Crusher prefers to keep his distance from Cole, so that he may launch a number of long-ranged attacks. He can pound the ground to unleash a lane of razor-sharp ice in Cole's direction, or summon jagged masses of ice to throw at Cole. If Cole gets too close to the Crusher, the Crusher summons an 180 degree wall of ice spikes around his location to knock Cole off of his feet.

WEAKNESS

When Cole can catch a Crusher in his sights, rockets serve as the most effective weapon in his arsenal. Pound the Crusher with rockets at mid-range, or hang back and use Rebound Rockets to tag and track the Crusher as it leaps across the rooftops of the Gas Works.

TITAN

The abominable Titan represents the final phase in the life cycle of an Ice Gang member. Growing massive in size with a thick crust of dense ice covering their bodies, Titans are tough cookies to fight. Titans have lost nearly all of their higher brain functioning at this point, and they have become mindless monsters of unrepressed rage. Bolts cannot pierce its icy exterior, forcing Cole to mix up his attacks with other powers.

ATTACKS

The Titan can perform the strongest attacks from its days as an Ice Heavy and Crusher. It fires deadly ice beams from both of its palms, tracking Cole across the battlefield, or lobs massive balls of ice to crush its foes. At close-range, the Titan can summon a wall of ice spikes in the area surrounding him.

WEAKNESS

While he is big and strong, the Titan is also slow and stupid. When possible, take the higher ground and pelt the Titan with rockets and grenades. Cole can quickly get behind cover before the Titan has a chance to retaliate.

For Cole MacGrath, killing enemies with a bit of style can be both fun and profitable. Completing stunts earns Cole additional experience points, which can be used to purchase new powers and abilities. Many of Cole's new powers require a set number of stunts to be completed before they can be purchased, and some stunts even affect Cole's Karma rating. Check out the list below for a complete list of the stunts that Cole can perform while cruising around New Marais.

Neutral Stunts

NAME	XP	Description
Take Down	Varies	Defeat an enemy. XP reward increases with the size of the enemy.
Impressive!	+5	Take down two enemies in one attack.
Amazing!	+5	Take down three enemies in one attack.
Astonishing!	+5	Take down four enemies in one attack.
Big Destruction	+5	Destroy a large object.
Blast Party	+10	Hit three enemies with one Blast attack.
Blast Riot	+25	Hit five enemies with one Blast attack.
Blast Shard	+5	Collect a Blast Shard.
Blast Shard Energy Storage Increased	+5	Collect enough Blast Shards to add another Power Core to Cole's energy gauge.
Bounce 'n Stick	+15	Stick a grenade to a human-sized enemy after it bounces off something.
CARnage	+15	Destroy four cars in four seconds.
Climbing Assault	+5	Kill an enemy while hanging from a ledge.
Dead Drop	+50	Collect a dead drop.
Dead Eye	+5	Score a direct hit on an enemy with a rocket.
Disabled Turret	+10	Disable an enemy machine gun turret.
Enviro Kill	+10	Kill an enemy using an environmental object.
Grenade Party	+10	Damage three enemies with a single grenade.
Head Shock	+1	Hit an enemy in the head with any bolt attack.
Hit Clueless Enemy	+5	Attack an enemy who is unaware of Cole's presence.
Hit Flying Enemy	+5	Hit an enemy with a bolt attack while the foe is in the air.
Precise Head Shock	+1	Blast an enemy in the head while in Precision Mode.
Rocket Party	+5	Hit three or more enemies with a single rocket.
Rubber Rocket	+5	Use a Blast attack to deflect an enemy rocket.
Special Delivery	+5	Kill an enemy by throwing an object with Kinetic Pulse.
Stick it to the Man	+10	Attach a sticky grenade to an enemy.
Tag!	+1	Hit an enemy with a bolt after firing a Redirect Rocket.
Watch Your Step	+15	Kill an enemy by knocking them off a high ledge.
Wet Landing	+5	Defeat an enemy by pushing them into deep water.
Wounded Kill	+1	Kill an enemy using a melee attack while they're on the ground.

Good Karma Stunts

NAME	XP	Description
Cold Shoulder	+1	Freeze an enemy with an ice attack.
Live Capture	+1	Arc Restrain a wounded enemy.
Healing Touch	+1	Heal a civilian.
Hostage Rescued	+5	Save a civilian from a mugging or an abduction.

Evil Karma Stunts

NAME	XP	Description
Bystander	+1	Kill a civilian. Requires an Evil Karma ranking of Thug or higher.
Drain	+1	Bio Leech a wounded enemy.
Elecution	+1	Arc Restrain an enemy, and then kill them.
Super Drain	+1	Kill an enemy with Ionic Drain.

InFamous 2 Trophies

NAME	Type	Description
InFamous 2 Platinum Trophy	Platinum	Collect all other InFamous 2 trophies.
Pain Builds Character	Gold	Finish the game on hard difficulty.
Just One More	Gold	Pick up all the Blast Shards scattered around New Marais.
With Great Power Comes Greater Power	Silver	Unlock and purchase all powers.
Shardcore	Silver	Pick up 50% of the Blast Shards scattered around New Marais.
Fight the Good Fight	Silver	Unlock the good ending.
Forging Your Own Path	Silver	Unlock the evil ending.
Land Lord	Silver	Take over the first island in New Marais.
It's My Town, Now	Silver	Take over the second island in New Marais.
Well inFormed	Silver	Collect all Dead Drops.
Arch Villain	Silver	Earn full negative Karma.
Incorruptible	Silver	Earn full positive Karma.
Behind the Curtain	Bronze	Collect 50% of the available Dead Drops.
Closed Casket Affair (Hidden)	Bronze	Give Bertrand what he wants.
A Streetcar Named "Boom!"	Bronze	Complete BOOM!
Quid Pro Kuo	Bronze	Complete Leading the Charge.
Playing Both Sides	Bronze	Complete Fooling the Rebels.
Ambulance Chaser	Bronze	Complete Hearts and Minds Campaign.
Status Kuo	Bronze	Choose Kuo in Storming the Fort.
Get Nix'ed (Hidden)	Bronze	Choose Nix in Storming the Fort.
Am I the Daddy?	Bronze	Complete Nix's New Family.
Exposure	Bronze	Complete Exposing Bertrand.
The Cleaner	Bronze	Complete the assassination side missions.
Frozen Asset	Bronze	Complete the ice conduit side missions.
Dazed and Defused	Bronze	Take down the Blast Shard Bomber.
Back to the Bayou	Bronze	Return to the swamp blockade.
Mountaineer	Bronze	Climb to the top of the three tallest buildings in New Marais.
Extreme Makeover	Bronze	Destroy 30 verandas or other large objects.
Watch That First Step	Bronze	Defeat an enemy by destroying the object they stand on.
Finish What You Started	Bronze	Perform 100 finishers or ultra melee combos.
Knockout in the Blackout	Bronze	Defeat 50 enemies in powered-down areas while no missions are active.
Go Long!	Bronze	Hurl 50 objects using the Kinetic Pulse ability.
Cole' Blooded	Bronze	Defeat 100 civilians.
Army of Me	Bronze	Defeat 300 enemies.
Hero to the People	Bronze	Stop 80 crimes in progress.
Nothing Can Bring Me Down	Bronze	Stay off the ground for 130 meters.
Return to Sender	Bronze	Send a helicopter's rockets back at it using any Blast ability.
Vehicular Manslaughter	Bronze	Defeat 25 enemies by throwing cars at them.
Take Them for a Spin	Bronze	Hit at least six cars in a single Ionic Vortex.
Shock and Awe	Bronze	Thunder Drop into a group of five or more enemies.
Thunder Flop	Bronze	Thunder Drop from the highest place in New Marais.
Head Hunter	Bronze	Use the Precision ability to rack up three head shots in rapid succession.
Discerning Taste	Bronze	Take down a street performer who is imitating a statue.
I'm as Shocked as You Are	Bronze	Defeat an enemy or civilian by stepping in water.
Don't Fence Me In	Bronze	Climb a chain link fence and rejoice.
Express Elevator	Bronze	Ascend 50 Vertical Launch Poles.
Heavy Hitter	Bronze	Use your Ionic Powers 30 times.
Matching Set	Bronze	Unlock and purchase a power of each type by performing stunts.
Level Up	Bronze	Create a new mission using the UGC level editor.
UGC Curious	Bronze	Play 10 user-generated missions.
UGC Veteran	Bronze	Play 25 user-generated missions.
Trail Blazer	Bronze	Play five user-generated missions under the Newest filter.

While most of the trophies in *InFamous 2* are fairly straightforward in their descriptions, there are a few ambiguous cases and exceptionally elusive awards that are worth discussing further. Here are a few hints and tips for some of the harder trophies.

▮▮▮ MOUNTAINEER

The description for the Mountaineer trophy reads: "Climb to the top of the three tallest buildings in New Marais." Sounds easy enough, but what are the three tallest buildings?

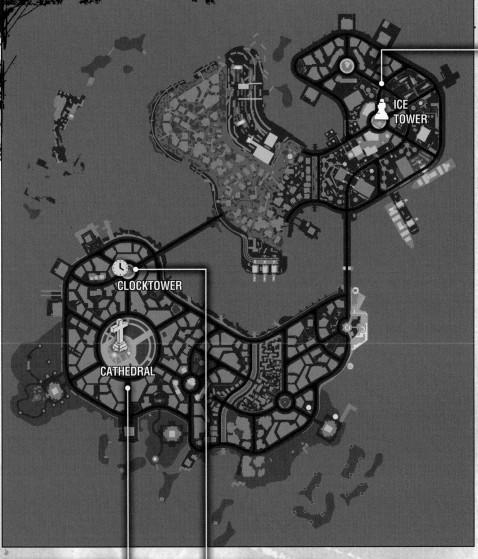

The final building is the Ice Tower, located in the Gas Works area on the second island. Climb all the way to the top of the tower, then use the Vertical Launch Poles to reach the antenna. Stand on the very top of the antenna to claim the trophy!

The next building is the cathedral, located just south of the clock tower. Cole must stand on the peak of either belfry to count this ascent toward the trophy.

The first building is the clock tower in the northwest area of the main island. Climb all the way up the tower and place Cole on the tip of the spike on the roof.

THUNDER FLOP

The Thunder Flop trophy can easily be earned while gunning for Mountaineer. Climb to the very top of the Ice Tower and stand on the upper part of the antenna. Choose a landing point on the ground and leap, then immediately press ⓞ to initiate the Thunder Drop once Cole is clear of the building.

WATCH FOR FALLING CONDUITS

If Cole hits a building or any of the ice mounds built up around the base of the Ice Tower, the trophy does not unlock. Be sure to pick a landing area that makes for a clear shot all the way down.

NOTHING CAN KEEP ME DOWN

Cole needs the Improved Static Thrusters upgrade to earn this trophy. He gains this ability after completing the "Good Gets Better" mission.

Here is another trophy that Cole can earn while he works toward Mountaineer. Climb to the very top of the cathedral on the main island of New Marais, and face Cole north, toward the clock tower.

Leap toward the clock tower and, at the peak of Cole's jump, hold **R1** to activate his Static Thrusters. Continue floating forward until Cole touches the street to unlock the trophy.

THE CLEANER

To earn this Evil Karma trophy, Cole must complete all three assassination side missions in New Marais. These missions are:

- Taking out the Trash (see page 44)
- The Hunt (see page 136)
- Assassin's Greed (see page 150)

FROZEN ASSET

This Good Karma trophy is earned by beating the Ice Soldier ally quest line that starts in Flood Town. The side missions Cole needs to complete are:

- Unlikely Allies (see page 149)
- Stay Frosty (see page 157)
- The Big Chill (see page 167)
- Mercy Kill (see page 169)

BACK TO THE BAYOU
REACH FOR IT!

Cole must have the Lightning Tether or Improved Static Thruster powers unlocked in order to earn this trophy.

For this trophy, Cole needs to return all the way to the swamp where he first entered New Marais. Head to the northwest corner of the first island and use the Lightning Tether to reach the tall electrical tower. Alternatively, Cole can float over from a nearby building or boat.

Retrace Cole's steps back to the beginning and claim the trophy!

I'M AS SHOCKED AS YOU ARE

Everyone knows water and electricity don't mix, but Cole can use that to his advantage to unlock this trophy.

Head into Flood Town, where there are enemies and civilians wading through shallow water everywhere. Jump into the water near someone and get out quick. Cole's natural charge does all the work.

KNOCKOUT IN THE BLACKOUT

There are two major opportunities to earn this trophy during the main story: before starting Powering up Ascension Parish (pg 61) or before starting Powering up Gas Works (pg 98).

Attempting to defeat 50 enemies in the powered-down areas of New Marais proves more difficult earlier in the game. Cole probably hasn't had a chance to increase his energy capacity by finding Blast Shards yet, leaving him with limited options in an area without plentiful power sources.

Follow the path of least resistance and enter the Gas Works area right after unlocking the second island. At this point in his quest, Cole should have more energy capacity, powers, and abilities. Take down 50 enemies, and unlock the trophy!

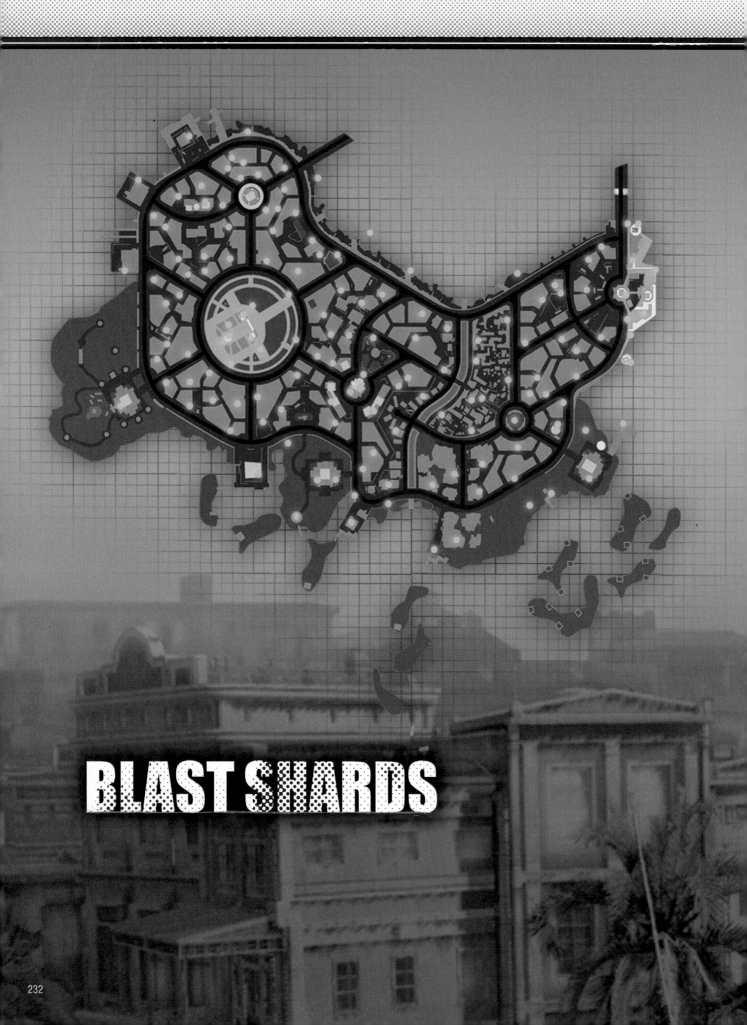

BLAST SHARDS

DEAD DROPS

Extras

Now that you've saved—or condemned—the city of New Marais, it's time to take a peek behind the curtain and witness some of the magic that made *inFAMOUS 2* a reality. Marvel at the concept art, and see how the characters and locations in New Marais reached their unique look. Then, go deeper into the game and gain valuable insight about the development of *inFAMOUS 2* with exclusive interviews with members of the Sucker Punch team. Enjoy, and thanks for playing!

KARL DECKARD
SENIOR SYSTEMS DESIGNER

What you actually do for Sucker Punch?

I am currently directing the design and production of the User-Generated Content component.

Aside from some much needed rest, what's next for Sucker Punch post-*inFAMOUS 2*?

In the near-term, we have a plan in place to continue providing killer content for UGC. We will continue to do so while designing our next game, which I am insanely excited about. Specifically, *transmission garbled* has the following core features…*static*… [TRANSMISSION ENDS]

Moral choices are a big part of the InFamous world. If you were given Cole's abilities, would you channel them for good or would you be corrupted by the power?

My heart is filled with goodness and joy! Right up until my second playthrough…

What mission (or kind of mission) is not in the main game that you hope players will create with the UGC tool set?

The goal of UGC is to allow people to express their creativity, so the high-level answer is any mission that allows them to do so. Personally, I like to see people designing non-standard missions that surprise me; casual mini-games, retro classics, artwork.

What's the most absurd mission the team created when experimenting with UGC?

A giant disco ball that turned rave-goers into zombies. Not many games you can say that about.

What is your favorite tool in UGC and why?

The Object Modifier is the clear winner for me. The notion of a single component that the designer can hook to nearly anything to modify the corresponding behavior of that component is very powerful. In the studio, we refer to it as "The One Ring to Rule Them All."

What tool do you think might be the most overlooked in UGC?

Anything that does not involve shooting things; people certainly enjoy shooting things. C'mon people, make a mission about collecting pretty flowers!

What you actually do for Sucker Punch?

I am responsible for the overall look of the game. I provide vision and guidance for the art team. I oversee visual development from the very first concept work done during pre-production, all the way through the production process, to final implementation in game.

Moral choices are a big part of the InFamous world. If you were given Cole's abilities, would you channel them for good or would you be corrupted by the power?

I'd try both…

Cole has access to a majority of his powers from the first game from the get-go. What was the process in developing Cole's new evolved powers for the sequel?

Since we're dealing with a sequel, the look and functionality of the majority of Cole's powers was already established, and we were at a great place to start from. With the development of new shaders and an FX engine pushed to its limits, we wanted the effects to feel more visceral, bigger and more dramatic—to pull you into the game, similar to a big-budget summer-blockbuster movie. For the lightning specifically, I wanted a more liquid-looking, plasma-like look and feel this time around.

MATHIAS LORENZ

ART DIRECTOR

What was the writing process like in developing the story for *inFAMOUS 2*? How did the script and the design of new enemies/characters mesh together?

The driving factor in creature design is a continuous back and forth between game design and character design, to integrate the gameplay requirements with a creature design that makes sense and is visually attractive. Once we have something that works within all those parameters, we'll integrate it into the underlying story-structure.

Conduits are characterized by elemental abilities. How did the team settle upon ice and fire/ oil as complementary powers for Cole's companions'?

This was mainly driven by design. Stylizing ice into good-focus-order and fire into bad-chaos-anarchy is really pretty straight forward, but has actually a solid structure, as it represents the super-ego and the id respectively, if you want to approach mythology from a Freudian angle. I've always seen Kuo more as the grown-up, the version of yourself who has to do the "things that are right" and take the responsible, long-term approach to a problem, thinking about the 'greater good.' Whereas Nix is the more childlike character, who rather carelessly pursues her own agenda of fun and instant gratification, thinking not too much about the consequences of her actions. Cole is, of course, stuck in the middle. I want to stress that we don't think about the companions in terms of good and evil so much as the two sides of a coin, each with pros and cons attached, just like in the real world…

Based on feedback from the first game, what elements of the core gameplay did you focus on improving the most going into the sequel?

Pakour and powers were our main focus this time around.

What kind of internal dialogue/debates occurred over the choice to essentially cast New Orleans as the game's setting in the form of New Marais?

New Orleans is the definitely one of the coolest cities in America, architecturally speaking, to explore. It is the perfect setting for a superhero who can climb and who does most of his work on rooftops.

What goals did the team have in mind moving forward in its depiction/interpretation of the Big Easy?

New Orleans has a lot of diversity in it, but in addition to that we also drew a lot of inspiration from other kinds of places in the south, as well. We also looked at a lot of European cities, like Paris, Rome, and Barcelona. The goal was to create a giant three-dimensional jungle gym for Cole to interact with, it's totally about the freedom to touch and interact with this huge sculptural city. We're not looking distinctively at one particular place for inspiration. It's more like we investigate a wide variety of stuff, and then we mix and match. And of course, on top of everything, you put your imagination to it. Because for a game, well, for any piece of entertainment, you want it to be bigger than life.

Why did you choose to depart from the more clearly separated districts that only opened in sequence with the restoration of power to the less hindered world of New Marais?

It's just a different type of gameplay-structure this time, to give the player the feeling of a fluid traversal through a more cohesive city. There certainly still are a lot of distinctly different neighborhoods. We wanted to make sure that when you move from one place to another that there's not just a tonal shift but an architectural one.

While using Cole's abilities can interact with and affect the city, what subtle effect do you most hope players will notice and appreciate?

Cole can now climb over fences…? ;)

DARREN BRIDGES
GAME DESIGNER

What you actually do for Sucker Punch?

Hero powers design, enemy combat design, and general combat balancing.

Aside from some much needed rest, what's next for Sucker Punch post-*inFAMOUS 2*?

We have lots of plans for UGC, and I'm super-excited to see the flood of content the user community will come up with. I expect there will be an evolving relationship between the awesome things users are creating and the new tools we can supply them to facilitate their ideas. This is new territory for us, and even after two years of working on the game, I can't wait to play it more once users start flexing their creativity.

Moral choices are a big part of the InFamous world. If you were given Cole's abilities, would you channel them for good or would you be corrupted by the power?

While I can't lift a car and throw it at someone's head, I believe that I (and most people I know) actually do have a lot of power. The reality is, if you earn enough money to take care of your own family's health and supplies and you still have time or money left over, you have a lot of the power Cole does. Want to cause an explosion? Buy an M-80. Want to literally save someone's life? Buy food or medicine for someone who lives in poverty or has been hit by a natural disaster. The choices I would make with Cole's powers are probably similar to the choices I've made with my life so far.

Cole has access to a majority of his powers from the first game from the get-go. What was the process in developing Cole's new evolved powers for the sequel?

We started by creating simple versions of a couple dozen new power ideas we had. We've found that it's a lot easier to evaluate something in game than on paper, so our approach is to prototype and try new things as quickly and simply as we can, and then use those prototypes to prove which ideas will work out. Once we had the simple versions running, we filtered it down to the ones that seemed most promising and kept working to flesh them out. Some of the first powers we developed for *inFAMOUS 2* were the Kinetic Pulse, Induction Launch, and Ionic Tornado.

How did you approach the issue of giving players a new power-base to build while still maintaining Cole's progression from the first game?

The first inFamous game was an origin story that sees Cole progress from a normal bike messenger to a near-demigod. At the beginning of *inFAMOUS 2*, Cole is already a well-known superhero or supervillain, and his trip to New Marais is a quest for power. Cole starts the game with all his navigational powers from inFamous, and basic (or "Alpha") versions of his combat powers. As you progress through the story and activate blast cores, you'll unlock several new versions of each class of power, like the Pincer, Artillery, and Magnum Bolts. In addition, you'll get to play with all of Cole's completely new power classes, like the Kinetic Pulse and the Ionic Vortex, as well as the shared powers he can get from Nix and Kuo. We wanted to make sure Cole started out as a powerhouse, but continued to grow throughout the story of *inFAMOUS 2*.

Conduits are characterized by elemental abilities. How did the team settle upon ice and fire/oil as complementary powers for Cole's companions'?

Our biggest priority was choosing themes that would enable us to create exciting gameplay. I personally love two aspects of ice: that you can create it anywhere, and that you can easily shatter it. This gives the ice soldiers lots of dynamic movement and shielding abilities, and it gives players more things to shatter and destroy. Ice and fire/oil also made sense for Karma: while Kuo uses ice to safely incapacitate enemies, Nix just blows them up.

Based on feedback from the first game, what elements of the core gameplay did you focus on improving the most going into the sequel?

Hand-to-hand combat was a huge focus for *inFAMOUS 2*. The original game emphasized ranged combat, but many players still ran up to enemies and punched them in the face. This is a very iconic superhero thing to do, so for *inFAMOUS 2* we set out to make the melee combat both visually exciting and viscerally satisfying. We also looked at new ways to incorporate Cole's electrical powers into his parkour movement throughout the city, which led to Car Jump, Induction Launch, improved Static Thrusters, and the Lightning Tether.

What mission (or kind of mission) is not in the main game that you hope players will create with the UGC tool set?

All the missions we make need to fit together in the canon story of the inFamous universe, so I'm excited to see what happens when you take away that restriction. I want to play a mission where you fight an army of Zekes, and each time you defeat one, he turns into a potted plant. In fact, I think I'm going to make that right now!

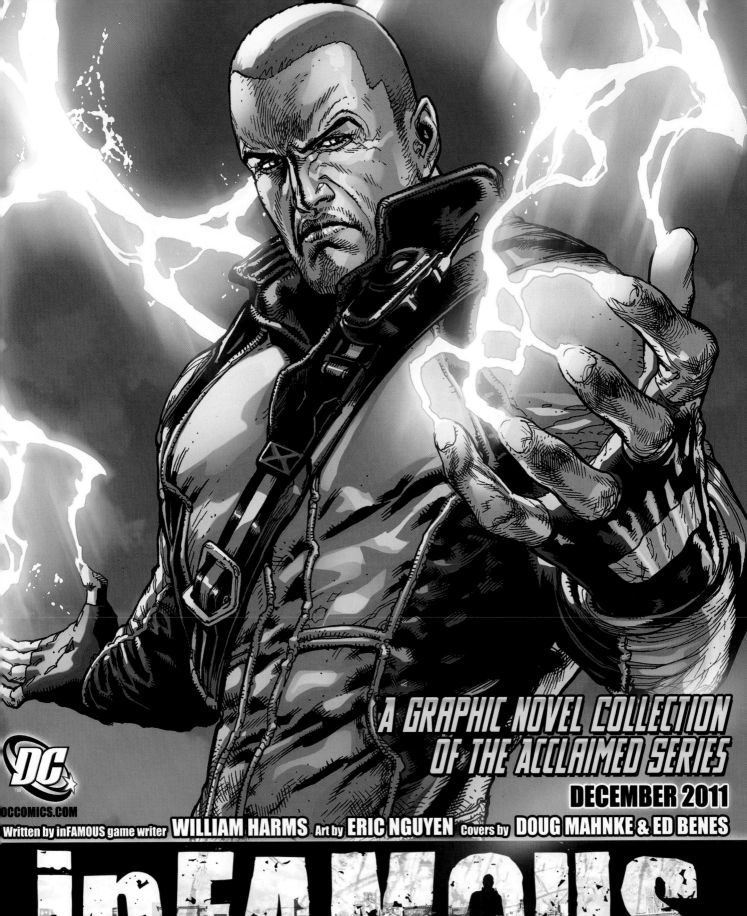

A GRAPHIC NOVEL COLLECTION OF THE ACCLAIMED SERIES

DECEMBER 2011

DCCOMICS.COM

Written by inFAMOUS game writer **WILLIAM HARMS** Art by **ERIC NGUYEN** Covers by **DOUG MAHNKE & ED BENES**

inFAMOUS

inFAMOUS 2

Official Strategy Guide

Written by Dean Leng and Josh Richardson of Off Base Productions

DK/BradyGames, a division of Penguin Group (USA) Inc.
800 East 96th Street, 3rd Floor
Indianapolis, IN 46240 The ratings icon is a registered trademark of the Entertainment Software Association. All other trademarks and trade names are properties of their respective owners.

Please be advised that the ESRB ratings icons, "EC", "E", "E10+", "T", "M", "AO", and "RP" are trademarks owned by the Entertainment Software Association, and may only be used with their permission and authority. For information regarding whether a product has been rated by the ESRB, please visit www.esrb.org. For permission to use the ratings icons, please contact the ESA at esrblicenseinfo@theesa.com.

ISBN: 978-0-7440-1319-1

Printing Code: The rightmost double-digit number is the year of the book's printing; the rightmost single-digit number is the number of the book's printing. For example, 11-1 shows that the first printing of the book occurred in 2011.

14 13 12 11   4 3 2 1

Printed in the USA.

BradyGAMES Staff

Publisher
Mike Degler

Editor-In-Chief
H. Leigh Davis

Trade and Digital Publisher
Brian Saliba

Licensing Manager
Christian Sumner

Operations Manager
Stacey Beheler

Credits

Senior Development Editor
Chris Hausermann

Book Designer
Carol Stamile

Production Designer
Tracy Wehmeyer

Editorial Assistant
Angie Lawler

BRADYGAMES WOULD LIKE TO THANK:

Ken Schramm, Greg Phillips, Dan Cole, Edward Pun, Chuck Lacson, and Wilson Cheng for creating an incredible gaming experience and helping us to create and shape this product.

THE AUTHORS WOULD LIKE TO THANK:

Stacy Burt, James Manion, and Sary & Vichhana Leng.